The Apple Way

Jeffrey L. Cruikshank

McGraw-Hill
New York Chicago San Francisco Lisbon
London Madrid Mexico City Milan New Delhi
San Juan Seoul Singapore Sydney Toronto

The *McGraw·Hill* Companies

Library of Congress Cataloging-in-Publication Data is on file.

Copyright © 2006 by McGraw-Hill. All rights reserved. Printed in the United States of America. Except as permitted under the United States Copyright Act of 1976, no part of this publication may be reproduced or distributed in any form or by any means, or stored in a database or retrieval system, without the prior written permission of the publisher.

1 2 3 4 5 6 7 8 9 0 FGR/FGR 0 1 9 8 7 6 5

ISBN 0-07-226233-8

Editorial and production services provided by TypeWriting, Acworth, GA.

McGraw-Hill books are available at special quantity discounts to use as premiums and sales promotions, or for use in corporate training programs. For more information, please write to the Director of Special Sales, McGraw-Hill, Two Penn Plaza, New York, NY 10121-2298. Or contact your local bookstore.

The Apple Way is in no way authorized or endorsed by or affiliated with Apple Computer, Inc., or Steve Jobs.

To Judy Kohn, who figured out Apple way before I did.

About the Author

Jeffrey L. Cruikshank was the co-founder of Kohn Cruikshank, Inc., a Boston-based consulting firm that served corporate and institutional clients for more than twelve years. In September of 2001, Kohn Cruikshank moved to Milton and became The Cruikshank Company, Inc.

Cruikshank is a graduate of Amherst College, and worked with a number of companies and schools in the Boston area in the 1970s and 1980s. In 1980, he became the editor of the *Harvard Business School Bulletin*, beginning a relationship with that school that has continued since then, and has led to many other engagements in the worlds of education and business.

In addition to helping shape key communications for dozens of public and private institutions, Cruikshank is the author or co-author of numerous books of interest to managers. These include histories of the Harvard Business School, New England Electric, Cummins Engine Company, The Weather Channel, and Perdue Farms. He has also written a book on corporations and architecture for Herman Miller, Inc.; the definitive guide to art in public places (*Going Public*); and books on numerous other subjects, ranging from logistics in the Gulf War (*Moving Mountains*) to entrepreneurship (*Low Risk, High Reward*) to the inner workings of the commercial real estate industry (*The Real Estate Game*). In 2005, he published his first murder mystery (*Murder at the B-School*).

Contents

Introduction

A Tale of Two Introductions

A foolish consistency is the hobgoblin of little minds, adored by little states-
men and philosophers and divines.

—Ralph Waldo Emerson

Apple thought they had it right, this time.

The date: January 19, 1983. *The place:* the Flint Center at De Anza
College, less than a mile down the road from Apple's headquarters on
Bandley Drive in Cupertino, California. *The event:* the formal unveiling of
Apple's new flagship product at the company's annual meeting.

The product was a computer, of course, and it was called the "Lisa,"
which—depending on who was doing the explaining—either stood for
"local integrated software architecture," or was the name of Apple
cofounder Steve Jobs's daughter, or both.[1]

The Lisa had been in development since the fall of 1978, when Jobs
began focusing on a new computer that would replace the aging Apple
II. At that time, Jobs envisioned a machine that would sell for $2,000, and
be aimed primarily at the business market. The new machine would be
only an evolutionary step beyond what Apple was already producing. In
other words, it would be another heavy, clunky, "small" machine—
"small" being only a relative term—with a built-in green-phosphor display, a more or less conventional user interface, and so on. Nevertheless,
Jobs had high hopes for the new machine, which he hoped would shore

up Apple's existing small-computer market, consisting mainly of educa-
tors and amateur computer buffs, and also begin to expand that base into
the business arena.[2]

So, planning began along those lines. Then, about a year later—in
November 1979—fate intervened. Against his better judgment, Jobs was
persuaded to visit the Xerox Palo Alto Research Center (PARC). The PARC
laboratories have since achieved legendary status as a place of astonishing innovation, a place of bubbling technological ferment. But back then,
it took some arm-twisting to get Jobs to stop by the sprawling, mod-
ernistic complex at 3333 Coyote Hill Road in nearby Palo Alto. By all
accounts, Jobs didn't think that stodgy old Xerox had much to teach
Apple Computer, which was then flying high: growing at astronomical
rates, getting ready for its second private placement, and generally (*pun
unavoidable*) the apple of Wall Street's eye.

And, there was a grain of truth in that assessment. Xerox had been a
fabled innovator, in its day—more or less inventing the field of photocopying, among other things—but its glory days seemed to be behind it.
As the world headed toward the paperless office, photocopying machines
were looking more and more like buggy whips. Worse, the competition
from Japan was intensifying: It was getting harder to make buggy whips
at a profit.

So, from Xerox's side of the table, there seemed to be good reasons
to cozy up to Apple, and even to the famously irascible Steve Jobs.
Maybe some of the innovations that had been languishing on PARC's lab-
oratory benches could find their way to market with Apple's help. At the
very least, assuming that the upstart Apple lived up to its growing buzz,
it couldn't hurt to get a piece of that private placement.

A deal was struck: Xerox would buy 100,000 shares of Apple for $10
a share (and would agree never to buy more than 5 percent of Apple,
which jealously guarded its independence). In return, Apple would get
to make two reconnaissance trips to PARC, looking for bright and mar-
ketable ideas.

Those trips took place in the last two months of 1979, and for the formerly disdainful Jobs, they were a revelation. Xerox's computer scientists
demonstrated an amazing machine—the Alto—that had many of the
characteristics that personal computer users would later come to take for
granted: things like a graphical user interface, or "GUI" (which allowed
the user to interact with the computer in ways other than typing in text

commands), bitmapping (a feat of code-writing that allowed for the merging of text and images), a novel input device called a "mouse," a networking capability, and a user-friendly interface featuring pop-up menus and moveable windows.

Most of these innovations had been sitting around PARC for quite some time—in fact, the Alto was already six years old, and the mouse dated back to the 1960s—and the PARC scientists had presented similar dog-and-pony shows to many previous delegations of corporate bigwigs. But unlike all those previous delegations, this one (headed by the newly humbled Jobs) understood exactly what they were seeing: the future of personal computing. The trick would be to put these innovations into an attractive and affordable package.

Enter the Lisa

Just over three years (which according to Apple translated into some 200 man-years of development efforts) and $50 million later, Apple unveiled the Lisa. The new machine certainly took its inspiration from the Alto, but it also went well beyond Xerox's pioneering device. Most notably, Alto was the desk; Lisa sat *on top of* the desk. On the hardware side, Lisa featured a one-button mouse—a significant improvement over Xerox's three-button model—a 5-megabyte hard drive, two floppy drives, and a 12-inch monochrome display. And, although Lisa was plug-ugly by today's standards—resembling the offspring of an unhappy mating between a TV set and a toaster—it was far and away the best-looking computer then on the market. As for peripherals, a new dot-matrix printer featured a revolutionary "what you see is what you get" function—captured in the acronym "WYSIWYG," pronounced "whizzywig"—meaning that for the first time, users could see on the screen what would actually show up on the printed page. Today, we take this for granted; back then, it was a breakthrough concept.

But the real surprises came on the software side. Lisa was the first commercially available computer with a GUI like the Alto's GUI.[3] Simply put, the user no longer had to enter text commands, but could direct the computer by pointing and clicking, clicking and dragging, and so on. Again, the "desktop" metaphor is taken for granted today, but in 1983, it represented a staggering breakthrough. Lisa's desktop featured pull down menus, windows, scrolling capabilities, a trash can, a clipboard (to facil-

Lisa's charms:
■ Intuitive
■ Versatile
■ Beautiful (but in her own way)

itate cutting and pasting), and integrated applications (meaning that the user could move easily from one software program to another). Those applications ranged from a spreadsheet program to word processing to drawing and graphing.

In other words, Lisa had almost everything.[4]

What *didn't* it have? First, Lisa didn't have a lot of friends in the all-important independent software-development community. If the question is, "what can you develop, for the machine that has everything?," the answer turns out to be, "not much."

Second, it didn't have compatibility with any other machine in the world. Whoever bought this dazzling new machine, therefore, would be committing himself or herself to an Apple-only universe. This raised an obvious question: How many risk-averse business people would pick Apple over, say, IBM?

Third, the Lisa's floppy drives were unreliable, necessitating an upgrade after only 6,500 machines had been sold. Worse, its Motorola 68000 processor, the beating heart of the new machine, simply wasn't up to the task of processing all that GUI-driven information. Lisa therefore earned the dubious distinction of becoming the first computer with its own knock-knock joke: *Knock knock. Who's there? (Wait 15 seconds) Lisa!*

Finally, and most important, Lisa didn't have a low price point. Instead of the $2,000 price tag initially ordered up by Jobs—who had been kept out of the Lisa development process by colleagues who thought the project too important to be entrusted to a fundamentally non-technical type like Jobs—Lisa went on the market at a staggering $9,995.

Lisa's fatal flaws:
■ No friends
■ Incompatible
■ Unreliable and slow-moving
■ A very expensive date

This necessitated the hiring of a new and dedicated sales force, whose work was greatly complicated by persistent rumors that Apple would soon release a similar machine for less than half the price of the Lisa. Apple strongly denied this at the time, but sales suffered. All across Apple's existing consumer base—computer users who were both loyal and savvy—people asked the same question: *Why buy a Lisa for full price, when you'll be able to get more or less the same thing for half price in six months?*

Exit the Lisa

Business is all about competition. So what was the competition doing in this same time period?

Two months after Lisa was unveiled, the year-old and Houston-based Compaq Computer released its new so-called "portable" computer. It weighed 28 pounds—a little more than half of what Lisa weighed—and sold for $3,590. True, it had no graphic capabilities and a stingy little 9-inch screen, but through a feat of reverse-engineering, it was 100 percent IBM-compatible. And because the IBM PC and its MS-DOS operating system were already starting to emerge as the standard for U.S. businesses, the Compaq had more than a little charm for budget-conscious IT types. In cubicles all across the country, nervous middle managers asked themselves the same question: *Hey, who's going to fault me for going with IBM, or the IBM clone?*

The rest, as they say, is history. In April 1985, Apple yanked the Lisa off the market, after selling an ungrand total of around 80,000 units in a year and a half. (Some estimates go as low as 60,000.) By way of comparison: The bland-but-functional IBM 5150 PC (introduced in September 1981, and listing for $3,000) sold almost 250,000 units in its *first month* on the market. There is a photograph—famous among computer buffs—of a bulldozer burying the last 2,700 unsold Lisas at a landfill in Logan, Utah, in 1989.[5] (The task required 880 cubic yards of fill, at $1.95 a yard.) Apple swallowed its pride, took a tax write-off, successfully fought off a lawsuit filed by Xerox—which claimed infringement of its GUI patents—unsuccessfully lodged a very similar suit against Microsoft, and moved on.[6]

A Story with a Happier Ending ... So Far ...

OK, now we fast-forward to the fall of 2001, when the very same company, Apple, introduced a very different kind of product. The date was Tuesday, October 21. The locale, this time, was Apple's headquarters. Again, the event featured Steve Jobs, now the company's CEO (although he got to that post by a somewhat bumpy path). The reporters and analysts in attendance had received a mysterious invitation from Apple the previous week. "This coming Tuesday," the invitation read, "Apple invites you to the unveiling of a breakthrough digital device. (Hint: it's *not* a Mac.)"[7]

So, what was this breakthrough device? As it turned out, it was a new hand-held digital music player called the "iPod."

A *what?*

Let's Reinvent an Industry

At the time, portable CD players like Sony's Walkman dominated the hand-held digital music playing market. Maybe "dominated" isn't a strong enough word: There were something like *300 million* Walkmen (and knock-off devices) out there on the streets. The Walkman name itself was so ubiquitous that despite Sony's strong efforts to protect its trademark, it was slowly turning into a generic, like "Kleenex" or "Band-Aid."[8] So did the world need a new way of listening to music through headphones?

And did the world need a digital music player that cost upwards of $400, when low-end Walkmen knock-offs were selling for under $50? Some observers didn't think so. They offered up various unflattering explanations of what "iPod" stood for: *Idiots price our devices. I'd prefer owning discs. I pretend it's an original device.*[9]

But other observers came down squarely on the side of the iPod: *Impressive piece of design* was another explanation of "iPod." And, as with many of Apple's products, the quality of the iPod's design revealed itself on many levels—some quickly and some not so quickly.

The first thing that struck people about the iPod was its tactile and visual qualities. Shaped something like an elongated and slightly squashed pack of cards, the white plastic iPod was light—six and a half ounces—but also felt pleasantly heavy in the palm of your hand, hefting like a small slab of platinum. (The player's stainless-steel backside underscored the subliminal precious-metal impression.) Remarkably, in an age of increasingly complex gadgetry, the iPod had almost no controls, other than a round wheel about the size of a half-dollar on its front face, situated beneath a tiny screen. It exuded an air of mystery, like a sleek and updated miniature of the obelisk in Stanley Kubrick's *2001: A Space Odyssey.* What *is* this thing? What does it do? How does it work?

iPod's charms:
- High functionality
- Elegant design
- PC-compatibility (although not from day one)
- Ties to other products/services
- Huge buzz

What the thing did, back in the fall of 2001, was put a universe of digital music in your pocket.

The iPod employed a high-speed FireWire connection to tie into an Apple computer, where it took orders from an Apple software package called "iTunes," introduced only nine months earlier. Remarkably, the tiny device, with its tiny 2.5-inch Toshiba hard drive, could store up to 1,000 songs. (That capacity has since been increased to *10,000* songs on higher-end models, or the equivalent of more than 600 hours of music.) It could copy an entire CD in less time than it takes to read this paragraph. In effect, it provided a way for music lovers to liberate their "juke box" from their computer, and take their music—and, incidentally, other kinds of computer files—on the road, organized in whatever way they preferred to have it organized.

True, CDs and Walkmen had been on the road for years. And true, most computers had CD-burning capabilities that let computer-savvy music lovers create their own CDs. (Somewhat surprisingly, Apple was late getting to this particular party.) But the iPod—in combination with the elegant iTunes software—made everything extraordinarily *obvious*, and effortless, for the first time. And using the iPod itself was stunningly easy. A circular moving scroll wheel let you first pick a function, and then—assuming you picked music—allowed you select songs by title, artist, or other categories. A push of the central button sent the tune into a pair of high-quality "ear buds," and that's all there was too it.

At that October 2001 meeting, Steve Jobs hinted that the iPod would soon be made compatible with Windows machines, which by then represented more than 95 percent of the PC market. That code-writing effort—performed mainly by independent, third-party developers—began in earnest the following month, and paid off in July 2002, with the introduction of the first PC-compatible iPods.[10] But meanwhile, something interesting was happening. Even without Windows compatibility, Apple sold 125,000 iPods by the end of 2001. Was it possible that Apple—the perennial also-ran, niche player in the PC world—might be onto something?

Apple didn't wait to find out. It kept improving the iPod—introducing improved controls and extending the limited battery life—and also pushed into closely related products and services. In April 2003, for example, the company unveiled its "third-generation" iPods (thinner, smaller, tougher, and with more memory), and also announced the opening of the "iTunes Music Store" (iTMS) for Mac users. The "music store" was in part a creative response to the burning issue of music piracy. For 99 cents, one could download a legal copy of a track, rather than illegally downloading it from a file-sharing network, but it was also a clever way of selling more iPods. It was an audacious move. "Apple, in a sense," noted the *New York Times*, "was willing to try and reinvent the entire music business in order to move iPods."[11]

Riding the Rocket

Only a month later, iTMS had sold its millionth song. And—far more important—by June 2003, Apple had sold its millionth iPod. In September, Apple announced that more than 10 million songs had been sold. (The pace of song sales now was accelerating to several million a month.) In January 2004, in the wake of the holiday retail season, Apple said that it had sold another million iPods since the previous summer. The pace of iPod sales continued to accelerate dramatically: the 3 millionth iPod was sold in May. Pretty soon, it was hard to walk down the street in a major U.S. city and *not* see someone sporting the sleek white headphones trailing down to the top of the white iPod that had come to be part of the increasingly iconic iPod look.

It was a virtuous circle: More iPods meant more song sales meant more iPod sales. In the early morning hours on July 12, 2004, iTMS sold its 100,000,000th download. Thanks in part due to a contest related to that milestone, something like 40,000 songs were sold in the final 10 minutes of the countdown to 100 million.

Pick almost any point on the spectrum over the ensuing months, and you find the same things: more songs in the iTMS (more than a million, by late 2004), more paid downloads (150 million by late 2004, at the rate of 4 million *per week*), and more iPods being sold (2 million between July and September 2004 alone, for a total of more than 6 million sold). By October 2004, Apple commanded an 82 percent share of all digital music players sold in the U.S., and a 92 percent share of all hard drive-based players. All other U.S. entrants—including products from Creative, Dell, and iRiver—had been effectively driven from the field. A little less than a year later, in August 2005, Japanese electronics maker D&M Holdings threw in the towel, announcing plans to discontinue its groundbreaking Rio PMP300 MP3 player.[12]

And then there were those *ads*. Created by TBWA/Chiat/Day, the "Silhouettes" campaign that kicked off in 2003 depicted all-black human forms holding white iPods and sporting white earplug-and-cord combinations, all against dazzling neon backdrops of lime green, lavender, milk-yellow, and pink. Between January and October 2004, according to *Media Week*, Apple spent something like $70 million advertising the iPod.[13] You couldn't open a magazine, turn on the TV, or ride the subway without bumping into the ubiquitous silhouettes.

The iPod rocket continued to soar, and Wall Street took notice. After hitting a dismal 2003 low of $16 a share, Apple stock started a dizzying climb, more than doubling by June 2004, and more than doubling again by November (when it reached $68.44 a share). Some analysts predicted that the company would hit hard times in the first quarter of 2005; in fact, the opposite was true. Apple shipped 5.3 million iPods in the quarter—up 558 percent over the first quarter of 2004—and also enjoyed a 42 percent increase in computer sales. Revenues were up 70 percent, year over year, and net income increased by *530 percent*. The company had $5 billion in the bank, with more money pouring in over the transom. "Apple is firing on all cylinders," Steve Jobs commented, at the risk of understatement.[14]

The cylinders continue to fire, as of this writing. In September 2005, Apple introduced the iPod "nano," a full-featured iPod that's thinner than a pencil, boasts a color screen, and holds 1,000 songs (or 25,000 photos)—all for between $199 and $249. And, on the same day, Apple also announced the introduction of the iTunes phone—the company's first tentative entry into the cut-throat cell phone business.[15]

The Apple Way

The same company, some of the same players, and some important, enduring philosophical threads—and yet, the outcomes of the Lisa and the iPod stories couldn't be more different.

You could conclude that the two launches had nothing in common. You could conclude that because they were separated by almost two decades, in an industry characterized by nothing so much as *rapid change*, that there are no lessons to be teased out of them.

But you would be wrong. Over the years, Apple learned from its mistakes and changed. As *The New Yorker* recently put it:

Even Apple Computer—once the most imperially self-reliant of companies—has changed. Steve Jobs used to fantasize about controlling everything down to the sand in Apple's computer chips. Today, Apple works contentedly with companies like Motorola and Hewlett-Packard.[16]

You can't do it by yourself, no matter how smart you are. Markets move too quickly, technologies grow too complex, and too many smart people are investing too much time and money in innovation. And, by the way, lots of those smart people are working in teams, trying to beat you out.

> You can't do it by yourself—no matter how smart you are.

Well, for Apple, this was hard-won wisdom. (Jobs doesn't give up on his fantasies easily.) That lesson—and many more like it—are captured in the following pages.

And just as important, some things about Apple "didn't" change. Consider the following list:

- Be intuitive.
- Be consistent.
- Conform to the ways in which people actually work.
- Have enough performance to do the jobs that need doing.
- Provide an open software and hardware architecture.
- Be reliable.
- Be pleasing and fit into an everyday work environment.[17]

Now consider the following Steve Jobs quote:

We don't underestimate people. We really did believe that people would want something this good, that they'd see the value in it. And that rather than making a far inferior product for a hundred dollars less, giving the people the product that they want and that will serve them for years, even though it's a little pricier. People are smart; they figure these things out.[18]

If someone asked you which of these two scraps of writing described the Lisa and which was about the iPod, there are probably enough clues to let you figure out which is which. (The bulleted list comprises the original specs for the Lisa, most likely determined by Jobs himself sometime around 1979. The Jobs quote, from 2003, refers to the iPod.) But what's interesting is how *interchangeable* they are, with only a few edits.

Sometimes stubbornness and consistency have served the company well; sometimes they haven't. The trouble with consistency is that it so easily shades over into what Emerson called a *foolish* consistency. Is it a good thing to consistently produce the best personal computers on the market—computers that generate an almost unnatural passion on the part of their users? Absolutely. Is it a good thing to give up market share, year after year, to companies whose products aren't as good as yours, but who understand that most people don't want to pay more for elegance of design or for functionality that they'll never need? Absolutely not. *People are smart; they figure these things out.* Those lessons, too, show up in subsequent chapters.

> Be consistent—right up to the point of foolishness. Then stop.

Although we've just looked at some ancient history (the Lisa) and some history in the making (the iPod, the iMusic Store), this is not a history book. There are at least a dozen good histories of Apple on the market—authorized and unauthorized, friendly and unfriendly—which I'll refer to and draw upon in subsequent chapters. No doubt the runaway success of the iPod will inspire still more histories. This is not the latest book in that series.

And, although Apple is a technology company, *The Apple Way* is not written for computer buffs. Instead, it is a book for managers who want to learn both from Apple's mistakes (which at times were life-threatening) as well as Apple's triumphs (which were dizzying, and served to confound the company's many critics).

Yes, it *is* being written on a PowerBook G4—that *big* mother—proudly shown off by the two-foot, eight-inch Mini-Me to the seven-foot, five-inch Yao Ming in the hilarious PowerBook TV ad. But although my family has something like a dozen Macs and two iPods distributed across a home, an office, and a few college campuses, I am not an Apple zealot.

> Vanilla is sometimes good, and sometimes bad. It all depends.

I like the plug-and-play nature of Macs; I like the fact that that they're not as subject to viruses as their PC counterparts; and I admire their consistently cutting-edge design. But I am less interested in the religious wars that rage between Mac fanatics and Windows devotees, and more interested in what we can learn from a company that maintains a sharp profile, in an era of increasingly bland, diversified, and homogenized companies.

I will present the lessons of *The Apple Way* in four basic categories:

- Make the product king.
- Make the customer king.
- Break the marketing mold.
- Fix your leaders and your plans.

Each of these categories includes several chapters that serve to illustrate facets of the central lesson. Note that these categories don't separate out perfectly. (Innovative marketing helps make the product king, for example.) But note that overlaps reflect the reality of business: Things splash over from one realm to the other, and you deal with it.

> Make the product king.
> Make the customer king.

Note, too, that these categories also aren't internally consistent. Can you make both the product king and the customer king? Probably not, but that's what Apple tries to do, time and time again.

Chapter 1

Marvels and Margins

Every prayer reduces itself to this: "Great God, grant that twice two be not four."

—Ivan Turgenev

This is the story of a company that—when it's good—is very, very good. And when it's bad, it flounders.

The good side of Apple Computer, Inc. is its products. They are good because they help people do their work more effectively and efficiently (in the case of the Macintosh computer), or because they help people enjoy life more (the iPod MP3 player), or both. Actually, these products aren't just good; they're great—*insanely great*—as Steve Jobs famously put it.[1]

The bad side of Apple is that it's not much of a *business*. "The mistake everyone makes is assuming that Apple is a real company," commented Regis McKenna. "But it is not. It never has been." McKenna was in a position to know. His firm did Apple's PR for 15 years, and—for better or worse—helped make the company what it was.[2]

Apple's strategy has been, consistently, a case of "too little too late." Until recently, its management has been weak at just the wrong moments. Its return to shareholders over time has been erratic, at best. A dollar invested in Apple in 1990 is worth (at this writing) about 75 cents, a 25 percent decline. The same dollar invested in the S&P 500 in the same period is worth about $1.75, a 75 percent increase.[3] In other words, even after all the excitement generated by the iPod, and the associated upsurge in Apple's stock, Apple isn't yet worth as much as it was a decade and a half ago. In 1990, Apple owned 10 percent of the worldwide personal computer market. Today, its market share is under 2 percent:

Apple's Market Share, 1984–2004

Year	Apple Share
1984	6%
1985	2.60%
1986	4.20%
1987	6%
1988	6%
1989	5%
1990	5%
1991	11.20%
1992	12%
1993	10%
1994	9.30%
1995	9%
1996	5.10%
1997	3.45%
1998	2.70%
1999	3.19%
2000	2.78%
2001	2.48%
2002	2.35%
2003	2.05%
2004	1.98%

Source: www.pegasus3d.com/totalshare0.gif

Apple's apologists point out that luxury automakers like BMW, Lexus, Jaguar, and others command similarly small market share, and no one is predicting that BMW (for example) is on the verge of extinction. So why pick on Apple?

They also point out that Apple is the only integrated hardware and software personal computer company still in operation today. They point to the good things that flow out of that unique degree of integra-

> Think about your market share: Are you really BMW, and if so, is that really good enough?

tion: simplicity of use, consistency across software applications, and so on.

This gets us back to our starting point: Yes, Apple makes great products. But in the long run, that may not be enough.

Aladdin Meets Casper

The Mac operating system (OS)—the code that runs the Mac computer—is an amazing feat of programming.

The OS is a bit like the genie that comes out when you rub the lamp—and *only* when you rub the lamp. Or, it's like the friendly ghost that haunts the old Victorian pile that you recently purchased: all pervasive, but never intrusive. Aladdin and Casper, at your service.

I can cite two examples from my own experience. First example: I purchased my first digital camera several years back. I asked the salesman what else I needed to buy to make the camera talk to my Mac. "Nothing," he said, with a shrug. This didn't seem possible. I had read something, somewhere, about how there was a device called a "dock" that had to sit between the camera and the computer. But, because he didn't seem to want to sell me anything else, I paid for my camera and left.

I took a couple dozen test shots, without much faith in the whole process. Then I plugged the camera into the back of my PowerBook using the cord that came with the camera, turned the camera on, and waited to see what would happen.

First, the little iPhoto icon at the bottom of my desktop screen started bouncing up and down lazily, as if it had just woken up from a nap. Then the iPhoto screen showed up, with the multicolor revolving pinwheel in the middle that tells me to be patient; my Mac is doing something. Then up came a little dialogue box that told me that there was a Canon PowerShot G2 attached to the computer, with 25 images on it; would I like the computer to download those images?

I hit the "OK" button.

Then another dialogue box asked if I'd like the Mac to erase the pictures from the Canon as it went along. Again, I hit "OK." A minute or two later, the photos were downloaded into a date-stamped folder, ready for attention from me, and the camera's memory card was empty—ready for my next photo shoot.

Second experience: My daughter's little white iBook started getting flakey in her senior year of college, after about three years of hard use. Since she was soon to go out into the workforce, we had the discussion that lots of Mac users have had over the years (especially in the dark days of the 1990s, when it looked like Apple truly was on the verge of extinction). *Time to switch to a Wintel machine?* In other words, is it time to join the 90-plus percent of the personal computing world that takes its marching orders from Windows and Intel?

Since she was then aiming at a teaching job, it didn't seem likely that she'd have to migrate to Wintel for her professional needs. (Schools tend to be Mac-friendly.) Plus, she really liked her iBook: small, smart, fast, intuitive. So, on a given Saturday morning in November, we decided to go buy another iBook.

The CompUSA salesman assured us that if we bought an accessory called a "FireWire," it would be easy to transfer files from the old iBook to the new one. "A *snap*," he promised. *Uh huh*, I said to myself. I'm no techie. I was already dreading what promised to be a terrible job—reloading software, moving files, recreating Internet transfer protocols, and so on. Mentally, I set aside the weekend.

When I got home, I plugged the FireWire—basically, Apple's name for an external bus standard called IEEE 1394, which is not interesting for our purposes—into the appropriate hole in the back of both iBooks. (There's only one hole it fits in, and anyway, there's an identical symbol on both the computer and the cord that tells you where the cable goes.) I turned both iBooks on, and held my breath.

Up came a dialogue box on the new machine, which said something to the effect of, "Oh, look. I see another machine just like this one, connected to this one. Would you like to recreate that machine on this one?" After checking two or three times to make sure I was copying from old to new, I hit the "yes" button. The little multicolored pinwheel spun around a few times; then another dialog box came up. It said something like, "This will take approximately an hour and 45 minutes. Please make sure both machines are plugged into an external power source." I did, and then hit "OK." Both machines started whirring quietly. There wasn't anything else to do, so I went for a walk.

An hour and a half later, I came back, and the second machine was an exact duplicate of the first, screen saver and all.

What do these two stories mean? It means that somebody out in Cupertino anticipated exactly these sequences of events, and *prewired* the computer to handle them in a way that even a technophobe could handle. And there must be thousands of similar stories that could be told. Unless you're a true computer nut, you're unlikely to even scratch the surface of what lies buried in the Mac OS. For example: Mac users tend to use a one-button mouse, because that's what Apple has favored for decades. Windows users are accustomed to a two-button mouse. So, what happens to those brave Windows users who buy an iPod, succumb to the so-called "halo effect," and buy a Mac as an (expensive!) iPod accessory?

Well, they can plug in a two-button mouse, and it will operate exactly as it did in the Windows environment. Why? Again, that's because somebody out in Cupertino *prewired* it to act that way. They anticipated the needs of these brave converts. Even some diehard Mac fanatics would be unaware that this capability lies buried in their own OS, extending a welcoming hand to those who venture in from the Dark Side.[4]

I asked a Windows fanatic in Chicago what she liked about the Windows OS. She liked the fact, she said, that her computer wasn't full of stuff that she wasn't ever going to use. She didn't want six million printer drivers on her machine, clogging things up; she enjoyed installing just the right printer drivers herself, and having everything work. She didn't like the machine thinking for her (or trying to think for her.) She *liked to do it herself*, even if that meant that—because the printer driver that came with the printer turned out to be outdated—she had to go on the Web, find and download the correct printer driver, and install it.

This struck me as very interesting. I used the word "fanatic" above. As Mac chronicler Scott Kelby has pointed out, you often hear the phrase "Mac fanatic," but you *never* hear the phrase "PC fanatic."[5] (You hear "PC user," if you hear anything.) But that's a little backwards. With some notable exceptions—some of whom we'll meet in Chapter 9, running Mac Users' Groups—Mac users aren't really "fanatical" about their machines at all. In fact, they have no interest in how computers work. They don't want to install printer drivers, ever. My friend in Chicago, *she's* the fanatic.

But back to the main point: All of these painless Mac experiences are possible because Apple controls both the hardware *and* the software.

Want to take a look behind the Dark Curtain and see how business is done in the Wintel environment? Consider the following piece of deep Internet technochat, which seems to have something to do with chipmaker Intel's determination to fix the shortcomings of laptops, circa 2002:

> *Deep down Intel knows the mobile experience is truly horrible, and it wants to fix it. We want one-inch thick laptops which last all day, but the technology doesn't get us there. Intel can't, like Apple, simply define some standards in a quick half-hour meeting, and email them to the hardware division for implementation. It needs to coerce and finesse its OEMs to arrive at the same destination. (Apple's power management is terrific, but then it doesn't have to play by the ACPI rules)...*
>
> *Microsoft has been so concerned with integration recently that the most obvious and incremental consumer benefits haven't gotten a look-in. This happens when companies navel-gaze for too long. At Microsoft, you can get rapid promotion for suggesting wheezes such as tying the MSDN subscription to Passport. But you get nothing for adding a 'Location Manager' to Windows: something that allows you to create a profile to unify your TCP/IP settings, printer preferences, and choice of networked drives, depending on where you are. Macintoshes have had it for years, and even Linux has a Location Manager these days, for heaven's sake.[6]*

Just to underscore the main points: If you're Intel, you can't simply call a half-hour meeting and solve a pressing user problem by defining some standards. (That's the sort of thing that Apple does.) And, if you're Microsoft, it seems, your focus on integration—and perhaps navel-gazing—distracts you from providing "incremental consumer benefits." The result for Windows users (again, circa early 2002) is that you don't have the kind of Location Manager that Macs have had onboard for years.

> The point: Macs are great because Apple controls every relevant aspect of the Mac experience.

Consistency and Continuity

For most people—not counting nerds—a computer is only a tool. It's something that you use to make a given job easier. If using the computer doesn't save time and aggravation, or if (God forbid) it actually makes the job *harder*, you're unlikely to use it.

Apple's approach over the years has been to make using a personal computer as easy and intuitive as possible—maybe in part out of altruism, but certainly out of the desire to sell more computers. The way it has achieved this has been to: 1) develop an operating system that anticipates most of the tasks that a user might ask it to carry out, and have a ready, "human-like" response to any such request, 2) establish a set of conventions to which all applications software packages have to conform, 3) tightly control the work of outside developers to make sure they follow those rules, and 4) design and build computers that are exquisitely well suited to deliver the goods.

What does all of this mean to the user? It means *easier*.

We've already talked about the joys of the Mac OS: Casper the Friendly Ghost, anticipating your every need.

As for consistency across applications, this is something that Mac users have the luxury of taking for granted, but it deserves special mention all the same. Simply put, if you're an outside developer and you want to write applications that will run on a Mac, you have to play by Apple's rules. (More on this interesting dynamic in the next chapter.) And Apple's rules are relentlessly aimed at *consistency* and *ease of use*.

> Consistency and continuity are all-important, to non-technoweenies.

If you're an experienced Mac user, even before you break the seals on your new software package, you know a whole lot about how to use it. You know how to install it. (Double-click on the desktop icon and sit back.) You know how to open a new file. ("File-open" on the pull-down menu—and always in the same place on that pull-down menu—or simply "Apple-O" on the keyboard.) You know the most important command of all: "Apple-Z", which undoes the bonehead mistake you just made. You know what a dialog box is going to look like, and what kinds of questions it's likely to ask you, and the range of responses you're likely to be presented with. You know how to save files, quit the program, and even force the program to shut down in the event that it freezes up on you.

In other words, you can more or less get away with not even looking at the manual that came with that new application. Well, OK; not true when it comes time to digging down into the deep complexities of Quark or

Photoshop; but if you've mastered a Mac spreadsheet program, you're in good shape to tackle a bookkeeping program, a tax application, or even a database-management program. That's why Apple manuals—for both its products and operating systems—are so short. You *know* that the first time you hit "Apple-S", for example, that combination of keys will *always* ask you what you want to call the document, where you want to put it, and in what format. (And every time you hit "Apple-S" after that, your computer will simply save the latest version of your document, no questions asked.)

Maybe there's a stray Wintel user who's wandered in, and is saying, "Well, what's so special about *that*? My machine does more or less the same thing from program to program." Two responses: First, "more or less" isn't the same as "always." (It's the *exceptions* that can make the Windows environment so frustrating.) And second, the only reason that the Windows environment is slouching toward consistency is because Apple set such a good example, many years ago.

It's a little like zoning. Boston has zoning; Houston does not. Boston has consistency of land use, where proposed individual land uses must fit into a bigger picture. Houston does not. The best planners, developers, and architects in Houston try to keep the bigger picture in mind, and make things better for users, even if they're not legally required to do so. They think it's a competitive advantage (and perhaps even that it's the "right" thing to do).

The Macintosh hardware reinforces this consistency. Stuff is almost always in the same place. If you know how to turn on one Mac, you know how to turn them all on. You know how to turn the sound up, down, or off; you know how to make the screen brighter or dimmer. You know what to expect from the track pad or, alternatively, where to plug in a mouse.

The other big bonus in the Apple approach is *continuity*. At least until the introduction of the OS X operating system (pronounced "Oh Ess Ten," for non-Mac nerds), there was a remarkable degree of continuity, from one generation of Macintosh to the next. Improvements to the OS were seamlessly incorporated in, rather than injected in, as Apple's President, John Sculley, explained to the *New York Times* in 1990:

> *Apple's principal strength has and will continue to be consistency. Programs designed to run on the original Macintosh in 1984 will run on Apple's most advanced machines, which is something that is not true of IBM and compatible machines.*[7]

This is less true today than in the past. (The transition to OS X has led to some awkward solutions, in the name of continuity with what's now called the "Mac Classic environment.") Nevertheless, the larger point still holds: It's still easy to use a Mac. And the main reason why it's still easy is that Apple still *does it all*. It controls the box, and it controls the core commands for the box, and it controls key aspects of the work of the outside people who write additional commands for the box. Good for us users, and sometimes good for Apple—but not always.

Chasing Gross Margin

Here's the problem in a nutshell: At least until very recently, Apple has been obsessed with a particular business measure: *gross profit margin.* This is simply revenues minus the cost of goods sold, expressed as a percentage of revenue. In other words, if a company sells $100 million worth of goods, and it cost $60 million to produce those goods, then

> Gross margin is a great measure—until the day that it isn't.

the company's gross profit on its sales is $40 million, and its gross profit margin is 40 percent ($40 million divided by $100 million).

Gross profit margin has been important for Apple in part because, just as for every other company, it measures how efficiently Apple is producing its goods. It has also been a key indicator because it reflects how quickly the company is able to turn over its inventory. In the personal computer industry, prices almost never go up; they almost always go down. The day a new product is put on the market, it starts becoming obsolete—sometimes at an alarming rate. Competitors jump in with (seemingly) similar products, offered at lower prices. Rumors may circulate that you're about to obsolete your own product. (This is one of the bad things that happened to the ill-fated Lisa, when rumors began to spread about a forthcoming Apple product with the same capabilities at half the price. The rumors were true: It was called "Macintosh.") For these reasons and others, the longer your product sits in a warehouse or in a retail outlet, the more downward pressure will be exerted on its price. If you're a PC manufacturer with high gross profit margins, it probably indicates that you're turning over your inventory at a healthy clip.

Of course, there's another way you can bulk up your gross profit margin: *Charge really high prices.* But this is only possible if you have some strong differentiator—one that makes people willing to pay a premium for the good or service that you're offering.

For Apple, this differentiator has been its unique OS, packaged in a distinctive box—elegantly designed, with user needs in mind, in a way that a Dell computer doesn't *pretend* to be—that reinforces the benefits of that OS. In the past, this one-two combination has worked well for Apple. In 1989, for example, Apple enjoyed a gross margin of 54 percent, almost 9 percentage points higher than Compaq's equivalent figure, even though Apple spent far more than Compaq on R&D.[8] Two years later, when industry-wide price-cutting drove everyone's margins down, Apple still turned in a respectable 40 percent gross margin. "Apple's unique Macintosh software," noted the *New York Times*, "has helped it avoid the worst of the PC industry price wars, where margins for competitors like Compaq and Dell had plunged below 30 percent."[9]

It only got worse, in the late 1990s, thanks to the relentless race to the bottom engaged in by the PC makers:

> *The ongoing price war in the IBM PC world was leading companies like Compaq to drop prices as much as 50 percent every six months. While the Macintosh could command a premium in the marketplace, that premium was shrinking, putting enormous pressure on A's margin.[10]*

And here comes the rub: The Macintosh environment has simply become less unique over the years. With each new generation of Microsoft's Windows OS, the behemoth from Redmond gets a little closer to creating an intuitive, user-friendly computing environment.

Meanwhile, at least until very recently, the inherent shortcomings of Apple's products—especially their high energy use and their slow processing speeds, dictated by the PowerPC chip—have been thrown into ever-sharper relief. In a 2001 response to a *Mac Observer* online article, a writer named Steve (who described himself as a "still loyal Mac fan that has been forced to use Windows cause it's better and cheaper"), sounded an ominous note:

> *The general comment about 2 years ago was 'Apples are good if you're doing graphics.' But now, even that comment is dead. Now it's 'Apples used to be good for graphics, but PCs have all the same*

software now, and they have 1 GHz PCs. Macs are twice as expen-
sive for half the MHz. You could get two PCs for the price of one
Mac, and they'd be just as fast."

Unfortunately, I believe this to be true. I don't care what kind
of speed tests Apple has posted. I just know from daily use of apps
like IE, Word, Freehand, and Photoshop that my PC is WAY faster
than my G4. Oh, and by the way, I'm talking about a PII, 400mhx
PC I built 3 years ago for $700.

Sorry, Apple. Unless OS X gets ported for use on PC boxes, I
think you're in for some dark times.[11]

Some of the steps that Apple has taken recently—including the introduction of the high-speed dual G5s and the spring 2005 announcement
by Steve Jobs that Apple would soon be embracing longtime arch-enemy
Intel and using Intel chips in future generations of Apples—speak to
these performance problems.

But for Apple, the larger questions still loom. Is the time-honored
strategy of pursuing gross margin now officially dead? Are iPods and
Mac minis—Apple's recent forays into consumer electronics and lower-
margin, higher-volume computers, respectively—the wave of the
future?

And, if not, what *is* the wave of the future? Will there be enough margin for future miracles?

Lessons in Marvels and Margins

At the end of each chapter in this book, I'll provide a shorthand summary of the managerial lessons contained therein. So, let's look at what I'll
call Apple's "lessons in marvels and margins":

- **Think about your market share: Are you really BMW, and if
  so, is that really good enough?** Apple and its apologists like to
  say that going from 10 percent market share to less than 2 percent
  market share in a decade is OK, because the Mac is a premium
  product. But, is that really good enough? Taking half steps to the
  wall in the wrong direction is unsustainable.
- **Macs are great because Apple controls every relevant aspect
  of the Mac experience.** So, what are the equivalent levers in your
  business? Who is using your product, and how? And what things

about their experience need to be controlled internally? How does "control" relate to "profit"?

- **Consistency and continuity are all-important, to non-tech-noweenies.** Even in the fast-moving world of high-tech, Apple has found ways to: 1) create consistency of user experience across multiple programs, and 2) allow for continuity from one generation of OS to the next.

- **Gross margin is a great measure—until the day that it isn't.** The world has changed. It's not clear whether Apple has changed along with it. A gross margin that depends on a highly differentiated product may turn out to be unsustainable—and therefore a trap.

- **Product shortcomings will whack your margins.** And we're not talking about catastrophic stuff like PowerBook batteries catching fire, here; we're talking about the kinds of chronic product inadequacies that invite unflattering comparisons and customer defections. If your chip leads to underwhelming processing speeds, for example, your spectacular graphic user interface may not be enough to make up for it. And if, meanwhile, your industry is engaged in cut-throat competition, and if, meanwhile, your OS edge is being narrowed by skilled competitors.

Chapter 2

Find the Future

∾o∾

Far-sighted as falcons, they looked down another future.
                                                    —W.H. Auden

A t first, writing a chapter about Apple as an innovator appears to be an easy task. But it isn't.

There's too much to say.

In fact, there are a thousand possible jumping-off points for the story. So let's arbitrarily pick the day in 1983 when Steve Jobs opened the first Mac divisional retreat with a dramatic little demonstration. Jobs was then running the Mac division, which was charged with coming up with the computer that became known as the "Macintosh." The people gathered around him were among Apple's most talented engineers and programmers. At Jobs's request, a pirate flag flew above the building, underscoring the renegade aspect of the Mac enterprise: *We break the rules.* Thinking like a pirate turns out to be a good mind-set for innovation.

Jobs opened the plastic bag that he was carrying, turned it upside down, and out onto the conference table slid a brown felt-covered object that looked something like an oversized desk diary, hinged along its long axis. But when Jobs opened the object, the onlookers saw something totally unexpected. One half was a mock-up of a keyboard. The other half was a simulated computer monitor, like a small TV screen. But *flat.*

"This is my dream of what we'll be making in the mid to late '80s," Jobs told his bemused colleagues. "We won't reach this on Mac One or

Mac Two, but it will be Mac Three. This will be the culmination of all this Mac stuff."[1]

There's no record of whether the Mac "pirates" took this particular demonstration to heart. But some eight

> Share the vision. Make it tangible. Make it visible.

years later, in 1991, Apple introduced three models of a machine it called the "PowerBook," a revolutionary notebook PC. It weighed around five pounds, and retailed for between $2,500 and $4,600, depending on the model.

The PowerBook wasn't the first laptop on the market (Compaq introduced its LTE portable in 1989, putting enormous pressure on Apple to respond), but it was the best. It featured a stunning LCD display, integrated palm rests, and a built-in trackball. Again, Apple's trackball wasn't entirely new; it was just *better*. "The best attempt by the Windows world," the PowerBook's Product Manager Bruce Gee later recalled, "was the funky trackball from Microsoft that attached to the side of the keyboard like a wart."[2]

No warts on the PowerBook. Almost overnight, it became the best-selling computer in the United States, with $1 billion in sales between 1991 and 1992. Thanks to the PowerBook, Apple passed IBM to become the market-share leader in the domestic PC industry.[3]

Steve Jobs looms large in this story. Curiously, he was never Apple's resident technical genius. (Steve Wozniak played that role first, and was succeeded by many others who were far more talented technically than Jobs.) But more than anyone else, Jobs had the uncanny ability to look into the future. As Apple's public relations guru Regis McKenna later put it:

> *I really think that Steve Jobs and [Intel's] Bob Noyce were two of the people that I've met in my life who really did envision the future. Not too many do . . . Steve came in, and I can remember him sitting in our little conference room and talking about children using computers, and teachers using computers, and business people using computers, which had to be in 1976, 1977, in that time frame.*[4]

> People + strategy + dollars = a window on the future

Jobs was not responsible for all of Apple's innovations. Nor did all of the company's innovations succeed on the level of the PowerBook. In fact, many of them bombed, and several of them bombed spectacularly. (Those stories will be told in the following pages.) But for most of its history, by combining dollars with people—sometimes strategically—Apple has found a way to look over the horizon and find the future.

Like What, for Example?

In 2002, Mac chronicler and enthusiast Scott Kelby came up with an interesting list of Apple "firsts."[5] These include, for example:

- The 3.5" floppy disk drive.
- Color graphics (on the Apple II).
- Built-in networking (technically, a NeXT innovation).
- Built-in wireless LAN (including dual built-in antennae).
- Built-in sound (of course, many of those old PCs could be taught to make noises, but you had to purchase and install a separate sound card).
- Easy access to the guts of the computer.
- The ability to hook up more than one monitor (not possible on PCs until the introduction of Windows 98).
- The personal digital assistant, or PDA (the ill-fated Newton, described below).
- Ubiquitous USB connectors (USB was, in fact, a PC invention, but nobody in that world picked it up until Apple did).
- FireWire (the wonderful cable and standard, referred to in Chapter 1, that permits huge flows of data directly from one computer to another, which is now universal among PCs).
- Elimination of tube-based monitors in favor of LCD flat-panel displays.
- Elimination of internal fans (in iMac and Cube) through self-cooling (mostly because Steve Jobs always hated fans in computers).

To this list could be added ancient breakthroughs (such as the first "computer in a box"; and the first commercially successful application of a graphical user interface [GUI]—integrating words and pictures—and all of the associated miracles of desktops, trash cans, etc.), and more recent innovations like the "iApplications" (iMovie, iTunes, etc.), and—of course—iPod and the iMusic Store, described in the Introduction.

Most of the media attention that recently has been focused on Apple has concentrated on the iPod phenomenon, but it's worth pointing out that 2004 (for example) was a pretty good year for innovation elsewhere in the Little Kingdom. That was the year that Apple introduced the iMac G5, an integrated brain-and-screen model that was only 2 inches thick (*where's the rest of it?*), sitting atop an anodized aluminum stand. (Dating back to his days at NeXT, Steve Jobs has always loved an elegant computer stand.)

Apple also premiered its Apple Cinema Display LCD monitors, which set a new standard for brightness, and for "readability" from an unprecedented range of angles. (Liquid crystal display monitors, especially cheap ones, tend to work only when viewed dead-on.) The iBook laptop—with sophisticated new wireless networking technology—also made its debut, leading to a 74 percent increase in Apple laptop sales.

Just missing my arbitrary 2004 window—as a result of being introduced in January 2005—was the "Mac mini," Apple's first credible assault on the super-low end of the computing. The Mini, which as Steve Jobs explained was a "BYODKM" machine (bring your own display, keyboard, and mouse), went on the market at prices starting at $499. It was another case of "Where's the rest of it?" The Mini is 6.5 inches square, 2 inches high, and weighs just under three pounds.[6]

As of this writing, Apple hasn't reported on Mini sales, except to comment that it is "very pleased with customer response." Independent analysts estimated that Apple sold something like 138,000 Minis in the first quarter of 2005, or approximately twice as many as most outside observers had predicted.[7]

A Hit and Two Misses

So, Apple is on a roll. It has found a way, in recent years, to connect ideas with markets. It wasn't always so. Sometimes Apple came up with great ideas and failed to follow through on them—despite strong market interest. Other times, the company ventured into truly visionary realms, only to come back from the frontier with its tail between its legs, beaten by the lack of a market.

In the former category is the Apple LaserWriter printer. Back in the mid 1980s, the daisy-wheel printer was considered state-of-the-art.

(Younger readers won't remember how awful these things really were. Older readers may recall the ungainly and expensive aftermarket hoods that were used to muffle the horrific clatter these dreadful printers generated.) In the spring of 1985, as part of a larger "Mac Office" package, Apple introduced its LaserWriter, a $7,000 machine capable of outputting text, charts, and drawings *all on the same page*, in a wide variety of type styles and sizes. Suddenly, office workers could put together and print out an almost infinite variety of publications, ranging from manuals to catalogues to newsletters to business forms—all from the desktop.[8] Taken for granted today, sure, but *astonishing* back then.

Guy Kawasaki, former head of developer "evangelizing" at Mac, and later a Silicon Valley marketing guru, confesses that, like many of his colleagues, he missed the LaserWriter boat:

> *The LaserWriter was the best part of the Mac Office. More than any other piece of hardware, it showed the distinct advantage of owning a Mac, and it saved Mac and enabled Apple to reemerge from [the financial calamities of] 1985. Everyone takes the LaserWriter for granted today, but most of Apple fought against its creation. Many people, myself included, thought it was nuts to design a $7K printer ... Ironically, most of Apple fought against the very thing that probably saved it.[9]*

Then, mysteriously, Apple simply ... *dropped* its wonderful invention. As part of a larger withdrawal from the field of computer peripherals, Apple abandoned the LaserWriter (and its big brother, the LaserWriter Plus) in February 1988. "They quietly slipped into the night," writes Scott Kelby. "Here one day, gone the next."[10]

In the category of visionaries coming home with their tails between their legs, Apple gave us the Newton (1993) and Pippin (1996). Newton, the so-called personal digital assistant referred to above, was a hand-held device championed by John Sculley. The Newton was a combination computing-and-communications device that was supposed to recognize cursive handwriting—input by means of a special pen—and also send and receive e-mails and faxes. "Supposed to" is the fatal phrase: Newton's shortcomings in the handwriting-

> The future isn't always welcome, and—without nurturing—it may not stick around.

recognition arena made it more or less a laughingstock, the butt of jokes on late-night TV. But, there were other problems, as well. Weighing in at about a pound, the size of a hardbound Steven King novel (big!), Newton was nowhere near as portable as it needed to be. And going on the market at $700—when less elegant but reasonably functional alternatives were selling at $300—also helped make Newton a tough sell.

Steve Jobs—the humbled and angry Apple visionary then in exile—was openly skeptical. "They are going to have trouble getting the volume up," he told the *New York Times*. "If Apple was doing really well, they would forward-price them, but there is no way they can sell enough Newtons at $700 and up."[11]

It's interesting to note what Jobs *didn't* say. He didn't say that Apple shouldn't be wasting its time out on the frontier. He knew from personal experience, however, that high-priced products brought back from the frontier often fail to find their market. And, given his proven talent at finding the future, he may even have had an inkling of the revolution that was to begin a scant three years later, when—in March 1996—a little company called Palm introduced its Pilot 1000 and Pilot 5000 organizers.

Pippin was yet another tantalizing disappointment. Pippin was a Nintendo-like game device, which plugged into a standard TV set and used a scaled-down version of the Mac operating system to run its games and—significantly—surf the Web, by means of a 14.4 kb modem. Apple's co-founder and true patron saint, Steve Wozniak, had pushed for Pippin, because he believed it would help refocus the company on children and education. (*Get to them through their games! Get to them on the Web!*)[12]

Launched in Japan in June 1995, Pippin sold 20,000 units almost overnight, and looked like it might become Apple's first successful foray into the consumer-electronics field. Then, even before Pippin could be introduced in the United States, sales dropped precipitously. Like Newton, it was far more expensive ($600) than competing systems like Sega ($300). True, the Sega system's visuals were clunky compared to Pippin, but Sega was cheap, and thousands of developers were already writing games for it.

> Being three years ahead of your market—and costing twice as much as your competitors—is a bad formula.

"In the end," former CEO Gil Amelio lamented, "Pippin just faded away, another missed opportunity." Well, not exactly: Amelio pulled the plug on Pippin before the end of 1996. "Apple essentially admitted that it had failed once again," as Michael S. Malone puts it. "It had the core of Larry Ellison's $500 Network Computer ready a year before the competition, and it had once again failed to follow through."[13]

The lesson? It's not just about finding the future; it's about following through, once you've found it. And here, more often than not, is where the money comes into play.

Follow the (R&D) Money

Innovation doesn't come from money; it comes from people. On the other hand, innovating without money is nearly impossible—especially in the high-tech realm—where competitors will pay what's necessary to steal your best technical and engineering talent. Holding on to that talent means paying competitive salaries. It also means spending enough money in interesting directions to keep the talent happy.

In its early years, Apple more or less spent what was necessary to get the R&D job done, almost without controls. (Many observers of that period describe the company as "lacking adult supervision"; nowhere was this more true than in R&D.) The arrival of John Sculley in 1983 as CEO—arguably, Apple's first full-time professional manager—might have signaled a more disciplined approach to spending for innovation. In fact, the opposite proved true. Sculley decided that Apple needed new products to survive, and launched a series of expensive research initiatives, including Newton. The corporate plan for 1991, for example, called for new products to be developed and introduced in every quarter.[14] As a result, Apple's R&D budget was proportionally much larger than those of its competitors. Compaq's R&D budget, for example, was only half as big, relative to sales.[15]

> Follow through! With no follow-through, the future can't work.

Sculley also invested in the infrastructure of innovation. In 1990, he built a new R&D complex at headquarters in Cupertino, in large part because he was having a hard time persuading his software designers to come into work. (They complained that the existing open-floor-with-cubicles plan was too noisy and distracting.) The *New York Times* wrote a generally laudatory account of the result:

> *This spirit is what Silicon Valley is supposed to be all about— quiet informality combined with intense commitment. What*

makes the scene unusual is that the building is designed for this type of interaction and that it provides plenty of private space for workers as well ...

The six-building R&D campus, which is partly occupied but won't have its full complement of 2,300 workers until later this year, represents a fundamental shift in the culture of a company founded in a garage 15 years ago by two bearded young men in blue jeans. The design marks the end of Apple's commitment to open-plan offices, which it has used in all R&D in the past.[16]

But as Sculley made these moves, he had the huge advantage of money in the bank. His successor, Michael Spindler, did not have this luxury. Within weeks of taking over as CEO in the summer of 1993, Spindler announced large-scale layoffs across the company—and also announced that R&D would be reduced to 6 percent of sales, more in line with industry norms.[17] But R&D crept back up under Spindler, topping $600 million in 1995. When Gil Amelio succeeded the short-lived Spindler in January 1996, his overall impression was that Apple's management had "let R&D run wild."[18] But Amelio's response was not to cut R&D significantly, but rather, to focus the company on better product planning, so that its R&D dollars would be spent in more productive directions. (See Figure 2.1.[19])

Amelio came and went within 500 days. (The March of the Apple CEOs will be described in detail in Chapter 12.) Steve Jobs, returning in the summer of 1997 to a sea of red ink, did what he had to do—which, among other things meant cutting R&D dollars by more than *half* from

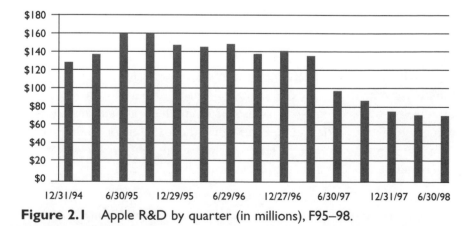

Figure 2.1   Apple R&D by quarter (in millions), F95–98.

their 1995 peak. (He also killed the Newton, which some took to be a case of vengeance, pure and simple, against nemesis John Sculley's pet project.) The Apple community trembled: Was this the beginning of the end of innovation at one of America's most innovative companies? Was even the visionary Steve Jobs (*Steve Jobs???*) willing to eat the seed corn, and forget about the future?

In a word: No. Even before the company's financial picture improved, Jobs began pumping money back into R&D. Between 2000 and 2002, for example, Apple's revenues fell from $8 billion to $5.7 billion. (Remember that this was in the heart of a sharp recession.) In that same period, however, the company's annual R&D spending increased from $380 million to $446 million.[20] This was still well below the lofty $600 million plus peaks of the mid 1990s, but it was a clear sign of recommitment to innovation.

> If you believe in the future, and your future lies in R&D, don't starve R&D.

One of the clearest pictures of Apple's R&D spending emerged from CFO Fred Anderson's speech at the U.S. 2003 Technology Conference. In the 2003 fiscal year, Anderson revealed, Apple's R&D spending was running at an annual rate of about $500 million, up some 42 percent from the dark days of 1999. Of that $500 million total, 49 percent was being spent on hardware development, 29 percent on the Mac operating system, and the remainder on applications.[21]

It's worth remembering that Apple is, at heart, a *hardware* company that also writes software. Fully half of its R&D dollars have to go into hardware-related innovation, an expense that a "pure" software company like Microsoft doesn't incur. At the same time, Apple absolutely *has* to keep upgrading its operating system hardware, an expense that the Dells of the world sidestep entirely. In the same year that Anderson spoke at the Technology Conference, Apple's sales were about a fifth of Dell's, and yet their R&D budgets were roughly the same, in absolute dollars. In other words, Apple was spending up to 8 percent of sales on R&D, while Dell was spending an unvarying 1.5 percent.[22]

This is both the bad news and the good news, all at once: Apple is *on the hook* to innovate, along multiple dimensions, in ways that neither the Microsofts nor the Dells of the world are. Even in the worst of times, those R&D dollars have to be found. And, because they are found, Apple continues to find the future.

Less Can Be More

Successful innovation requires not only money and people, but also a *strategy*. Sometimes, thinking strategically means doing more with less—especially when, as we've seen, R&D dollars tend to stay in parallel with revenues. And this, in turn, often means deciding to do less.

Apple always prided itself on being responsive to customer needs—although, as we will see in later chapters, it wasn't always particularly good at figuring out what those needs might be. By the mid 1990s, main-

> Being forced to spend R&D dollars is a bad thing. And a good thing.

ly in the name of responsiveness, Apple featured an astoundingly complicated product line. With something like 80 models and variations, turning over at a rapid clip, no one—not even the people who were supposed to be selling the machines out there in the retail world—could keep up. As former Apple CEO Gil Amelio recalled the situation:

> *[The] attitude was, 'If a customer wants it, we have to build it.' …What we were really building was confusion. Customers came to buy and left bewildered. And the cost of inventory and maintaining these many products in the distribution channel was deflating our profit margins.*[23]

Amelio didn't last long enough in the CEO's office to effect significant changes in this realm. But his successor, Steve Jobs, did. Perceiving exactly the same problems as Amelio before him, Jobs came up with an exquisitely simple grid for product planning—and, by extension, for innovation. "We sell consumer products and professionally oriented products," he told his colleagues. "We need a desktop offering and a portable offering in each of those two categories." So the math was easy: Two times two equals four. As Jobs explained in 1998:

> *If we could make four great product platforms, that's all we need. We can put our A team on every single one of them, instead of having a B or C team on any. We can turn them out much faster. So that's what we set out to do.*[24]

Following this simple plan, the "A team" set out to innovate in four (and only four) areas. The first result was a desktop for the professional market, the Power Mac G3, which was twice as fast as comparable Wintel machines and sold more than a million units in its first year on the market. Next came the PowerBook G3 (professional/portable), also highly successful, to the extent that Apple wasn't able to keep up with demand for the larger-screen model.

The consumer side of the two-times-two equation was even more successful. On August 15, 1998, Apple started shipping the phenomenally popular iMac, the desktop product that first began to persuade people that Jobs might actually be able to reverse Apple's declining fortunes. "One price, one model, one box, one decision," said Jobs of his phenomenally popular innovation.[25] (There was more than one color, but consumers seemed prepared to deal with at least this level of choice.) Last, but not least, came the iBook: the consumer portable introduced in 1999 that can be seen as the embodiment of the vision that Jobs first sketched out at that Mac divisional retreat, way back in 1983. With its titanium-clad counterpart, the TiBook, the iBook sold almost a million units in 2001, almost twice the volume of peak-year PowerBook sales.[26]

Successful innovation combines inspiration, resources, *and* strategy.

Sleeping Well

At the center of the innovation story, as noted above, is the elusive and enigmatic figure of Steve Jobs.

Less important figures in the history of Apple have written books explaining their point of view; Jobs has not. But, he has given us occasional glimpses of how he thinks about innovation, and the challenge of looking into the future. In a 1995 interview most notable for his obvious hostility to Apple—from which he had been displaced by his former mentor, John Sculley—Jobs marveled aloud at the innovative traditions of his native California, and especially of the San Francisco/Berkeley/ Bay Area:

> *You've got the invention of the integrated circuit, the invention of the microprocessor, the invention of semi-conductor memory, the invention of the modern hard drive, the invention of the floppy disk drive, the invention of the personal computer, [the] invention of genetic engineering, the invention of object-oriented technology, the invention of graphical user interfaces at PARC, followed by Apple, the invention of networking. All that happened in this Bay Area. It's incredible...*

I mean, this is where the beatnik happened, in San Francisco
… This is where the hippie movement happened. This is the only
place in America where rock and roll really happened …

You've also had Stanford and Berkeley, two awesome univer-
sities, drawing smart people from all over the world and deposit-
ing them in this clean, sunny, nice place where there's a whole
bunch of other smart people and pretty good food. And at times,
a lot of drugs and all of that. So they stayed.

There's a lot of human capital pouring in. Really smart peo-
ple. People seem pretty bright here, relative to the rest of the coun-
try. People seem pretty open-minded here relative to the rest of the
country…[27]

So, *context* is critical, as Jobs sees it. Innovation happens when great people congregate, bounce off each other. (Good weather and pretty good food also help.) But equally important is *mind-set*—the determination, as Jobs put it, "to express something of what [you] perceive to be the truth around [you] so that others can benefit from it." Innovation is simply the fruit of that determination. Lots of people at Apple, Jobs explained, straddled the distinction between "artist" and "scientist." They were computer jocks, but they could have been poets:

If you study these people a little bit more, what you'll find is that
in this particular time, in the '70s and '80s, the best people in com-
puters would have normally been poets and writers and musi-
cians. Almost all of them were musicians. A lot of them were poets
on the side. They went into computers because it was so com-
pelling. It was fresh and few. It was a new medium of expression
for their creative talents. The feelings and the passion that people
put into it were completely indistinguishable from a poet or a
painter. Many of the people were introspective, inward people who
expressed how they felt about other people, or the rest of humani-
ty in general, in their work—work that other people would use.
People put a lot of love into these products, and a lot of expression
of their appreciation came to these things.[28]

Three years later, at the 1998 Seybold Conference—an annual confab of Web-based publishers, which represents a critically important market to Apple—Jobs took a question from the audience. The questioner asked, in so many words, when Jobs would feel comfortable about

Apple's future. When would he feel that he had turned the company around?

Jobs, then a little more than a year into his second incarnation at Apple, thought about the question for a moment. Then, in his typical fashion, he turned the *question* around. Our goal, he said—adopting his customary first-person-plural voice—isn't to turn the company around according to a set schedule. Our goal is to make the better products that we know are out there to be made. It is to make the *best* products:

> *The reason a lot of us are at Apple is to make the best computers in the world, and make the best software in the world. We know that we've got some stuff that [is] the best right now. But it can be so much better. So we don't come to work every day thinking, 'Well, when are we going to turn Apple around?' We come to work every day knowing we know how to make even better products.*
>
> *So that's what's driving us. The turnaround is just one milestone on a long road, and it's not for us to declare. Somebody else can decide when that happens. But we're out to make the best products in the world. And we'll sleep well when we do that.*[29]

Making the best products in the world—and sleeping well—means many things. It means working within known boundaries, and making existing products just a little bit better: design, manufacturing, and so on. It means pushing at those boundaries—putting a new idea in an old context, or an old idea in a new context. But most important, it means *finding the future*. And, although Apple hasn't always delivered on its discoveries, it can certainly claim to have found the future far more often than most other corporations.

Lessons from the Future

What puts Apple in a class with the other great innovators—legendary organizations like Xerox, Sony, and Bell Labs? There are at least seven lessons that Apple has learned, over time:

- **Share the vision. Make it tangible. Make it visible.** Years after the fact—after Steve Jobs was gone from Apple, and before he came back—R&D people at the company remembered the mock-up of a computer that became the PowerBook: the best-selling computer ever, up to that point.

- **People + strategy + dollars = a window on the future.** To inno-vate successfully, you need the right people, the right strategy, and adequate resources.

- **The future isn't always welcome, and—without nurturing—it may not stick around.** Some of the best ideas in history have been pooh-poohed by the people who should have been their best friends. Some great products have left a willing market sim-ply through neglect.

- **Being three years ahead of your market—and costing twice as much as your competitors—is a bad formula.** Ask the peo-ple who believed (and in some cases, *still* believe!) in the Newton. Ask the people who hoped that Pippin would beat Sega.

- **Follow through!** With no follow-through, the future can't work.

- **If you believe in the future, and your future lies in R&D, don't starve R&D.** To the extent that Apple has succeeded, it is mostly the result of brilliant innovations—plus some good market-ing, and some occasional management.

- **Being forced to spend R&D dollars is a bad thing.** And a good thing. Apple's R&D budget is approximately a tenth of Microsoft's. Half of Apple's R&D budget goes to hardware. So, Apple can only spend a twentieth as much as Microsoft on software development, in any given year. But is that hardware money well spent? Well, watch the iPods and Mac minis flying out of the Apple Stores.

Chapter 3

Take Their Breath Away

I know what I want and I know what they want.

—Steve Jobs

This is a chapter about something called "design." As I'll use the term here, design won't include the development and defense of a unique operating system, which is the subject of the next chapter. This chapter focuses on the process whereby a product *takes form*.

Maybe this doesn't sound like a big enough topic for a whole chapter. Don't things take the form that they're supposed to take, based on what they're supposed to do? Doesn't a toaster, for example, have a couple of slots in the top, and a big knob or lever of some sort to get the toast to go up and down?

Yes and no. Yes, form follows function, as the architects say. Toasters definitely need slots and knobs to do their job. And yes, some computer makers have decided not to worry much about the design of their products, past the purely functional. (Based on what we're going to stuff inside it, how big does it have to be? How heavy does that turn out to be? What's the price point that results? Is that OK?)

> Form follows function. Except when it leads function, or runs alongside it.

On the other hand, design can be more than function-following. It can be political. It can be subversive. It can be didactic. It can be seductive. It can be a differentiator in a market (personal computers) that has long been woefully underdifferentiated.

Over the years, Apple's designs have been all of those things. And in the last decade or so—more or less coincident with Steve Jobs's return to the company—Apple has emerged as the source of some of the most sophisticated industrial designs in the world, and that has helped keep the company alive.

Take 2002, for example. In that year, the iMac won the gold medal in the prestigious Industrial Design Excellence Awards (IDEA) Computer Products category. ("Apple does it again!" enthused the judges. "Innovation, ease of use, aesthetics and fit and finish are all expected from Apple. The new iMac exceeds expectations in each of these dimensions. The iMac is a paradigm shift that will be copied but is unlikely to be surpassed.")

Also in 2002, iPod won "best of best" from Design Zentrum Nordrhein Westfalen, Essen, Germany. (*The user interface is functional, ergonomic, and logical; titles are selected using a scrollwheel according to playlist, song, or artist.*") And in the same year, the iBook also won "best of best." ("When are computers really made for people? Design and technology are crucial in deciding that ... The design of the Apple iBook facilitates a very uncomplicated relationship with the user.") And Germans—as we will see—know good design.[1]

As in the previous chapter, Steve Jobs plays an enormously important role in the Apple design story. He was, and is, a fanatic for telling detail—

> Finding the future isn't enough. You also have to deliver it.

every telling detail. He is never content to "find the future" and let someone else deliver it. To an almost astonishing degree, he has participated—and participates today—in determining how big the future will be, what it will be made of, the colors it will be available in (if it's black, *which* black), its expansion and connectivity capabilities, and so on. He doesn't always get it right, but he gets it right, very right, more often than most.

Design: From Naked to Normative

Because Apple has become synonymous with world-class industrial design, it might seem that this was always the case. Not true. Apple's first product, the Apple I, was actually sold without a case. Purchasers (mostly hobbyists, and therefore likely to have a workshop in the basement or the garage) bought Steve Wozniak's elegant circuit board and built their own enclosure for it—boxes that ranged from simple wooden contraptions to riveted metal containers.[2]

This wasn't the way the other Steve—Jobs, the less technically oriented of the two—wanted it. He already had developed strong ideas about how this new machine should present itself to the world. Among his relatively few personal possessions were several boxes made out of an exotic light-colored wood called *koa*, and Jobs decided that he wanted koa cases for the Apple I. When this proved prohibitively expensive, Jobs gave up, and in 1976, the Apple I went out into the world naked.[3]

The Apple II, which went on sale in 1977, represented Jobs's first design statement. Jobs felt strongly that the *appearance* of the computer played a key role in how the customer would think about, and therefore use, the computer. (Function follows form.) He wanted people to think of the Apple II as an appliance—something familiar and friendly, like a toaster oven, rather than

> If your product is inherently scary, go to great lengths to make it look friendly.

something mysterious and hostile. He haunted the aisles of Macy's, studying the design of appliances: what worked, what didn't. He hired industrial designer Jerry Manock to design a box for an appliance that had never existed before, but still had to look like it had always been there. He argued with Wozniak about the *height* of the new computer; Woz wanted expansion slots for the hobbyist, which required vertical space; Jobs knew the home user couldn't care less about expansion slots.

Jobs lost the argument, and the Apple II wound up taller than he wanted (and you could *still* buy a naked one). But he also won a few battles. At his insistence, the Apple II came in a molded plastic case, the first computer ever delivered in a plastic box, rather than a sheet-metal enclosure. And, far more important, the Apple II looked like someone had *cared* about how it would sit on a desk and how a user would interact with it. This is taken for granted today, but in 1977, it was unprecedented. *Byte* magazine called it "elegantly styled," and likened it to an "overgrown pocket calculator," which for *Byte* was probably high praise.

But Steve Jobs didn't get the chance to fully exercise his design vision until the creation of the Macintosh (1984). Significantly, this was after he and Woz were running separate divisions in the company—the Mac and Apple II divisions, respectively—and Jobs now had significantly more running room. His active exclusion from the Lisa project also motivated him to show his stuff, which he did, with a vengeance. The Mac (also designed by Jerry Manock, along with Terry Oyama) was a startling departure from everything that had gone before it. The screen and "brain" came packaged together in a single unit, which meant both fewer cables and a far more coherent look. Yes, the Mac looked like the vaguely familiar appliance that Jobs had been aiming to build all along. But it also had a jaunty, friendly, almost *human* cast. It had a little recessed handgrip on top that practically *invited* you to pick it up and put it someplace else. Its off-center floppy disk port, with a wider opening on one end to facilitate insertion and removal of disks, looked slightly cartoony, as if the Mac was just about to whisper something very funny to you.

The Mac's design, according to Terry Oyama, wasn't a "Jobs design," and yet, it was:

> *Even though Steve didn't draw any of the lines, his ideas and inspiration made the design what it is. To be honest, we didn't know what it meant for a computer to be "friendly" until Steve told us.*[4]

There's another side to the Mac design story, though, which illustrates the risks and complexities inherent in letting one (brilliant) person call all the shots. Jobs knew exactly how he wanted people to use his invention—*friendly, toaster oven, nonthreatening*—and he "designed in" features that made it difficult to use the Mac in any other way. You couldn't open up the Mac case without a special screwdriver. If you *did* get inside the case (thereby voiding the warranty!), you found you couldn't add expansion cards, or even more memory.

Part of this rigidity grew out of the recent Lisa disaster. (*See the Introduction.*) With its 1 MB storage capacity, Lisa was too expensive and didn't sell: dead on arrival. Jobs, determined not to make the same mistake with his own baby, mandated that the Mac could only have 128 kB of random access memory (RAM). This was in part to protect the price point—originally supposed to be under $1,000, but creeping toward the eventual $2,500—but it was also about *control*. The Mac's design was normative: *Here's how I will be used.* Again,

> Even a know-it-all doesn't necessarily know it all. Even a genius know-it-all.

function follows form. Jobs explicitly forbade his design team to even build in the capacity for more memory, somewhere down the road. But the Mac's principal hardware engineer, Burrell Smith, surreptitiously defied Jobs, building in space for up to 512 kB of RAM.

When the Mac went on the market in January 1984, it quickly became clear that its memory was far too limited. Burrell Smith's "secret compartment" was soon discovered, and within seven months, Apple had a 512-kB RAM Mac on the market.

The Jobs Aesthetic

Steve Jobs is often likened to Henry Ford, and the parallels can be eerie. They were both young, naïve, and inexperienced when they burst upon their respective scenes. They both began with powerful visions of how their products would change the world and then made those visions come to life. Both were focused on *customer needs*, and yet, both were quite willing to tell the customer what he or she needed. Ford would sell you any color Model T you wanted, as long as it was black. Jobs wouldn't countenance a hard drive in his Mac, because Jobs knew, *in his bones*, that a friendly toaster oven shouldn't need a hard drive.

There are also important differences between Ford and Jobs. Ford innovated mainly as a *manufacturer*; he didn't care much about design and similar fripperies. He was a single-minded and small-minded person: an anti-Semitic former race car driver who took his inspiration from the disassembly lines of local meat-packing plants. Ford turned a horse-drawn carriage into a horseless carriage. He didn't give a damn about what color the carriage might be—at least until Alfred Sloan's General Motors, with its profusion of product choices, started eating his lunch in the 1920s.

Jobs was something very different. It seems that he was born with an impulse toward perfectionism, which meant that he had to *follow through*, worrying about every last detail of his creations. Nothing less than perfect was good enough. John Sculley recalls a story from the early Mac days:

> *Little details obsessed Steve. Time and time again, the engineers would come back to him, saying they couldn't design a piece of plastic to conform to the odd shape of the Macintosh computer case, which Steve insisted had to be all one piece. Its construction represented a manufacturing breakthrough.*

'Steve, we can't do it. It's too complex,' one of the industrial design engineers told him.

'I don't buy that,' he snapped. 'If you can't do it, I'll find someone else who can.'

Eventually, it was done—but it took something like 15 separate forming tools to make one piece of injection molding for the case.[5]

So, Jobs knew what "perfection" looked like. But *how*? He was basically a nerdy kid from a middle-class nerdy background who didn't get very far through Reed College. He had no training whatsoever in art, architecture, or industrial design. So, where did his singular vision come from?

The answer seems to be that Jobs, almost completely self-taught, was an amazingly quick study. For inspiration for the Apple II, he roamed the product aisles at Macy's. He scrutinized how companies with a reputation for high-end hardware worked their magic. In Apple's early days, for example, the company shared a building with Sony's regional sales office. Jobs, writes Alan Deutschman, took full advantage of this proximity:

Steve would come over and look with great interest at Sony's marketing materials, its letterheads and logos and graphics, the paraphernalia of its corporate identity. He would feel the paper stock to get a sense of its weight and quality. He had an obsession with the visual and the physical, but his judgment was not yet highly developed. He had the impulse for aesthetic perfectionism, but not the unshakable self-confidence that he needed to achieve it.[6]

So, he kept studying, dissecting, absorbing. He scrutinized high-end German products—including Braun appliances, Bösendorfer pianos, BMW motorcycles, Porsche and Mercedes cars—trying to figure out exactly what made them so pleasing to touch, to use, to drive. John Sculley recalls finding Jobs strolling through the Apple parking lot one day, studying the cars he was finding there. "Over the years," he said to Sculley, as he pointed at a nearby Mercedes, "they've made the lines softer but the details starker. That's what we have to do with the Mac."[7]

How to become an aesthete:
1. Pay attention
2. Get help

But Jobs apparently realized that, on his own, he couldn't attain the lofty heights occupied by the likes of Sony, Braun, and

Porsche. Therefore, early in 1982, he organized a competition to find and hire a world-class industrial designer to push Apple to the next level. Based on a review of industrial design magazines, Apple asked a small number of leading designers to enter the competition in an industrial design "bake-off." The winner, as it turned out, was a relatively unknown German named Hartmut Esslinger. In the spring of 1983, Esslinger moved to California, set up a company called frogdesign, Inc., and signed an exclusive contract with Apple to provide design services.[8]

The contract was rich—$100,000 a month, plus billable time and expenses—but frogdesign put a stamp on Apple that endures to this day. The designers selected distinctive typefaces, grids, and colors, and rolled them out across the company in a thoroughgoing onslaught. Everything from products to collateral materials to owner's manuals got the frogdesign treatment. Nothing was too mundane to be left imperfect. "We want to make books that are so gorgeous," explained Chris Espinosa, **Don't go halfway with your aesthetic. Go all the way.** the original manager of writers for the Mac instruction manuals, "that you read once and then keep on your shelf because they look so great."[9] Lots of people at Apple at that time would have said the same sort of thing, more or less cheerfully.

This was only possible because of the close relationship between Jobs and Esslinger. Esslinger reported directly to Jobs, and both shared and shaped his client's tastes. Nominally, CEO John Sculley was in charge of the company at this point. But Mac division head Steve Jobs was in charge of taking your breath away.

Designing without Jobs

Jobs left Apple in September 1985, in an unhappy rupture with John Sculley. Apple, facing severe budget constraints, began trying to renegotiate its expensive contract with frogdesign (and began paying its monthly bills late). Eventually, Esslinger gave up on Apple and went to work with Jobs at his new company: NeXT Computer.

Jobs's successor as head of product development was a colorful Frenchman named Jean-Louis Gassée. Gassée didn't subscribe to Jobs's notion of appliances styled (and priced) for the masses. Instead, he—like the doomed and soon-to-depart John Sculley—looked for ever more ways to push Apple's prices up and increase its gross margins. Gassée encouraged Apple's engineers to build more bells and whistles into the Mac, in part to increase its appeal to a corporate audience (and push up those margins!). This was good, in some ways: Only high margins could underwrite the R&D that was needed to keep Apple competitive. But as designer Charles Eames was fond of saying, creative constraints actually *help* designers do their work. Pulling out the stops, and cozying up to an unresponsive corporate audience didn't help. They contributed to Apple's becalming in the later 1980s, and its decline in the 1990s.

A scruffy young English designer named Jonathan Ive joined the company in 1992. He had come full of high hopes, expecting to find the Apple of Steve Jobs's day, but he was sorely disappointed. The company, he later recalled, "seemed to have lost what had once been a very clear sense of identify and purpose. Apple had started trying to compete to an agenda set by an industry that had never shared its goals."[10]

In the absence of a powerful leader with a strong aesthetic sense, Apple continued to flounder in the first half of the 1990s, and come up with limp designs for limp machines. It is instructive, and more than a little depressing, to read CEO Gil Amelio's account of a dinner he attended, sometime in the 1995–96 period, with Hollywood talent agent Jeff Berg:

> *I was impressed with Berg's knowledge of Apple; he surprised me with his sanguine comments on issues he thought I should keep in mind to make the company successful—continuing to improve the technology while developing the user experience. He pushed hard, as well, on the idea of industrial design—making our products sexy looking. This was a notion I gravitated to quickly, because I agreed totally: A computer that's great looking is a real plus in the marketplace. (In accepting the idea, I was unknowingly paying homage to one of the wiser of Steve Jobs's approaches.)*[11]

Well, yeah. A computer that's great looking is a real plus in the marketplace. But this earnest, plodding interpretation—*sexy looking, great looking*—doesn't come close to capturing what Jobs's relentless perfectionism was all about. In Amelio's defense, this wasn't exactly working in his wheelhouse. But as CEO, it fell to him to fix Apple's problem. And in the design realm, he discovered that he was struggling with a toxic legacy created by a decade of green-eyeshade types and freestanding, self-absorbed engineers:

*I found it highly frustrating that I could not get the Apple engi-
neers to appreciate design. They were so tuned in to performance,
features, operating systems, and speed that I had more pushback
on industrial design than any of the other [consumer-facing val-
ues], which frankly surprises me to this day, since Apple R&D is
filled with engineers and engineering managers [who are] among
the most visual and creative people I've ever met.[12]*

All in all, this was a bizarre circumstance, like a nonmusician telling
the members of the philharmonic to *appreciate the score* a bit, please.
When Amelio tried to bring what he considered to be an exciting new
desktop computer to market—code-named "Spartacus" and featuring a
dazzling brain-and-screen combination perched atop an elegant curved-
metal stand—he met strenuous resistance from Apple engineers, who
said the machine's relatively slow CD-ROM drive would doom it in the
marketplace. Spartacus was, in Amelio's estimation, "industrial design fit
to be displayed at the Museum of Modern Art," and engineers were
squelching it for alleged performance shortcomings that (at least as
Amelio saw it) customers would never even notice.

By the time Spartacus got to market—as the limited edition, 20th-
anniversary Mac; both overpriced and underpowered—other companies
had gotten there before it, effectively dooming it to the oblivion of the
also-rans.

Back to the Future, Again

Almost as soon as he returned to Apple in the summer of 1997, Jobs was
spotted carrying around a piece of white molded foam that looked like a
cross between a TV monitor and an oversized bicycle helmet. This, as it
turned out, was a mock-up for a new computer that Jobs eventually
named the "iMac" (with the "i" standing for "Internet," which was a bit of
creative marketing).

The designer of that machine, Jonathan Ive, couldn't have been happier. The company he *thought* he had joined in 1992 was suddenly coming out of hiding, and—happily—calling on his own design skills:

*This only changed when Steve Jobs returned to the company. By
reestablishing the core values he had established at the beginning,
Apple again pursued a direction which was clear and different*

*from any other company's. Design and innovation formed an
important part of this new direction.[13]*

Originally, the iMac was conceived as a super-low-end network computer, along the lines envisioned by Jobs's friend (and Oracle CEO) Larry
Ellison. In many ways, it was a reversion to Jobs's original conception of
the Mac: a stripped-down, consumer-
friendly appliance. Like the original Mac,
the iMac went through a gradual price-
creep, but Jobs stubbornly stuck with his
vision of an all-in-one machine. The indus-
try was telling him that all-in-one was poison, but Jobs didn't believe it.
"I know what I want," he told a friend, "and I know what they want."[14]

**If you know what they
want, *give* it to them.
Ignore the skeptics.**

The translucent blue iMac (followed by iMacs in four other translucent colors) was an instant hit. Something like 278,000 units jumped off
the shelves in the six weeks between June 15, 1998, and the end of July,
and Apple had trouble meeting the demand.

The world applauded. Well, *most* of the world. One hold-out was the
Wall Street Journal, which complained that the iMac wasn't all that innovative and that, anyway, Steve Jobs was up against some pretty lame
competition:

> *Apple Computer chief Steve Jobs is being hailed as a bold revolu-
> tionary for introducing a new model of the company's hot iMac
> computer that comes in five bright colors, instead of the pallid
> beige that marks most of the world's PCs. This move follows his
> scandalous decision last year to clad the original iMac in a
> translucent blue case.*
>
> *Mr. Jobs, who is currently reviving Apple with good design
> and clever marketing, is indeed a revolutionary in the computer
> business. But he achieved that distinction for truly innovative
> products earlier in his career, not for selling colored computers.
> His iMac is a good machine that sells well, but it's hardly a break-
> through under its curvy covers. The attention he has drawn for the
> iMac says more about the computer industry's abysmal lack of
> design ingenuity than it does about him.*
>
> *In what other biz would it be a big deal to offer your products
> in colors, or with rounded contours? Imagine this news flash:*

'Ford Motor disclosed today that it will offer its new cars in a variety of colors and shapes.' Duh. Mr. Jobs deserves credit for his new design, but in his business, out-designing competitors is hardly a big challenge . . .

In general, however, the PC industry gives little or no thought to good design. It behaves less like the current Ford Motor Co., and more like that automaker in its early days, when it bragged that it only built cars in black. And the lack of color and style is only the most obvious of the industry's design lapses.

Point taken. But what the *Journal* wasn't saying was that "good design and clever marketing" was increasingly critical to Apple's very survival. Like the tortoise in the fable, Bill Gates in the years before the iMac's introduction had been slowly closing the gap between Apple's fleet operating system and Microsoft's own clunky knock-off. Windows 95—the first really good Microsoft operating system—had gone a long way toward making *every other computer in the world* competitive with Apple computers.

So, Apple was, and is, forced to innovate noisily at the margins. This sometimes led to bad mistakes—design for the sake of design, form following form. An example is the mouse that originally shipped with the first million-or-so iMacs:

It looked good—it just didn't work worth a darn. Take away its good looks, and it's what you would imagine a Soviet-era mouse would be like—clunky and awkward. It was shaped like a hockey puck (which should have tipped somebody off), and because it was perfectly round, you never knew which way was up when you grabbed it . . . Third-party vendors almost immediately began creating slip-on covers you could put over your heinous hockey puck to make it work like a regular mouse.[15]

In other words, an "unworkable concession to aesthetics," as one writer put it, and therefore a minor disaster.[16] Belatedly, Apple ditched the hockey puck in favor of an optical mouse, and the tempest subsided.

But the larger point still pertains: Apple must push the envelope, take risks, and continue to take our breath away. It's a high-wire act. Great design alone won't cut it; it takes great design tied to a great user concept, floated by a not-unreasonable price. The G4 Cube, a dismal failure, was introduced in 2000 and taken off the market in 2001, the same year that a Cube was acquired by the Museum of Modern Art in New York. (It was one of six Apple products acquired that year for MOMA's permanent collection.) Steve Jobs, contacted by the *New York Times*, said that while he was "surprised and honored" at MOMA's move to acquire the Cube, "the reason we care about design has more to do with touching the everyday lives of users."

Innovate: but don't force it.

The Cube, reported the *Times*, "radiated a Zen-like calm, but sales did not live up to expectations," for which Jobs provided a surprisingly unvarnished explanation:

> 'That was not a failure of design,' Mr. Jobs said. 'It was a failure of concept. We targeted the Cube at a professional audience. We thought they would rather have something small on the desk than expandability and we were wrong. It was a wrong concept—fabulously implemented.'[17]

"I know what I want," Jobs says, "and I know what they want"— except that nobody's perfect—even a perfectionist.

The Sleek Shall Inherit the Earth

As of this writing, Apple is again riding high, and spectacular industrial design plays a huge role in its current success. As *BusinessWeek* recently noted, Apple is nearly unique among contemporary technology companies in doing all of its own design in-house, at its Cupertino campus. Other companies have outsourced most or all of their product-design function, counting on outsourced design manufacturers (ODMs) to come up with products that—with minor tinkering and adapting—will fit into their product lines.

Not Apple. The company (read "Steve Jobs") apparently believes that having all the experts in the same place—the mechanical, electrical, software, and industrial engineers, as well as the product designers—leads to a more holistic perspective on product development. A critical mass of talent makes existing products better, and opens the door to entirely new products. For example, when

Assembling a critical mass of design talent may beat outsourcing. Just ask Steve Jobs.

it became clear that the iPod needed a "baby brother"—a smaller $100 flash-memory-based model, rather than the high-end $300 and $400 models—Apple's designers figured out a way to cut the iPod's circuit board in half and stack the two halves on top of one another. This configuration used height that was already needed for the battery, but cut the Shuffle's width roughly in half.[18] Neat. Not a solution that would have emerged from an ODM in the Far East.

In all of this, as noted earlier, Steve Jobs plays a surprisingly hands-on role. He sweats the big stuff. He sweats the small stuff. He sweats everything.

Which leads us back, again, to the joys and terrors of having *one person* play such a prominent role in the fate of a company, especially in a realm as subjective as design. Alan Deutschman makes the case that Apple was relatively late getting to the compact disk, read-write (CD-RW) party in large part because Steve Jobs himself was out of touch with a younger generation's tastes and priorities. (Does a billionaire with his own Gulfstream V jet have to steal music over the Internet? No.) Similarly, suggests Deutschman, Apple flourishes when Jobs follows his fine-tuned market nose in the direction of a playful, friendly, consumer-appliance aesthetic (the Mac, the iMac)—but hits the rocks when the CEO exercises his *own* aesthetic, which is "austere, rarified, minimalist, cold, refined: the understated taste of an aloof elitist."[19] This is the realm of the ill-fated NeXT computer, and the G4 Cube that bore more than a passing resemblance to that earlier cube.

The good news for Apple, of course, may be that little item called iPod, which—in an austere, rarified, and minimalist way—gives that younger generation a *really cool* (but not cold) way to party down.

Lessons in Taking Their Breath Away

So what do three decades of consistently amazing industrial design teach us? At least eight things:

- **Form follows function. Except when it leads function, or runs alongside it.** Apple sometimes observes the time-honored maxim of form following function. And other times, including some of Apple's biggest successes, form *dictates* function, or at least is a coequal.

- **Finding the future isn't enough.** You also have to deliver it. Steve Jobs's relentless perfectionism is the medium that brings the future to life. No, he's not easy to work with, but he delivers.
- **If your product is inherently scary, go to great lengths to make it look friendly.** The personal computer, as Jobs saw it, had to look like a consumer appliance to win over the consumer. Even the most exotic Apple products are, at heart, appliances.
- **Even a know-it-all doesn't necessarily know it all. Even a genius know-it-all.** A compelling vision can be blinding. Sometimes the visionary needs a little myopia around just to keep good options open.
- **How to become an aesthete: pay attention, and get help.** Study the world around you, and hire a good coach. Start with the classical center, and work your way out toward the avant-garde edges. Be aware that you'll begin as a conservative (a fan of, say, Victorian-era gingerbread), and get wackier over time (becoming, say, a fan of Frank Gehry).
- **Don't go halfway with your aesthetic.** Go all the way. The great design companies of the world build their brands through a *relentless* application of their aesthetic. Go for broke.
- **If you know what they want, give it to them. Ignore the skeptics.** The boo-birds are always out there. If your gut is talking— and if your gut has a reasonable track record—follow your gut.
- **Innovate, but don't force it.** Otherwise, you'll wind up with a mouse that looks—and works—like a hockey puck. Take their breath away, but as a result of their cursing at you.

Chapter 4

Guard the Family Jewels

It was not a bosom to repose upon,
but it was a capital bosom to hang jewels upon.

—Charles Dickens

Imagine that you're a brilliant software engineer at Apple in the early 1980s. Let's say your name is Andy Hertzfeld. (Apologies to Andy Hertzfeld, who is in fact a real person.[1]) Your title on your business card is "Software Wizard." One of your jobs is to write the code that will enable the Macintosh—Apple's still under-deep-cover computer, scheduled for release in a year or two—to display something called a "scroll bar."

The scroll bar is the seemingly simple little tool on the right-hand side of the computer screen that lets the user move quickly from the top of the screen to the bottom and back again. It's something that we take for granted today, but back when the Macintosh was still only a gleam in Steve Jobs's eye, the scroll bar was a pain in Andy Hertzfeld's neck—*your* neck.

So, you sit down and write 80 dense pages of computer code, exploring all the ways that you could conceivably invent this "scroll bar" thing. This takes you several months, notable mostly for sleepless nights and bad food. Then you throw away three-quarters of your work, as you whittle down your solution to a state of elegant simplicity. Then you take a deep breath, and ask your boss, Steve Jobs, to take a look.

There is a chance that your boss will call everybody over to admire your work product. That will feel great.

There is also the possibility that your boss will call your work a *piece of shit* and storm around in a rage. That won't feel so good.[2]

Change without Change

"Elegantly simple" were the watchwords that Jobs used to describe the Mac, as he envisioned it. But simplicity was (and is) a deceptive concept, in the world of computer code. Sometimes the "simplest" code is the most complicated. This was true for the Mac operating system (OS), which had to fit within the 128 kilobytes (kB) of read-only memory (ROM) that Jobs had allocated to that system.

> "Simple" may be incredibly complicated.

The operating system, simply put, is the software that tells the hardware what to do, on a basic level: *on, off, restart*, and so on. It manages the computer's life-support systems. In other words, it's the equivalent of the medulla oblongata, the part of the brain that controls heartbeat and respiration. *Applications* software programs, by contrast, sit one step further out from the core. They tell the OS what to do. They are the cerebrums—the conscious brains—and they are the subject of the next chapter.

But, if you're a hardware maker like Apple, the OS is the family jewels. It's what makes your computer different from all those other ones out there. It's why IBM's long-ago decision to hand over responsibility for its PC operating systems to upstart Microsoft was so astounding, and fateful. *Here, Bill; here are the keys to the treasury.* But it was fateful only in retrospect, of course. Who knew that PCs were more than a toy?

It costs somewhere between $500 million and $1 billion to develop an OS from scratch for a PC. (There are a lot of expensive person-hours in there, in addition to the Jolt Cola and Twinkies.) If only for that reason, you'd want your billion-dollar OS to last a long time. In addition, though, you'd want your OS to be durable for two other reasons. First, as will be explained in the next chapter, you want to encourage outside developers to write applications that run on your OS. The

> Make a product that forces change but protects continuity.

more frequently you change the OS in fundamental ways—ways that require big changes in the applications packages—the crankier those developers are going to get.

Second, if you're a hardware company like Apple, you want to encourage your existing customer base to *buy a new computer* every two or three years. (This has historically been a problem for Apple, whose machines have tended to be at least a little more durable than the average PC, and therefore slower to turn into doorstops, boat anchors, or landfill.) From an OS standpoint, this entails striking a tricky balance. You want to introduce enough new features to persuade those buyers that it's time to upgrade hardware, as well as software, but you have to give those buyers *continuity* from one generation of OS to the next. Otherwise, they'll risk losing access to all those files they generated using your old OS, and they may lose the use of their favorite applications.

The Mac OS that Hertzfeld and others invented in the first half of the 1980s, dubbed System 1.0, consisted of six files and required 216 kB of random access memory (RAM). In RAM terms, Jobs's band of self-styled "pirates" had crammed a brilliant, graphics-based OS into an amazingly small amount of space—a marvel of compact and compelling software engineering. Contrast this with the specs that Apple came up with for System OS X (pronounced oh-ess-ten), released in September 2000. At least in its beta form, OS X required 128 *megabytes* of RAM, or roughly a thousand times as much RAM.[3]

In the intervening 15 years, obviously, "elegantly simple" went by the boards. Things got about a thousand times more complicated, in fact.

Dark Kernels

One reason why things got more complicated, as will also be explained in the next chapter, is that Microsoft managed to wangle a license from Apple in the mid 1980s to build the Mac graphical user interface (GUI) into new Microsoft applications—and gradually, into the "Windows" environment itself. Therefore, shortly after the arrival of the Mac in 1984, Microsoft began making the transition from the relatively dreadful DOS environment to a crude GUI of its own—a move that can more or less be dated to the fall of 1987, with the introduction of Windows 2.0.[4]

To many in the industry, and at least some in Cupertino, it was already clear that Apple would have to run hard to stay ahead of the legions from Redmond. The Mac OS would have to get better, and better, and better—while not changing *too* much, for reasons stated above—just to maintain its lead over Windows. Windows 3.0 (May 1990) closed the gap slightly (and sold an astounding 10 million copies). Windows 3.1 (April 1992) got a little closer to the GUI target (and sold another 3 million copies). It was like looking in your rear view and seeing an increasingly well-heeled tortoise gaining on you. It was like Butch Cassidy seeing the relentless trackers over his shoulder, and nervously asking the Sundance Kid, "Who *are* those guys?"

And a little later, remember, the Kid says, "They could surrender to us, but I wouldn't count on that."

Then, in August 1995, came a truly bad moment for Apple. That's when Microsoft released Windows 95, a GUI that really did start to approximate the Mac look and feel. True, the dark DOS kernel was still lurking there in the middle of Windows 95, but the Windows interface quickly chased DOS from the screen, and left the user looking

> Don't wait for the other guy to surrender. Especially if it's Microsoft.

at, well, an ugly and still somewhat counterintuitive sort of Mac. Mac users took to putting derisive bumper stickers on their cars ("Windows 95 = Macintosh 89"), but it was a clear case of whistling past the graveyard. *Word is closing in. They could surrender to us, but I wouldn't count on that.*

But Mac, meanwhile, had some dark-kernel problems of its own. One was the result of Steve Jobs's parsimonious approach to memory, back when he and his team were putting the original Mac System 1.0 together. To conserve space, Jobs decided *not* to "partition" the computer's memory in a way that would have separated out the OS from the applications. (This would have required more code, more memory, more power, a bigger box, and the steeper price tag that Jobs was trying to avoid. The fate of the overpriced Lisa was still in the front of everyone's minds.) The result? Every time an application program crashed, the OS would crash as well. It was a little like having the main circuit breaker in your house flip to the "off" position every time a light bulb blew.

No, this wasn't such a big problem for the first generation of Macs, with their relatively simple applications. But the situation got worse and worse in the decade between 1985 and 1995, as both the OS and apps in general got more complicated.[5]

Macs *crashed*, and crashed like crazy—annoying, frustrating, and sometimes scary. Work that had been completed before the crash but not yet saved to disk disappeared in the crash. Mac users got used to shutting their frozen computers down, rebooting, and holding their breath to see how much damage had been done. And just to make sure *everybody* wound up unhappy, a little dialogue box would come on the screen upon rebooting, informing you that your computer had been turned off improperly (nice use of the passive voice, suggesting that you yourself might have had something to do with this improper outcome!) and that from now on, you should try to behave yourself, please, while the blameless Mac picked itself up and dusted itself off and checked itself for any damage that you might have done to it. (Well, not in exactly those words, but take it from me, it *felt* like that.)

And there was yet another dark kernel in the Mac OS by the mid '90s, called "System 7." In March 1994, Apple launched its "PowerMac" series, based on IBM's powerful PowerPC microprocessor, which promised to make the Mac move up to *eight times* faster than previous generations of Macs. But, as short-lived CEO Gil Amelio later recalled, it didn't work out exactly that way:

> *Apple's OS suffered from problems tracing back to the company's transition to the newer generation PowerPC machines. The Mac OS had been modified to accommodate the changeover, but so that it would run on older machines as well, the new software version depended heavily on "emulation"—which works by making hot new software behave like its clunky predecessor—and was so unstable that users worldwide were suffering the frustration of frequent crashes and lockups. A series of quick fixes would have overcome the problems, which would have been chalked up to the customary new software bugs and soon forgotten. Instead, Apple engineering managers shifted most of their programmers to work on the next-generation OS, Copland, figuring that its release would erase the need to fix the problems in the earlier version. The System 7 problems had never been fixed and weren't being addressed as a top priority.[6]*

The PowerPC solution settled upon—modifying the Mac OS—was itself a tacit admission of failure. In 1991, former rivals Apple and IBM created a joint venture, called Kaleida, to come up with a new cross-platform multimedia development environment that would enable next-generation Macs and IBM PCs to run *all* popular varieties of software. It didn't work, and in 1995, after a half-billion dollars had been invested in the effort, the two companies called it quits.[7]

So, both of the dark kernels (no partitioning, emulation) persisted, and both contributed to those infernal crashes for which Macs increasingly were becoming notorious.

No WIMPs Here: Phil and Bob

We'll return to that next-generation OS that Amelio referred to—Copland—shortly. But first we need to step sideways and consider alternatives to the so-called "WIMP" approach: windows, icons, mouse, and pull-down menus.

Xerox developed the fundamentals of the WIMP approach—the GUI that we use today—which Apple borrowed from Xerox, and Microsoft in turn borrowed from Apple. Because that GUI has gotten better and better, and simply because it's been *around* so long, we tend to take it for granted. But today's GUI is not necessarily God-given. Visionaries both at Apple and Microsoft (yes, visionaries at Microsoft) both tried on for size radically different ways of getting computers to serve their users.

In 1987, for example, Apple produced a high-end five-minute videotape entitled "The Knowledge Navigator," which featured a university professor (flannel shirt, horn-rimmed glasses, etc.) working in his study. He is shown interacting with a flat device on his desk that features a bow-tie sporting character, Phil, on its screen.

> Is today's solution God-given, or simply force of habit?

(The user could supposedly choose between a cartoon Phil and a humanoid Phil, although neither Phil ever made it beyond the concept stage.) Phil, according to the video, was an intelligent guide who would help the professor prepare for a talk and organize his schedule for the day. The professor would ask Phil spoken questions (no keyboard involved) and Phil would go get the answer. Phil could also arrange video phone calls, facilitate collaborative manipulation of work on the desktop, and lots of other useful things, a sort of virtual butler-valet-batman for professorial types.[8]

Microsoft's version was "Utopia," alternatively known as "Bob." In its first and emphatically last incarnation (released in 1995), it featured a cartoon Golden Retriever named Rover who—like Phil—was eager to serve his master. The user located Rover in an appropriate room in the "Home" and put him to work on the desired tasks. (The Home was apparently owned by an off-screen presence named Bob; some skeptics said that Bob's real name was "Bill.") "I'm just one of a scrumptious gang of Personal Guides here to help you find your way in the Home," Rover announced in an opening pop-up screen. "Give us all a try if you want, or stick with me. The choice is yours!"[9]

Bob was clunky and condescending—nauseatingly so, in fact—but the program grew out of several years of research by two Stanford University professors, who interviewed hundreds of people about their preferences for interacting with computers. It "sat on top of" Windows 3.1, and apparently was intended to serve as a warm-up for a more sophisticated version that might sit on top of Windows 95. "Bob" was offered as a $100 premium package for home users: a steep price, especially when you could get a Mac that was far easier to deal with than Rover.

Also in Rover's "scrumptious gang" pop-up were two choices: *Onward, Rover!* and *Forget It.* Most people chose to *forget it.*

But down in Cupertino, people were still focused on intelligent agents and entirely new ways of getting computers to do useful things, which of course would mean dramatically different operating systems. Donald A. Norman, then head of Apple's user interface design group, said in 1995 that usability enhancements in the forthcoming Copland OS would take intelligent agents a huge step forward. It would be an "active interface," he told the *New York Times*, in which the user would increasingly be able to say to the computer, "Do it for me."[10]

> Sometimes the tried-and-true is better than all the known alternatives. But keep looking.

But both Phil and Bob/Rover illustrate the perils of drifting too far from the tried and true, when it comes to operating systems. Phil—had he come to life—would have required a start-from-scratch OS effort, and presumably a dramatically different set of applications—hard on the heels of apps rewrites for both the Lisa and the Mac. The developer community would have howled.

And although Bob/Rover actually made it out into the world, computer users found the cloying overlay program not helpful, but obnoxious. Oh, *puh-leeze*, said the purchasers of Windows 3.1. And Bob/Rover was buried out behind the Home.

Send in the Clones

Now we need to take a look at a fundamental OS-related choice that Apple made at least three times—and made it wrong either once, twice, or three times—depending on your point of view.

Microsoft achieved its near-total dominance of the world PC market by licensing its OS software far and wide. Apple, by contrast, steadfastly refused to license its OS to other hardware companies, on the theory that: a) it would give up end-to-end control of the user experience, and b) it would inevitably face margin pressures if low-end "clone" makers—that is, producers of cheap machines that ran on a license Mac OS—came into the market. And, in fact, there was evidence to support both contentions. A principal reason why the Mac experience was so "elegantly simple" was that one company made every single decision about that experience, from hardware through software. And, as for margins, when Compaq entered the market with its low-priced clone of the IBM PC, it signaled the beginning of the end for Big Blue in the PC marketplace.

On June 25, 1985, Bill Gates—brilliant, ambitious, and on the move—sent Apple CEO John Sculley a memo in which he advocated strongly that Apple license its OS to between three and five companies so that it could begin to manufacture "Mac compatibles" ("compatible" being a gentler word than "clone"). By adopting a closed architecture, Gates argued, Apple had made a serious mistake. It couldn't marshal the resources internally to make the Mac OS an industry standard, and it wouldn't get the kind of independent investment and support that were also needed to create a standard. Both Apple and IBM made mistakes, Gates continued, but something like *100 times* as much engineering resources could be brought to bear on IBM's mistakes, especially when "independent support" was taken into account. The flip side of great margins, Gates pointed out, was that corporations saw the Mac as a risky choice, in terms of both price and

> When your arch-rival offers a strategic suggestion, listen carefully.

choice. Apple had reinforced that perception of riskiness by being slow to bring out better operating software, larger-memory machines, bigger screens, and so on. It was a depressing list, all in all.

Apple had no choice, said Gates; it had to open up:

As the independent investment in a "standard" architecture grows, so does the momentum for that architecture. The industry has reached the point where it is now impossible for Apple to create a standard out of their innovative technology without support from, and the resulting credibility of other personal computer manufacturers. Thus, Apple must open the Macintosh architecture to have the independent support required to gain momentum and establish a standard.[11]

Gates was right. But, despite the fact that Apple had never competed in the low-end market, which suggested that the field was wide open for a Mac compatible in that particular segment, Sculley couldn't bring himself to pull the trigger. (Instead, he tried to license the operating-system technology and create a universal standard for Apple's "Newton" personal digital assistant, which was a notable flop.[12]) His successor, Michael Spindler, finally signed a Mac OS licensing agreement with Power Computing Corporation in 1995, but by then, it was far too late. The horse was out of the barn. Any chance of establishing the Mac OS as an industry standard had long since vanished.

Spindler's successor, Gil Amelio, thus inherited a tangled clone situation. It got more tangled the more he looked at it. Feisty little Power Computing had sized up the situation and had decided to go after the *high* end of the market: the desktop publishing end. Amelio was amazed to discover that Apple was netting something like $50 for each Power Computing clone that was sold, and thereby giving up something like *10 times* that much profit if it had sold a high-margin Apple computer (and OS) to the same customer:

I couldn't fathom how the fees had originally been established or what anyone had been thinking to allow Apple to come out so short. Perhaps after more than six years of fighting the battle of licensing, the war-weary Apple executives driving the program had been so excited about finally getting some licenses lined up that they neglected to ask finance to churn the numbers and see if they made any sense. We were caught in a licensing vise: losing sales to the clones, and making a pittance in license fees that came nowhere near balancing the scale.[13]

So, the solution that Bill Gates had put in front of Apple a full decade earlier—a way to leverage the cost of developing and maintaining an OS over a much broader base of users and a way to bring outside dollars to bear on both hardware and software challenges—was now closed to Apple. Short term, Amelio began trying to renegotiate the licensing agreements. But, whatever Apple would do in the long-term, it would have to do entirely on its own.

From Salvation to Dribbleware

So, what was this "Copland" OS that Gil Amelio and Donald Norman were talking about? Might this not be Apple's response to the serious challenge then being mounted by the Great Tortoise, Microsoft, and therefore represent the Little Kingdom's salvation? Might this not sidestep the whole thorny issue of clones, by putting an absolutely irresistible new machine in front of the world and unilaterally seizing back all that lost market share?

In a word, "no."

Copland was one of two major Mac OS projects begun around 1993. Scheduled to be delivered before Windows 95 hit the market, it was viewed as a transition to the more ambitious "Gershwin" OS that was to follow, sometime in the 1998 time period. Copland would solve some of the worst dark kernels of the Mac OS—the lack of memory partitioning, and the need to dumb down the PowerPC chip through emulation, in particular—but at the same time would still be fully "backwards compatible" with System 7 machines. Gershwin would be the Great Leap Forward.

The problem was, Apple couldn't seem to get Copland *finished*. From almost his first day on the job as CEO—February 5, 1996—Gil Amelio started trying to get a handle on the state of Copland. What he discovered was discouraging, to say the least: The all-important OS was "still just a collection of separate pieces, each being worked on by a different team, with what appeared to be an innocent expectation that it would all somehow miraculously come together."[14] Independent software developers were scheduled to receive Copland in beta form in May 1996, but that deadline came and went. The new release date, Amelio was told, was July 1996—although that new date didn't appear to be any more reliable than the first. Meanwhile, decisions were being made that struck Amelio as thoroughly wrong-headed—including the decision *not* to build memory protection into Copland:

> *Despite all the reasons for at last including full memory protec-*
> *tion, the Copland team had decided not to include it—a decision*
> *urged by marketing and salespeople, for whom any new operat-*
> *ing system that couldn't run on every Mac, no matter how ancient*
> *a machine, was breaking faith with Mac owners. Instead the*
> *Copland team had devised a pseudo protection scheme, which in*
> *truth left the problem basically uncorrected. It became devastat-*
> *ingly clear to me that sales were controlling technology, based on*
> *their short-term thinking.*[15]

So Amelio and his company were standing on what was almost liter-ally a "burning platform." Something like 500 engineers were working on Copland, and something north of $500 million had been spent on it—and Apple had precious little to show for all that effort.

With a growing sense of desperation, Amelio took drastic steps in several directions. First, he directed his technical staff to pare off bits and pieces of Copland to be included in a new OS upgrade, to be called "System 8."[16] And **If you can't unveil, dribble.** rather than wait for the whole Copland package to be completed, Apple would send it out in bits and pieces. As the *Wall Street Journal* reported:

> *The technique, dubbed "dribbleware," has become common on*
> *the Internet, where updates to application programs are sent out*
> *on a continual basis. Apple's move, though, is thought to be the*
> *first time it is being tried with an entire operating system. Each*
> *new section that is shipped would perform a portion of the tasks*
> *the operating system must handle, though presumably better than*
> *they were being handled in the previous version of the software.*[17]

Meanwhile, Amelio went shopping for a wholly new OS—from the outside. Hat in hand, he called Bill Gates up in Redmond, and asked if Microsoft would be willing to create a new Mac OS based on Microsoft's new NT system. Gates, Amelio later recalled, didn't attempt to contain his excitement. (*Lord of the entire universe! At last!*) Squads of Microsoft techies arrived in Cupertino to size up the opportunity. But, even after their intensive investigation, Microsoft seemed inclined to minimize the technical problems inherent in bringing the Apple GUI into the NT environment, at least as Amelio saw it. So, he kept shopping. He initiated conversations with Jean Paul Gassée, the former Apple head of research who had been fired by CEO John Sculley in 1991, and who had used his severance pay to start his own OS-oriented software company: Be, Inc. Gassée was eager to sell to Apple, but—after extensive talks—Amelio concluded that the price was too high for an OS that, after six years of trying, was still largely unfinished.[18]

And so, fatefully, Amelio made an overture to another former Apple employee, Steve Jobs, to enquire whether Jobs might consider renting or selling *his* OS to his former company.

The NeXT Solution

Several good books have been written about this particular soap opera, and I won't attempt to retell the entire unlikely saga in this context. Suffice it to say that when Sculley and the Apple board demoted Jobs in 1985, he left in a huff and took with him five key Apple employees. His stated intention was to set up a company called NeXT, Inc., which aimed to produce a high-end computer aimed primarily at the education market. Apple sued to stop what it saw as a raid on its assets—human and intellectual—but the suit was quietly dropped. (Suing one of the patron Saint Stevens was seen as a bad PR move.)

The NeXT computer, as it turned out, was both better and worse than Jobs's previous creation: the Mac. Introduced in 1988, its GUI was even snazzier than the Mac's; it ran like a "bat out of hell," and it was visually stunning. In short, it was way ahead of its time. But the company recorded almost no sales—only 50,000 over four years, thanks in part to the high price tag—and the venture drained Jobs's personal wealth to an alarming extent. NeXT gave up on selling hardware in 1990, and concentrated on refining its high-powered OS.

Just like Gates and Gassée before him, Jobs seemed eager to help solve Apple's OS-related problems. According to Amelio, Jobs urged Amelio to take the whole package:

> *If you think there's something for you in NeXT, I'll structure any kind of deal you want—license the software, sell you the compa-*

ny, whatever you want … When you take a close look, you'll decide you want more than my software. You'll want to buy the whole company and take all the people.[19]

"All the people," of course, would seem to include the CEO himself: Steve Jobs.[20] Several of Amelio's intimates cautioned him against welcoming the Machiavellian co-founder back into the Apple fold, but Amelio— by all accounts a regular guy, something like the neighborhood barber in manner and mien—seemed convinced that he could manage the mercurial Jobs effectively.

In any case, Apple needed a new OS, and Jobs had the best in town.

On December 20, 1996—just three weeks short of the all-important MacWorld trade show in San Francisco—Apple announced that it was acquiring NeXT for $350 million in cash and stock, and would assume some $50 million in NeXT debt. Jobs would return in a limited capacity, as "adviser to the chairman," and would report directly to Amelio. "This may end up being like the *Star Trek* movie where Captain Kirk and his crew come back to take the helm of the Starship Enterprise one last time," commented one industry analyst, in an observation that turned out to be amazingly prescient.[21]

> If you bring Captain Kirk onto the bridge, keep an eye on your seat.

Here begins yet another soap opera: the story of how Steve Jobs allegedly maneuvered Gil Amelio out of the captain's chair and claimed it for himself. Again, I'll leave that bizarre story to the legions of Apple historians who have gone before.[22] Suffice it to say that Jobs was effectively running the company within six months. And as a result, it fell to him to make sense of the acquisition of his former company by his *former* former company.

One of the first things he did was to stop licensing the Mac OS to the clone-makers. He arranged to buy the assets of Power Computing for $110 million, effectively shutting that competitor down, but permitted Taiwan-based Umax Data Systems to keep selling low-end clones in Asia, a business that Umax exited on its own in 1998.[23]

Next, he tried to make sense of the tangle that was Copland, System 8, and the NeXT OS. It made some sense to stick with the Apple GUI, rather than NeXT's. (After all, Apple *had* acquired NeXT, rather than vice versa.) But bigger questions loomed. One of these was what to do with UNIX, the beating heart of the NeXT OS.

We need to do a little techno-archaeology to make sense out of this. UNIX was an OS created at Bell Labs in the late 1960s. It had full memory protection and, because it was written in the C programming language, was machine-agnostic. (UNIX didn't care what kind of machine it ran on, in other words.) This was fundamentally different from OSs like the Mac, which were written in something called "straight assembly." UNIX was (and is) the best option for multi-user PC OSs—even better than Windows NT, which claimed to be the best OS for this increasingly important application.

Throughout the later 1990s, independent developers were coming up with ways to inject UNIX into Macs, mainly to help themselves develop in the welcoming Mac environment—or, more accurately—in a *stable* welcoming Mac environment. "You'll learn to hate DOS and Windows even more," wrote one developer to his colleagues in this period. "Mac OS is elegant and integrated, but UNIX is elegant, integrated, and extremely stable."

"For ease of use," this same developer wrote, "Mac OS rules. For scalability and reliability, UNIX rules."[24]

Apple fans, fearful of the technological takeover of the company by Jobs and his NeXT colleagues, worried that UNIX wasn't good enough. After all, it was a bulky, aging technology. It was losing ground (or *seemed* to be losing ground) to Windows NT. It lacked the vital capability to speed up in computers that had more than one processor. Didn't Apple need a home run, after all the Copland disappointments? Wouldn't people throw up their hands, concluding that Apple had finally lost it?[25]

Fixing It by Degrees: From Rhapsody to OS X

The technological takeover of Apple by NeXT was real enough. Only a few days after the transaction was completed—in early January 1997—NeXT's chief software designer, Avidis Tevanian, Jr., laid down the law to his new Apple colleagues. "No more dinking around," Apple's soon-to-be-named senior vice president of software engineering told them. "No more working on what's cool, rather than what's urgently needed."[26]

If it was a threat, it surely wasn't an *idle* threat. Within weeks, Copland was officially dead, and many of the Apple engineers who had worked on it were gone. The code name for the new Mac OS would be Rhapsody, and Apple would get there not through a Big Bang, but by degrees. Between that contentious January morning and the fall of 1999, Apple released five upgrades of its OS, following a schedule of a major release each year and a minor upgrade six months later. Little by little, Tevanian's team fixed the problems that had long plagued the Mac OS, picked up and incorporated useful bits of Copland, and also added new features that weren't available even in Microsoft's formidable NT OS, such as effortless Internet file sharing, improved security, and better search tools.

> Again: better to dribble than to postpone the unveiling indefinitely.

But the best was still to come. On September 13, 2000, Apple released a beta version of its OS X operating system software, the first fundamentally new Mac OS in just over 15 years. OS X, unlike its Mac predecessors, was UNIX-based. (No real surprise, there: Avidis Tevanian had been a UNIX champion and developer dating back to his days as a graduate student at Carnegie Mellon.) The prime directive for OS X—besides flash, speed, and flexibility, of course—was *stability*. And on this count, the new UNIX-based OS succeeded brilliantly. It simply didn't crash. Applications imploded, as usual, with the Mac then throwing up a little window announcing that "the application [fill in the blank] has unexpectedly quit." But, that telltale clock in the upper right-hand corner of the screen—where generations of Mac users had learned to direct their eyeballs even as their hearts were sinking—was still ticking off the seconds. (Frozen clocks don't tick.) Hit the magic key combination (option-apple-escape), the dead application is flushed, and the Mac is still chugging away.

This is a *big deal*.

Of course, this wasn't the end of the Mac OS story, only the first line in the next chapter. Remember the well-heeled tortoise, and the trackers chasing Butch and Sundance? Apple had to keep making OS X better. (It released five versions of OS X between 2000 and 2005.) Meanwhile, it also had to persuade people to *adopt* the new OS, which was fundamentally different from what they were accustomed to. Software developers had to be wooed and won, a task made easier by the increased sales of several hot new Mac products, including the iMac, which suddenly started driving up software sales. Jobs and his colleagues were convinced that, despite the risks inherent in the move into the unfamiliar, they were on the right track. When a "certain key vendor" up the coast in Redmond began grumbling noises about the low sales volume of its "Office for Mac/OS X" package, Apple politely suggested that dropping the $499 price on the software suite might help solve that particular problem.[27]

Curiously enough, OS X seems to have begun making inroads in neighborhoods that Apple had tacitly written off. "OS X is designed to meet all customer needs," said Philip Schiller, Apple's VP of worldwide marketing, at the time of OS X's release, "from the consumer to the educator to the desktop professional."[28] Notably absent from Schiller's list is corporate America. But data released by Jupiter Research in mid 2005 suggested that Apple might be making inroads into that market, as well:

> *The report found that 17 percent of businesses with 250 employees or more were running Mac OS X on their desktop computers. Twenty-one percent of businesses that had 10,000 or more employees used Mac OS X on their desktop.*
>
> *Mac OS X Server is also doing well with businesses. Nine percent of companies with 250 employees or more used Mac OS X Server, while 14 percent of companies with 10,000 employees or more used Apple's Server software.*[29]

Steve Jobs, for one, has no doubt about the virtues of OS X, which he considers to be the "most advanced operating system on the planet." It was nothing short of a "brain transplant," he told a rapt audience of developers in 2005—a revolution that "set Apple up for the next 20 years."[30]

Well, maybe not *20* years. That would be pushing it. But a brain transplant? Absolutely.

Lessons from the Family Jewels

So what can we learn from this story, which begins with a pain in the neck and ends with a brain transplant? At least nine things:

- **"Simple" may be incredibly complicated.** Going for simplicity isn't easy. And, at least in the OS field, it may foreclose future options. It's the *trade-off* that's key.
- **Make a product that forces change but protects continuity.** Here's a neat trick: Build enough planned obsolescence into your product so that people will keep coming back for more, which in part means bringing along all their old files and folders.

- **Don't wait for the other guy to surrender, especially if it's Microsoft.** What can you do—even if you're terminally out-gunned—to hold your turf? How fast can you innovate, and in which direction?
- **Is today's solution God-given, or simply force of habit?** It's human nature: We think that what is, is what's meant to be. But in many cases, it's not.
- **Sometimes the tried-and-true is better than all the known alternatives. But keep looking.** Obviously, this is the flip side of the previous point. OK, so Rover isn't an acceptable alternative. What is?
- **When your archrival offers a strategic suggestion, listen carefully.** I don't know about you, but if I ran a computer hardware company and Bill Gates wrote me a thoughtful memo, I'd memorize it.
- **If you can't unveil, dribble.** A bad image, to be sure. But if you have only half the dinner ready and your guests are hungry, start serving.
- **If you bring Captain Kirk onto the bridge, keep an eye on your seat.** You always saw that trait in Captain Kirk—that naked aggression—so you can't say you were surprised.
- **Again, better to dribble than to postpone indefinitely.** The diner who is hungry too long loses faith. Bring on the appetizers, as you talk about how great those entrées are going to be.

Chapter 5

Keep Your Friends (Reasonably) Close to You

Hunger is the best sauce in the world.

—Miguel Cervantes

Being a member of the community of independent developers for the Mac—the people who write the applications that make the Mac useful to the user—is a classic glass-half-full/glass-half-empty situation.

Glass half full: Total sales of software for Macs amount to something like $13 billion a year. If all those developers worked for the same company, that company would land somewhere in the middle ranks of the domestic U.S. Fortune 500. Yes, this would be well below software colossus Microsoft (#46, with $36.8 billion in 2004 revenues), but it would be respectably above the only other software company on the Big List: Oracle (#226, with $10.1 billion in 2004 revenues).[1] From the half-full perspective, there's gold in those hills.

Glass half empty: The installed base of Wintel machines is a billion machines, give or take a couple of tens of millions. The installed base of Macs is about 25 million, or about one-fortieth as big. No independent developer in his or her right mind would choose to write applications for one buyer when—with

> Is the glass half full, or half empty, or both?

more or less the same amount of effort—he or she could be writing for 40 buyers. Therefore, not only is there no gold in those hills, but all independent Mac developers are out of their minds.

Both perspectives are absolutely right, except for the blanket charge of mental instability, of course. Nobody, not even mighty Microsoft, turns up their noses at their share of Mac software sales. And, many developers find ways to coin money by aiming at the Mac users community, usually by developing programs that run on *both* Wintel and Mac operating systems. Here's some recent testimony from one such developer, screen-named "Emmanuel":

> *Why develop on Mac? Well, [despite Apple having] less than 5 percent of the market share ... I make just over 50 percent of my sales on Mac OS X. It did take effort to make "real" Mac applications and not just quick ports of PC games; the games were planned from the start to work on both platforms, and then were adapted to Mac OS specifics like Apple-Q and bundling. I can say first-hand that for a business like mine, it's really worth the effort, both in terms of sales and in terms of satisfaction: the Mac community of gamers is fantastic. I get e-mails all the time suggesting valid features. Even support e-mails are very courteous.[2]*

Sounds pretty good, right? You get half of your revenues for not a whole lot of extra work, and free good ideas from courteous people. But the problem, for Apple, has always been that the isolated success story isn't enough to support a multi-billion dollar computer maker. As the feel and functionality of the Windows operating system (OS) creeps ever closer to that of the Mac OS, the *application* is what makes the difference to more and more users. "So Problem Number 1 for Apple," says Harvard Business School Professor David Yoffie, "is how do you ever attract a large number of developers? Sure, you can always attract a small number. But how do you attract enough to make the platform competitive?"[3]

Apple understands this key challenge, even though it hasn't always *acted* as if it understood it. It tries reasonably hard to keep its friends close to it while also understanding that a little dose of *hunger*, now and then, isn't necessarily a bad thing, even for a friend.

What Does This Machine *Do?*

Before October 1979, that was the key question about the Apple II, Steve Wozniak's brilliant innovation. It turned on; it lit up. But it didn't actually do very much that was useful.

Then, in October 1979, Personal Software, Inc., of Sunnyvale, California, released a program called VisiCalc. It was the brainchild of a Harvard Business School student named Dan Bricklin, who was given to daydreaming in Room 108 of Aldrich Hall at the Business School. (First-year students like Bricklin spent their *whole year* in the same room, with the same 90 people. Sometimes the mind wandered.) Bricklin was a computer programmer who had decided to get a new career track going. In his B-school classes, he had learned that many companies did their financial forecasting, production planning, and contingency testing *by hand*—using specialized blackboards that sometimes extended across several rooms. The blackboards had rows and columns that marked off cells, which marched from left to right endlessly, out the door, and around the corner. Hapless data dweebs would manually enter data in these cells. Then a lord of commerce would change an assumption somewhere on one of the blackboards. Then the dweebs had to change every other cell affected by that changed assumption *by hand,* calculating as they went. It was something out of Dickens and Charlie Chaplin, all at once.[4]

Bricklin, daydreaming and staring at his T1 Business Analyst calculator, started visualizing a "heads-up" jet-fighter cockpit, in which he could move his calculator around by means of a mouse—he had seen a demonstration by mouse inventor Doug Engelbart—punch in numbers, get sums that would update automatically. "Eventually," Bricklin recalls, "my vision became more realistic." He began steering his budding application toward the best personal computer then on the market: the Apple II.[5]

The ad in the September 1979 issue of *Personal Computing* began by keying off the energy crises of the late 1970s: "Solve your personal energy crisis," read the headline. "Let VisiCalc power do the work." The copy then explained the concept that soon would become known as the electronic spreadsheet.

Say you're a business manager and want to project your annual sales. Using the calculator, pencil, and paper method, you'd lay out 12 months across a sheet and fill in lines and columns of figures on products, outlets, salespeople, etc. You'd calculate by hand the subtotals and summary figures. Then you'd start revising, erasing, and recalculating. With VisiCalc, you simply fill in the same figures on an electronic "sheet of paper" and let the computer do the work. The ad read:

Once you see VisiCalc in action, you'll think of many more uses for its power. Ask your dealer for a demonstration and discover how VisiCalc can help you in your professional work and personal life.
*   You might find that VisiCalc alone is reason enough to own a personal computer.[6]*

You might indeed. Consumers didn't necessarily see how VisiCalc would fit into their personal lives, but businesspeople got the "professional work" part. And, even though Corporate frowned upon it—the bean counters wanted all bean counting done on the mainframe, by the guys in the white coats—Apple IIs began popping up on desks all across corporate America.

What does this machine do? With Bricklin's stunning little application, it helped you try on alternative futures for size. And if the computer never did anything else, future sizing would have a good enough answer for many, many people. Future-sizing executives—something like 12,000 a month, after VisiCalc caught on—made VisiCalc the first runaway bestselling software program: the first killer app.[7] And sales of the formerly baffling Apple

> The person who makes your product useful is your friend. Your good friend.

II (*why would you want one of these things?*) jumped from 35,000 units in 1979 to 78,000 in 1980 to 210,000 in 1981. By 1984—the year the Macintosh was introduced—unit sales had reached a million.[8] VisiCalc, all by itself, accounted for something like one in five of those sales.

Bricklin and his partners got rich selling their magical software. Apple got rich selling the magical machine that ran the magical software. Apple could have gotten *a lot richer* if it had ponied up the $1 million needed to buy the rights to VisiCalc, but President Mike Markkula decided that the price was too high, especially since Apple was now investing heavily in its next-generation machine, the Apple III.

It was a fateful moment: Apple had a clear shot at turning itself into a software giant, and it backed away. From that point on, its fortunes rested in large part on the goodwill of external developers, including an increasingly assertive little company up in Redmond, Washington.

The Elephant Sits Where It Wants to Sit

Bill Gates enters this particular part of the story in 1982, when Steve Jobs learned that Microsoft was trying to break into the applications side of the software business. (Up to that point, Microsoft dealt mainly in operating systems and programming languages.) Jobs and Apple CEO John Sculley approached Gates and told him of a wonderful new machine that Apple was working on—code named

> When dealing with an elephant, write tight contracts and move faster than the elephant.

the "Macintosh"—and suggested that maybe Microsoft might want to develop some applications for the soon-to-be-amazing Mac. Gates agreed readily, and Microsoft soon came up with several outstanding programs for the Mac, including Word, Multiplan (later Excel), and File (the Ur-forebear of Access)—all programs that ultimately made their way into the PC universe.

While this was going on, the Lisa was bombing horribly in the marketplace. The machine's high price was one problem, but the lack of applications software (other than Apple's own limited selection of preloads) was another factor contributing to Lisa's ultimate resting place: the landfill. By the time the Mac was ready to be introduced—in early 1984, about a year behind schedule—Bill Gates decided he wanted to strike a better deal with Apple. He now had the clout: His company was growing fast, thanks in part to the spectacular success of the IBM PC that ran on his licensed MS DOS program. Meanwhile, Apple had failed to line up enough additional outside developers to offset Microsoft's developing muscles. The balance of power had shifted in Microsoft's favor.

Gates made an extraordinary demand. In return for releasing the sparkling new Microsoft apps, he wanted the right to use the Mac OS, and particularly those elements that defined its graphic user interface (GUI), in Microsoft's PC-oriented products. If Apple didn't give Microsoft the necessary permissions, Gates would simply sit on his apps. Facing an untenable situation, Apple caved, and agreed that Microsoft could dip into the family jewels.

It was yet another fateful decision. Microsoft later drew on this treasure trove to come up with a product called "Windows 1.0", an OS that looked suspiciously like the Mac "windows" environment, only clunkier. Apple sued, but the courts bought Microsoft's argument that Windows was an *application*, rather than an operating system, and

> When you hand over the family jewels, kiss them goodbye.

that the behemoth from Redmond had a valid license from Apple to use Apple's GUI in this particular way.

Once more, this time connecting the dots a little more tightly, Apple needed apps from Microsoft. Microsoft "convinced" Apple to license elements of its distinctive OS, including its look and feel, for use in MS/PC applications. The ultimate result was Windows 1.0: Microsoft's first baby step toward achieving parity with the Mac OS. Those wonderful Microsoft apps were indeed wonderful, but they turned out to be enormously costly to Apple in the long run.

There's another subplot to this episode, which is tangentially related to our story. Apple at that point was about to release its own version of the BASIC programming language for the Mac, called MacBASIC. The manuals were printed; one of the beta versions had been turned over to Dartmouth College for use in an introductory programming class; the train was leaving the station. But Gates absolutely did not want this sophisticated competition for his own version of BASIC for Mac, which was then under intensive development. He let Sculley and Jobs know that if they went ahead with the release of MacBASIC, he would stop working with Apple altogether—and, by the way, refuse to renew the MS-BASIC license for the Apple II, set to expire in September 1985. Since the Apple II was then carrying the company on its shoulders, this could have meant sudden death for Apple.

Again, Apple caved. It called in all the betas, sold MacBASIC to Microsoft for a dollar—which turned out to be a burial fee—and waited for the arrival of MS-BASIC for Mac. It was, arguably, the worst deal in Apple's history. When MS-BASIC finally did become available, it turned out to be not as good as MacBASIC. The language made few friends in the programming community, was only fitfully supported by Microsoft, and was itself pulled off the market within a few years.[9]

So, the Mac came to market with the benefit of some great Microsoft applications (which, as noted, were later ported back into the PC world, to the delight of IBM and Compaq users everywhere, and made PCs far more appealing). But, from a programmer's point of view, the Mac remained hard to work with. Its limited memory had to be carefully managed. It had all that GUI stuff (i.e., windows, icons, menus) that had to be managed through something called an "event loop." And users could choose what they wanted to be doing at any given point in time, an approach called "mode-lessness," as opposed to the older and simpler way of mode-based programming. True, this made things easier for users, but harder for programmers. It was a change in a way of thinking that confused many, and drove some away. "In truth," says former developer David Every, "the Mac was easier to write good GUI programs for than trying to do it all yourself. But since most of us were doing simpler command-line stuff, it *felt* harder."[10]

The memory issue proved critical, and it reflected a bigger problem: the "load it up and seal it up tight" mentality—Steve Jobs's mentality—that lay behind the new machine. As John Sculley later recalled:

> *The lack of memory, however, grew into a significant disadvantage because it made it difficult for programmers to write software for the Mac. The easier it is for the user, the more complex it is for the programmer to write for. It didn't help that Apple hadn't yet published software tools to make it easier for them to write programs. Henry Singleton, the only board director who did a lot of programming himself, began to complain about the difficulty in programming the Mac.*
>
> *'It's crazy that we have a computer out there that nobody can program,' he told Steve at board meetings. 'How do people program a Mac?'*
>
> *'They program on Lisas,' Steve would explain. 'But we're going to fix that. It's not going to be a big problem.'*
>
> *Nonetheless, some developers who intended to create Mac software simply gave up; others found the complexity slowed the pace of the development, causing long delays in getting to market.[11]*

All true, and we'll pick up some of these threads later. But the lack of a BASIC programming language surely helped stamp the *hard to program* label on the Macintosh's elegant forehead.

As one developer later put it, "Thanks, Uncle Bill."[12] And, for that matter, Uncle John and Uncle Steve.

Evangelizing 101

Life goes on. The Mac arrived with its very expensive Microsoft apps, and Apple continued to look for additional independent developers—both to soup up lagging Mac sales and to offset mighty Microsoft's growing power. Toward that end, they enlisted a colorful character named Guy Kawasaki to proselytize in the developer community.

For all the reasons listed above, ranging from lack of memory to lack of developer's tools, it was a tough sell. Kawasaki had to persuade developers to invest scarce resources in a new unproven platform that faced fierce competition in the marketplace, including competition from multiple Apple machines. This puzzled and worried CEO John Sculley, who saw his own company trying to get business applications written for four different Apple platforms (Apples II and III, Lisa, and the Mac) while archrival IBM was settling on a single standard.[13]

But Kawasaki proved a persistent salesman, even when facing a skeptical developer, or one with a long list of concessions that he or she hoped to extort from Apple. And here's where the *strengths* of the Mac came into play:

> *[We] would rub our chins, ask them to wait until they had seen a demo, and then blast into a performance with early copies of MacPaint, MacWrite,etc. ... either their jaws would drop to the floor, their eyes would pop out, and they would have to wipe the sweat off their foreheads, or we'd go back to Cupertino.[14]*

It worked, at least often enough—the library of Mac titles increased to more than 600 by 1985—and the circle became virtuous.[15] When the formidable PageMaker program exploded on the scene in the summer of 1985, it helped ignite the desktop publishing revolution. More Mac sales meant more Apple investments in improved Macs. A half year later, in January 1986, Apple released the Mac Plus, finally offering a machine that was powerful and flexible enough for both developers and high-end consumers.

Work with your friends to close the virtuous circle.

Developing in the Time of Troubles

But despite improving hardware, several things worked against Apple, in the increasingly difficult decade between the mid 1980s and the mid 1990s.

First, Microsoft's power continued to grow. (Maybe the right image is of that cute baby alligator that you bring home as a pet, which then gets *unsettlingly* big, and then *scary* big.) Rather than weaning itself from Redmond, Apple became *more* dependent on the unabashedly aggressive Bill Gates. This wasn't all bad, of course—those MS-Mac applications continued to help sell Macs—but having Uncle Bill calling your shots for you was unnerving. The folks up in Redmond began referring to Cupertino as "R&D South," and innovations in the Mac OS often showed up shortly thereafter in

> The bigger the alligator, the less responsive the alligator.

the Microsoft OS. Independent developers tracked these kinds of tea leaves carefully, as they decided where to place their bets.

Microsoft continued to be (and still is today) the biggest provider of applications for the Mac. But it began to look as if Microsoft was paying a whole lot more attention to its "Windows" applications than their Mac counterparts. By the late 1980s and early 1990s, the Mac programs were coming out a year after the Windows versions. Documents in Word—the emerging word-processing standard—opened almost instantaneously on Wintel machines; they could take 30 seconds (i.e., forever) to open on a Mac. But despite the fact that Microsoft was then grossing between $200 million and $300 million a year on its Mac applications, there was no particular urgency to *fix* any of these problems.

Hey: Where else was Apple going to go?

As you read the following passage from Gil Amelio's account of his short tenure as CEO of Apple in the dark days of 1995–96, put yourself in the shoes of that bet-placing developer:

> *I was hot to nail down terms that would allow Microsoft to openly endorse the Mac platform. Going public with a Microsoft endorsement in my pocket would mean I could serenade the major software suppliers and have a much better chance of keeping them in the Apple tent. The developers were continuing to lose confidence in the future of Apple and the Mac; if they began to leave in large enough numbers, it would be time to turn out the lights and fold the tent.*
>
> *If I couldn't get an agreement with Bill, at least I wanted an endorsement from him: "The Mac's a great product and we'll continue to develop software for it." Just a statement like that from the leader of the world's greatest software company could be enough to shift the balance for some developers, giving a lot of the Apple faithful confidence that staying with the Mac still made sense.[16]*

Not wrong, exactly, but *embarrassing*. And we've already seen how going with hat in hand up to Redmond plays out. This time, Gates told Amelio that he would give no such endorsement unless Apple kicked the

Netscape Internet browser out of the Mac tent, and replaced it with—you guessed it—Internet Explorer, which happened to be the Microsoft Internet browser. Even then, Gates coolly told Amelio, he wouldn't *guarantee* that an endorsement of the Mac would be forthcoming.

But, there were other self-inflicted wounds, as well. In the gross-margin-conscious Sculley era, for example, Apple got in the habit of treating its independent developers as a *revenue stream*, rather than a vital, critical, indispensable external partner. This is exactly backwards, if you're trying to grow your own developer's community. It is a little like a politician trying to charge reporters for interviews, or a hostess charging guests for bringing the potluck supper: not good for the symbiosis.

And, finally, back in the perceptual realm, Apple's troubles tended to be exaggerated in strange ways, which in turn exaggerated the growing sense that writing software for the Mac was a fool's errand. In the mid 1990s, a Washington, D.C.-based trade association, the Software Publishers Association (SPA), released a series of reports that seemed to show Mac software sales in a nosedive. SPA reported in 1995, for example, that Mac software sales were down 14 percent from the previous year (from $1.22 billion to $1.05 billion). *Abandon ship!*

> Don't charge the guests who bring the pot-luck supper.

It turned out, though, that these figures were based on sales *projections*, rather than actual 1995 sales. In 1996, the real 1995 sales figures were compiled—and showed a 45 percent increase, to $1.52 billion.[17] *Whoa, don't abandon ship!*

But again, put yourself in the shoes of a developer with limited resources. Which figure is more motivational to you, negative 14 or positive 45?

The Scope of the Problem

It's probably worth diving into the details for a minute, here. In 1995, when Heidi Roizen joined Apple as the new VP of developer relations, she came in as the head of an internal organization of some 300 people and a budget of $75 million. The organization was divided into five subgroups: Evangelism, Developer Support, Developer Marketing, the Developer Press, Developer University, and International Developer Relations. Their job: Foster good relations with 12,000 independent developers around the world—and build ties with new ones—all in the context of a company (apparently) going down the chute.

Roizen, then in her late 30s, was eminently qualified for the job. She had already worked at Apple in the public relations area. She subsequently had founded her own Mac-oriented software company, T/Maker, a publisher of clip art and children's games. Her company was located only five miles from Apple headquarters in Cupertino. And yet, no one from Apple had bothered to pay a visit when T/Maker began to drift away from the Mac platform.[18] *Anybody home, in the Little Kingdom?* Roizen had written some of T/Maker's code herself, so she understood the developer mentality firsthand. For a somewhat tongue-in-cheek view of that mentality, let's look at the opening paragraphs of a 1999 account by David K. Every, with the catchy title of "Developers Are a Bunch of Mamby-Pamby Whiners":

> *Let's face it, developers (like myself) are a bunch of whining geeks that want it all, yesterday, without bugs—that is, when we are asking Apple to deliver to us. When we deliver to customers, we want to include fewer features, have more time to do so, and a little leeway with "undocumented features." That's just the way developers are …*
>
> *Developers always want more, for free, and [want] Apple to smile while giving it to us. Anything less and there is going to be developers whining—take it with a large grain of salt. When developers stop whining, they are apathetic or have decided that it doesn't do any good—both bad indicators for a platform. So by that measure, the Mac is a raging success …[19]*

OK, so Every is exaggerating a little to make a point. But he illustrates the delicate balance that Heidi Roizen (and her predecessors and successors) have always had to strike: between treating developers like gods, and treating them like a bunch of whining geeks. It's about keeping them *reasonably* happy. Here's another developer's perspective from April 1996, in which author Don Crabb welcomes Roizen on board:

> *The last few months have been tough ones for the Mac developer community. As I am writing this … Apple has been pronounced dead by the know-nothing general press (if you ever thought* BusinessWeek *would get a clue, you can forget it once and for all)*

... [and] more than a thousand Apple employees have been let go (and while many needed letting go, badly, many were tight with developers) ...

Although DR cannot fix all the marketing and technical problems that Apple has suffered the last two years, it's now poised to be what it should have always been—the key organization in the company. Apple has tried being a marketing driven company and bombed. It has tried being a technology driven company and bombed. Perhaps it's time Apple tries being a developer-driven co? ... But for Apple to become developer-driven, it's going to have to trust us more than it's ever been willing to. It's got to get us on board much faster when it comes to new technologies.

Apple needs to start using us as a resource, not a revenue source. Apple needs to develop the right mechanisms by which we can be made part of the extended internal developer teams for all key Apple technologies ...

Crabb offered Roisen several specific suggestions, including:

- *Make entry-level developer support free, to encourage more Generation Xers to develop on the Mac.*
- *Lower the prices for all other developer support levels and increase each level's exposure to Apple engineers.*
- *Cut the price of developer tools to the bone. Sell them for cost, if necessary.[20]*

These were prescriptions that Apple eventually took to heart. (Eventually, Microsoft—instead of Apple—got the reputation for being cheap, hard-nosed, and wrong-headed toward its developers.) Heidi Roizen didn't stick it out, though. She lasted less than two years in the hot seat. She felt overwhelmed by the sheer scale of the problem, she later confessed, and also felt she was shortchanging her two young children. ("I was working every waking hour," she told an interviewer. "I was sneaking off between courses at dinnertime to check my e-mail."[21]) The Perils-of-Pauline state of Apple at that time, she confessed, also intensified the pressure she felt.

And, one more factor probably influenced Roizen's thinking: the return of Steve Jobs to the company in the summer of 1997. She considered Jobs a friend—but even so. "Steve is not a person you can feel comfortable with," she told an interviewer several years after the fact. Bill

Gates, Roizen's other mogul friend, is easy; Jobs is not: "With Steve you have this feeling that you are being judged."[22]

Kissing and Making Up

On many fronts, Jobs had his work cut out for him, but developer relations were among the most important fronts.

Jobs assumed that the combination of the spiffy new iMac and a highly visible ad campaign ("Think Different") would go a long way toward reinforcing wavering developers, and help bring new ones aboard. But he also made sure that key accounts had their own "evangelists" looking after them. Those accounts soon noticed a difference:

> *According to a senior exec at Adobe Systems, which sold around $300 million in Macintosh software each year, "In the last few years it was impossible for any developer to work with them. We couldn't rely on anything they said. We were absolutely convinced they were going to die." However, he continued, there had been "a 180-degree turnaround" since Jobs had taken charge.[23]*

Part of the problem that Jobs faced was the near-constant migration from one Apple OS to the next, as described in the last chapter. Apple's OS was more nearly 15 years old, and badly needed a thoroughgoing overhaul. The problem was that any such overhaul threatened to leave behind the applications that would only run on the outmoded OS. Surely, a number of developers would abandon Mac, under this unwelcome pressure to reinvest. For several years, therefore, Apple took a gradualist, step-by-step approach to introducing its new operating system (OS X). Although this was intended to help developers, it wound up annoying many. "Another year, another OS strategy," complained one:

> *In '96, the future was Copland. Last year it was Rhapsody. Now it's Carbon and Mac OS X ...*
>
> *Given the twists and turns of recent years, it's hardly surprising that the WWDC audience reacted to the new plan with a certain reserve. While Jobs's speech was generally well received, the applause was hardly thunderous ...[24]*

The "WWDC," of course, is Apple's Worldwide Developers' Conference, held in the spring of each year. The 1996 and 1997 WWDCs were highly charged—first because Apple seemed to be sinking beneath the waves, and second because of all those OS twists and turns. But Jobs's assiduous courting of the developers—including the introduction of powerful new development tools at a fair price—gradually paid off. So did his candor about his company's recent shortcomings. As he told the assembled developers in 1998:

> *The first person I actually called when I got back to Apple was my old friend John Warnock, who runs Adobe. I said, "John, tell me about all the craziness of working with Apple, and how we can sort this out." We began a dialogue about how Apple could work better with its developers that turned out to be very fruitful. Adobe, I think, represented many developers, in that it wasn't getting what it wanted out of Apple. It was starting to deinvest. I'm very pleased to say that with Adobe and all of our developers, we've really turned that around in the last year.[25]*

Far more important, though, was the simple fact that by the late 1990s, it was clear that Apple's head was still above water—and in fact, that the company might even be poised for a major rebound.

Jobs was in the habit of inviting heads of development companies on stage at the WWDC to give first-hand testimonials. The 1998 conference was no exception. One of the testifiers was Tom Gill, chief technical officer of Quark, publisher of a high-end desktop publishing package of the same name:

> *When Steve took over Apple a year and some ago, I didn't know him really well. He came to me and said, 'Tim, what is the one thing that I can possibly do for you that will help you at Quark do the best job that you can for us at Apple?' I'm sure he was expecting me to say that you should make the system 27 percent faster, or something. But what I said was, 'Become profitable.' Thank you very much. It is the coolest gift you could possibly have given me.*
>
> *Because Apple is very important to all of us. Actually, when I was up here on stage last year, someone observed … that I was emotional. I really was. And the reason is I can program both on Mac and Windows. So I'm bi. But I really want to come out of the closet and tell you all that I have five computers at home, and they're all Macs.*

So it was a very emotional thing. Because Mac has been very, very important to all of us. It's made the publishing industry what it is. And I cannot tell you how impressed I am with what Apple has done for themselves as a company, in terms of financial performance ...[26]

So yes, it's nice to be wooed. (Those who have been wooed by Steve Jobs himself—the master of the "reality distortion field"—agree it's an especially heady experience.) But it's even nicer to be wooed by someone you love—and who seems likely to stick around for a while.

Lessons in Keeping Your Friends (Reasonably) Close

The trick in dealing with vital vendors is to keep them close enough, but not *too* close. When it comes time to throw your 15-year-old toolbox out the window and introduce a stunning new set of tools, for example, you have to woo—and throw. Here are seven other lessons from Apple's relations with its developers:

- **Is the glass half full, half empty, or both?** How you answer this question—particularly if you're on the vendor side—may make all the difference to the Mother Ship.
- **The person who makes your product useful is your friend. Your *good* friend.** Lots of products find their niches only after their companion product arrives. The horseless carriage needed the pneumatic tire, and vice versa. So, Henry Ford and Harvey Firestone took good care of each other.
- **When dealing with an elephant, write tight contracts and move faster than the elephant.** How much bigger than you is your biggest supplier? If the balance of power is out of whack, tight contracts may be in order—and may not be enough.
- **When you hand over the family jewels, kiss them good-bye.** There are good reasons why people don't divulge the secret recipe: It won't stay secret. So, what information absolutely has to stay in-house?
- **Work with your friends to close the virtuous circle.** Software sells, computers sells; more software sells more computers.

- **The bigger the alligator, the less responsive the alligator.** If Bill Gates has taught us anything—besides having a brilliant business model, of course—it's that the biggest alligators get to set their own agendas.
- **Don't charge the guests who bring the potluck supper.** That's not how symbiosis is supposed to work. We *help* each other.

Chapter 6

Keep Your Promises

Where seldom is heard a discouraging word
And the skies are not cloudy all day.
                              —Brewster Higley, *Home on the Range*

Manufacturers make all kinds of promises, both explicit and implicit. They promise, for example, to save the world by means of this new whiz-bang widget (WBW; *explicit*, often in the context of a press conference or other media event). They promise to produce this wonderful new WBW at a quality level that will satisfy their customers (*implicit*), and to stand behind it in terms of returns and repairs (*explicit*, generally in a warranty). And they promise to make the wonderful new WBW available to those who want to buy it, within a reasonable time frame (*implicit*).

Almost no manufacturers keep all of their promises. Hey, stuff happens. The last regulatory roadblock can't be cleared. The factory burns down; the creek rises. The software can't quite get debugged. China buys up the entire world's supply of Metal X or Chemical Y, and as a result, manufacturing the WBW at a profit simply becomes impossible—at least for the time being. Or, the WBW actually goes out into the world on schedule, but design flaws begin to pop up, and the thing needs to get fixed.

People—even people in the media—are generally forgiving of the kinds of broken promises that grow out of "stuff happening," as long as no one actually gets hurt. Nobody's perfect, right? You take your best shot, and you behave honorably when something doesn't work out exactly as planned.

People are far less tolerant when promises get broken if it later appears that, from the outset, *they couldn't possibly have been kept*. A promise that can't possibly be kept is a lie, and no one likes being lied to. People are intolerant of corner-cutting design, of slipshod manufacturing, of products that don't ship in time for Christmas—even though that promise was made—and of warranties that spring leaks when they're put under pressure.

Over the past several decades, Apple has broken lots of promises, and has hurt itself badly in the process. Some of these broken promises fall into the "stuff happens" category; others have been less forgivable. But Apple pays a bigger price than most companies when it breaks a promise in either category. Why? First, because Apple has consistently tried to set a higher standard in an industry not always known for delivering the goods. (The term "vaporware" captures this problem.) One reason you pay more for a Mac, at least in theory, is that it will last a long time and work great—and, conversely, it won't catch fire, or blow up, or do any one of a number of other bad things.

> Apple pays a higher price when it breaks its promises.

And second, Apple pays a bigger price when it breaks promises because—for better or worse—people have such *strong attachments* to the Little Kingdom. When a total stranger misbehaves, we tend to minimize the importance of that behavior. But when a close friend, or a family member, or a lover misbehaves, God forbid! We feel positively betrayed. *I expected better of you!*

And when we are betrayed, we tend to get mad. "For 'tis the sport," wrote Shakespeare in *Hamlet*, "to have the engineer hoist with his own petard." Translated to present-day usage, that means something like, "We won't necessarily feel bad if the bomber gets blown up by his own bomb."

What gets people mad? Stuff that wasn't there and couldn't have been, stuff that was there but shouldn't have been, and stuff that could have been there but wasn't. Let's look at some examples.

Stuff that Couldn't Have Been There

When the Mac made its splashy debut in 1984 (see Chapter 10), it created expectations among the media and in the broader business community that Apple would make a similar splash in subsequent years. The problem was, the company simply didn't have the goods in 1985. But, rather than just take a pass, and live to fight another day, Apple cobbled something together. It promised to deliver stuff that, under the rosiest of scenarios, couldn't have been there.

> A wild exaggeration can be the worst kind of broken promise.

The vision that Apple decided to put forth, in that year, was "Macintosh Office." All in all, it was a good idea—in fact, a powerful concept that became a reality not so long afterwards, and which today we take for granted. Relatively small groups of people—"workgroups," Apple called them, coining a useful phrase—would use the four key components of the Macintosh Office to work together productively. These four components were Macs, software applications, laser printers, and something called the "AppleTalk Network," which served to tie the users together.[1]

At a media extravaganza on January 23, 1985, Apple executives ballyhooed Macintosh Office. Mac XLs! LaserWriter printers! The new Lotus "Jazz" program (the Mac version of the runaway success Lotus 1-2-3)! AppleTalk! Up to a total of 32 computers and peripherals working together on the same network! And look—even IBM PCs will be able hook up!

But, even on that festive day, there were hints of trouble. "We've got so much to do," a shaken Mac engineering manager was overheard to say, after the event, "and it's all such a mess!"[2]

What was such a mess? Well, for one thing, the AppleTalk plug-in card that was supposed to welcome those benighted IBM PCs onto the network wasn't ready yet. Even more critical, the AppleTalk file server—the hardware/software combination that was needed to enable people to share data and communicate directly with each other—was nowhere near ready. No small omission: That file server, recalls the then-CEO, John Sculley, was the beating heart of the AppleTalk network:

> *Steve [Jobs] told us the hardware was working in prototype form, but we had no software that worked. We also had a phenomenal product in a laser printer, dubbed the LaserWriter, but we weren't sure we could convince people that a Mac and a LaserWriter were enough to constitute a real event.*
>
> *The Mac was starved for business software. We were really getting by with mirrors at that point.*

Unfortunately, we weren't doing it well. Unlike 1984, the
Macintosh Office event became mere hype.[3]

Sculley later claimed that his own technological naiveté prevented
him from understanding that the VCR-like box that Jobs had been showing him was just that—a plastic box—that couldn't do *anything* without
the requisite software. But the tacit admission in Sculley's own account
(that he worried that a Mac and a LaserWriter alone wouldn't cut it, as the
stuff of a whoop-de-doo) undercuts the notion that an evil wizard misled
the hapless CEO.

At first, the press focused on the fact that the AppleTalk network had
significant limitations for the business user. Transmitting at 230K bps, it
was 10 times slower than the "PC Network" that IBM had just announced,
and 50 times slower than Xerox's Ethernet. As a result, reported the *New
York Times*, "Apple will not try to wire entire corporations—a task it will
leave to IBM and AT&T—but will try to connect its networks to the larger networks."[4] In other words, even in the rosiest of scenarios, Macintosh
Office would still leave Apple a bit player in the corporate IT market.

Gradually, though, the media focused in on the *real* fatal flow of
Macintosh Office: *There was no there there.* John Sculley provides a surprisingly candid assessment of what followed:

> *As the months wore on, our critics knew our announcement was
> contrived and premature. The media turned against us. We'd cre-
> ated the anti-event. It was like anti-matter; it swung the other way
> on us.[5]*

Are we supposed to infer that Sculley was surprised by this reaction
to a "contrived and premature anti-event?" said Sculley, who had previously headed up marketing for several of PepsiCo's most successful
divisions?

Lost in the unpleasant wake of the Macintosh Office disappointments
was the truly spectacular success of the LaserWriter. Although not really
an "Apple" technology, per se—in fact, the LaserWriter was basically a
repackaged Canon product—the reasonably affordable, sit-on-your-desk-
top printer made possible a whole new industry: desktop publishing. It
was the missing link (unless, of course, you needed that AppleTalk file
server). In fact, some people argue that Steve Jobs's biggest contribution
to Apple, in his first tour of duty with the company, was his stubborn

advocacy of the LaserWriter, which people up to and including the Apple board had wanted nothing to do with.

Balance the "visionary" with the "true."

Obviously, big-picture thinking is critical, in the context of a high-tech industry. If you can't see the blue sky, you're dead. And maybe sometimes you even have to lead *reality* a little bit with your vision (and hope that reality comes along at a reasonable pace). But at the same time, as the *New York Times* commented a bit caustically in 1989, you have to strike a *balance*:

The company has tried to seduce customers with visions of innovative products that will not be on the shelves for decades. The gap between the vision and the reality of the existing products may hurt Apple by creating a credibility gap, some analysts say.[6]

Of course, it didn't take decades for the missing pieces of AppleTalk to arrive. It only took two years, but they were two *very long* years.

Stuff that Was There, but Shouldn't Have Been

Then, you have the category of products that made their way to market, but shouldn't have been allowed to do so.

Gil Amelio, John Sculley's successor once removed, opened one of the chapters in his account of his days at the helm of Apple with a hair-raising story, one that reflects well on the patience of one of Apple's Japanese customers, but no so well on the company itself. One day, Amelio recalled, the Apple office in Japan phoned in to Cupertino to report a problem. One of their customers had experienced "a little difficulty" with a Mac, and wanted help with the cost of repairs.

Repairs to his *home*, that is:

A team from Apple Japan had gone to take a look and found that, for reasons nobody would ever be able to explain, the monitor on this man's Power Macintosh had exploded, demolishing half the room—walls, ceiling, furniture. Fortunately he wasn't at the keyboard at the time of the explosion.[7]

Apple rebuilt the house, wondering if this might prove to be only the first in a series of home demolitions initiated by Power Macs. It didn't; but there were plenty of other problems to worry about, when it came to quality control. A year earlier, for example—in March 1995—the Model 5300 PowerBooks were wowing the visitors at a Chicago trade show, right up to the point when the new and relatively untested batteries in several of them overheated and caught fire, earning it the unpleasant nickname of the "HindenBook." Michael Spindler, then the CEO, had to halt production on the 5300 and recall the units that were already out there, stripping retail shelves of Apple's hottest (literally) portable.[8]

And 1995 also happened to be a year when the personal computer market in general—and the laptop market in particular—absolutely *took off*. So: no supply, and an absolutely juiced-up demand. By the end of October 1995, Apple had a $1 billion backlog, meaning that roughly a million would-be customers were now being forced to sit on their hands, waiting for their computers to be delivered. (See the section Stuff that Could Have Been There, but Wasn't, below.)

But the woes of the 5300—described by Spindler's successor Gil Amelio as the worst product Apple ever produced—were far from over.

> **A defective product is a broken promise.**

The pins that connected the computer's power cord to the AC input were exposed and fragile, making them prone to breaking off (and leaving the user with no way to recharge the machine). The plastic bezel that held the 5300's screen in place tended to fall off, exposing the fragile edge of that very expensive component—and so on, and so on.

And this was part of a bigger, and equally depressing, picture. In the early days of the Mac—back when margins were robust, in the later 1980s—Apple's computers were built like the proverbial brick outhouses. But, by the early 1990s, under increasing margin pressure, more and more corners were cut. In addition, the growing popularity of laptops—which generally lead more dangerous lives than their desktop counterparts—meant that the percentage of "troublesome" computers went up every year on its own, in addition to whatever problems a lack of quality control created. But the quality-control picture was getting worse, year by year. The company that had earned a standout reputation in its industry for high-quality engineering and manufacturing was now putting that reputation in peril. As Amelio assumed the helm in early 1996, warranty complaints were running as high as *10 percent*—an almost nauseating pace.

Reluctantly, Amelio ordered yet another massive recall of the 5300. Amelio hoped that the "fix" would take one month; it wound up tak-

ing four. So, between May and August of
1996, Apple once again was starved for
laptop product, and remained so until the
next-generation laptop, the 1400, finally
became available. The drought was

> The only thing worse
> than recalling that
> defective product is *not*
> recalling it.

embarrassing, to say the least. When Whoopi Goldberg wanted a
PowerBook for her nephew, she had to get Amelio himself on the
phone to get the order filled.

Eventually, the 1400s came to market, as a critical product placement
in *Mission Impossible* created new demand for Apple products. But the
damage was done: "Apple's worldwide market share dropped from 6 percent to 3 percent on Amelio's watch," reported a Harvard Business School
research team. "In the core education market, the company's market
share fell from 41 percent to 27 percent."[9]

Meanwhile, Amelio tried to reinject quality into the company's design
and manufacturing areas. But here he ran up against some of the same
cultural problems that Sculley and Spindler before him had encountered.
As far back as February 1991, Apple had implemented an "Apple Quality
Management" program (AQM), based on the "Plan-Do-Check-Act" programs then in vogue in manufacturing firms. But the director of AQM
reported that he was meeting resistance from the company's engineers,
who either felt that as creative types, they didn't need a process, or that
other companies had little to teach the one-of-a-kind Apple. A number of
AQM classes were canceled due to lack of interest.[10]

By the time Amelio pulled the 5300 off the market for the second time,
there were some 650 Apple staffers working on "quality," broadly defined.
Whereas competitors were spending between 1 and 2 percent of revenues
on their quality efforts, Apple was spending between 5 and 6 percent—
not even counting the runaway warranty costs. The problem, Amelio gradually realized, was that Apple was using its quality dollars to fix design
and engineering problems, a kind of "secondary engineering organization"
that took half-baked products the rest of the way through to completion.
When people complained about the huge resources being sucked up by
"quality," they were in fact looking at disguised engineering costs.

In May 1996, Amelio broke into that cycle by separating out several
related functions—operations, manufacturing, quality control, and so
on—and by appointing a quality czar to head up the "Apple Reliability
and Quality Assurance Group." The czar was Mike Connor, former head

Quality can turn around quickly—if you *make* it turn around quickly.

of product development for a division of ADP, and also a highly decorated combat veteran—the sort of guy, concluded Amelio, who would not let his underlings cut corners. Connor reported to Apple's chief technical officer, who reported to Amelio, except that at the time of the reorganization, Amelio himself was the interim CTO. So, the organization understood that Connor's voice would be heard loud and clear in the corner office.

Amelio's quality assurance division turned out to be short-lived. Connor resigned in September 1997, when the recently returned Steve Jobs dissolved his group.[11] But according to Amelio, his impact had already been felt. "In a mere eight months," Amelio wrote, "Apple led the industry in every quality category."[12] In one of his last public statements as CEO, he proudly noted that there had been a 90 percent decrease in warranty claims on the PowerBook 1400.[13] In other words, Apple was relearning how to put good stuff on the market, and how to keep bad stuff *off* the market.

Compared to home demolitions and trade-show fires, the quality issues during Jobs's second stint at Apple (that is, beginning in the summer of 1997) have been relatively trivial. Lots of PowerBook AC adaptors from the late 1990s (including several of mine) were recalled and replaced. Some AppleVision monitors seem to have failed prematurely. The celebrated/infamous G4 cube either did or didn't develop cracks (or cosmetic blemishes) that either did or didn't go all the way through its stunning clear plastic housing. The fourth-generation iPods either do or don't have strange audio quirks, and my daughter's iPod failed either because it failed (bad design? bad fabrication?) or because someone dropped it. More seriously, a 2003 lawsuit alleged that Apple had misrepresented the playtime and lifespan of the iPod's battery. After some legal wrangling, Apple agreed to give qualifying iPod owners up to $50 in cash or credit—and in some cases, a new iPod.[14]

The negative chatter on the web notwithstanding—Google "apple quality control," and brace yourself—Apple seems to have regained its balance. Today, it gets high marks from *Consumer Reports* for both reliability and support—in fact, the *highest* marks, in every category. For example: The second-best desktop brand after Apple, Dell, is 25 percent more likely to experience some kind of hardware failure than a Mac. Gateway and Compaq laptops are 50 percent more likely to fail than Macs.[15]

Sure, there's always something to gripe about. After four years of hard service, my first G4's screen went ominously dark a few months back—not *black*, exactly, but very, very dark. If you shot a flashlight beam through the white apple logo from behind, you could make out what was on the screen. *Screen failure*, I gulped; *very bad*. Figure $600, at least. The local Apple Store took a cursory look and said it had to go back to California for repairs. Pack it up, ship it out, and wait. Turns out—nerd readers will shake their heads at the obviousness of all this— that the problem was that my battery was failing and was delivering not quite enough juice to light up the screen. So I paid $300 for a $100 battery, and a lot of postage and insurance.

Gripe: Maybe the Apple Store could have done this level of troubleshooting, and sold me a battery, and saved me $200.

Non-gripe: That little G4 is back in business, happily running OS X and doing whatever else I ask it to do.

Stuff that Could Have Been There, but Wasn't

Our last category has already been introduced above, in the context of Whoopi Goldberg's nephew's PowerBook: Products that were promised to customers, could have been there, and therefore *should* have been there. In 1997, *Wired* published a story called "101 Ways to Save Apple," which included the following nugget of advice for Apple's management:

> **9. Fire the people who forecast product demand.** *In 1996, you had a million dollars in back orders for the PowerBook 1400, while the warehouses were full of unsold Performas.*[16]

Unfortunately, it's rarely as easy as that. Until fairly recently, Apple relied largely on the people in its distribution channel (store clerks at CompUSA, for example) to help predict demand. But that's almost always a case of "steering by one's wake," maybe with a slug of emotion or wishful thinking thrown in, as well. A great product, or a lousy economy, can change all the calculations overnight. One reason why Steve Jobs took the audacious step of setting up the Apple Stores' retail network, as described in Chapter 8, was to try to get better ground-level information about product demand.

And the ability to get the right stuff in the stores at the right time, the ability to keep those kinds of promises, also grows out of internal

Promise-keeping often involves getting good information and using it wisely.

capabilities and inclinations. People have to be market-driven. Yes, they have to be committed to creating great stuff, but they also have to be willing (no, *eager*) to carry their vision through to a successful product introduction. *Real artists ship*, Steve Jobs used to tell his band of Macintosh "pirates." There's a time to invent, and a time to get the invention out the door.

This hasn't always been the case at Apple. As noted in Chapter 4, Apple engineers in the late 1980s and early 1990s were accustomed to working on what they wanted to work on—what was *cool*—rather than what was on the top of the company's agenda. "Nice work if you can get it," Gil Amelio later commented sardonically, "but not what the company needed."[17]

In addition, at the other end of the pipeline, the Apple sales force had gotten in the habit of exercising a *de facto* veto over the introduction of products that they didn't think they could sell. In other words, commented Amelio, "a technology the R&D guys were enthusiastically working on would turn out to be a product the salespeople had absolutely no intention of selling."[18] *Uh oh!*

The point is not to hand over entire responsibility for product development and introduction to the engineers. Rather, the point is to get the entire creative team, out to and including the sales force, pulling in the same direction. Amelio attempted to do this by creating separate product divisions, each with its own divisional general manager, who would have responsibility for getting sales on board (or, conversely, getting Engineering off of its wacky idea). Of course, this scheme has its own perils, especially if one division emerges as the "favorite child." In the Sculley era, Steve Jobs's Mac division was so obviously the favored child—favored over Steve Wozniak's Apple II division—that Woz quit the company in a huff. (Big loss!)

It's the CEO's job to broker these kinds of tugs and pulls. And, in the context of a technology company, it's also the CEO's job to get down in the trenches and steer product development. At least through the mid 1990s, Apple had the disadvantage of relatively hands-off CEOs, and the people in the middle ranks at Apple *liked* it that way. As Gil Amelio recalls:

It still amazes me to this day that Apple people were astonished the CEO would want to "get his hands dirty" by being involved in decisions on new product strategy. There are very few decisions more important to a company than its product decisions. I can't figure out why any CEO would leave these essential product decisions entirely to other people.[19]

Obviously, Apple doesn't have the problem of a hands-off CEO today. (Steve Jobs's hands are plenty dirty, in the good sense.) But if Apple is going to continue to deliver on the promise of the Macintosh platform over the next several decades, it's going to need a steady stream of leaders with this same ability, and commitment.

A Tough Industry for Promise-Keeping

A confession: the back half of that previous sentence was borrowed from Prescription #6 in the previously mentioned 1997 *Wired* article, entitled "101 Ways to Save Apple." Here's that Prescription #6 in its entirety:

> **6. Apologize.** *You've let down many devoted users and did not deliver on the promise of the Macintosh platform.[20]*

I'm not aware of any other companies that get publicly scolded in just this way. There appears to be a certain amount of, well, *emotion* involved. In later chapters, we'll explore the double-edged sword of the Apple cult. People who love you will: 1) let you get away with murder, and 2) scrutinize your every step jealously. And as noted earlier, when your lover betrays you, it feels really bad. *I was devoted to you, but you let me down. You didn't deliver on your promises.*

The thing about falling in love with a computer maker is that when you do so, you're likely to get let down, because the ground under your feet—and under the computer-maker's feet—is both highly complex and highly unstable.

Complex? According to a leaked internal Microsoft memo, when Windows 2000 was shipped on February 17, 2000, it had something like 63,000 known "potential defects." The Mac community (and the larger community of Microsoft bashers) gleefully pounced upon this as evidence of the basic perfidy of Microsoft—63,000 bugs, and they still shipped it! Microsoft responded with indignation, saying that in fact, of those 63,000 potential defects, only 21,000 were really "postponed" bugs, which the company saw as real problems that would have to be dealt with. The other 27,000 potential defects were merely things that the

Falling in love with a high-tech company is likely to be a frustrating experience.

developers had agreed would need some attention, eventually, in categories like feature requests, confusing phrases in the documentation, ideas for possible future enhancements, and so on.[21]

My point here is not to pick on Microsoft, but to underscore the promise-keeping implications of selling a product with so many unresolved issues attached to it. "Our customers do not want us to sell them products with over 63,000 potential known defects," as the author of the leaked memo phrased it.[22] Right. But there comes a time, as one Windows columnist commented, when you have to "freeze the code and ship it." *Real artists ship.*

The second problem is the inherent instability of the industry, and its products. Explains Macophile Scott Kelby:

> *Shortly after you buy your Mac, not only is the price of the model you just bought going to drop, but Apple is going to either:*
>
> *a. Increase the speed,*
> *b. Add more RAM,*
> *c. Add a bigger hard drive, or more likely,*
> *d. Do all of the above.[23]*

If computer-makers promise you a stable future, in other words, they're promising something they can't, and *shouldn't*, deliver.

Lessons in Promise-Keeping

In 1985, by ballyhooing Macintosh Office, Apple promised far more than it could deliver, and paid the price. Early in 2002, Apple took the unusual step of announcing—well in advance of MacWorld Tokyo, scheduled for March—that there would be *no new computers* introduced at the show.[24] Better to give people the straight story, up front, than to let them feel that you've broken some sort of promise to them.

What other lessons in promise-keeping can be gleaned from this quick tour of widgets and warranties? Here are eight:

- **Apple pays a higher price when it breaks its promises.** We like the story of the little engine that could. We *don't* like to think that the little engine cut a corner, or lied to us, in getting up the mountain and down the other side.

- **A wild exaggeration can be the worst kind of broken promise.** People figure it out, and they make you pay for it.
- **Balance the visionary with the true.** Especially from a high-tech company, and especially from an innovative high-tech company, people expect a little embroidery at the margins of the vision. They just want the main story to be mainly true.
- **A defective product is a broken promise.** After you break this kind of promise, the only question is, can you fix it fast enough, and on fair enough terms, to make up for the damage to your relations and reputation?
- **The only thing worse than recalling that defective product is *not* recalling it.** The U.S. automakers have earned a reputation for being slow to recall. Sure, it's expensive, and you don't like to see the word "recall" in close proximity with the company or product name. But the alternative can be far worse. If the 5300—the HindenBook!—is going to *catch fire*, call it in!
- **Quality can turn around quickly—if you *make* it turn around quickly.** Of course, this is easier if you have a lapsed tradition of quality, as did Apple. It's a little bit like coaxing a lawn back to life: Good roots make the job much easier.
- **Promise-keeping often involves getting good information, and using it wisely.** If you don't have an ear to the ground, you'll wind up sitting on high inventories (thereby annoying Wall Street) and stuffing your channels with unwanted product (thereby annoying your channels).
- **Falling in love with a high-tech company is likely to be a frustrating experience.** Most of the time, they can't give you what you want. They break their promises.

Chapter 7

Build the Cult

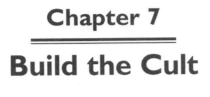

There go the people. I must follow them, for I am their leader.
—Alexandre Ledru-Rollin, French revolutionary

An interesting book with an interesting title was published recently: *The Cult of Mac.* The book's cover photo depicted the back of what appears to be a close-cropped male head. Shaved into the young man's already short haircut, extending nearly from ear to ear, is a pretty good rendition of the ubiquitous apple-with-a-bite-taken-out Apple logo.[1]

Let's face it: There aren't a lot of other products that inspire this kind of loyalty. Harley-Davidson fans have been known to tattoo that company's shield logo onto various body parts. But that's about it, really: Macs and motorcycles. Only Apple and Harley inspire people to become free (and in some cases, permanent) walking billboards for their products.

What's this all about?

It's about two things. First, it's about a user's boundless dedication to a product that he or she (let's face it again: usually "he") feels is *far superior* to anything else that's out there. It's about people deriving their own identity, at least in part, from their use of that product. *I ride a Harley; therefore, I am. I work on a PowerBook G4 driving an Apple Cinema Display; therefore, I am.*

But it's also about a smart company—Apple, in this case—carefully cultivating its user base to make up for its small market share and its traditional deficiencies in marketing and distribution. "Building the cult" has been a by-product of good products; it has also been the result of a very deliberate, and successful, corporate strategy.

And, to a large extent, it's the reason why Apple is still in business today.

The Roots of the Cult

First, let's put at ease any Windows users who might be reading this book. I'm using "cult" as shorthand for the twin phenomena described above: diehard users intersecting with corporate strategy. There is no evil Kool-Aid and no sacred text. On a regular basis, the Supreme Wizard makes it clear that he is of flesh and blood. As one author puts it:

> *Whatever the mainstream media, and magazines like* Forbes, *would like you to believe, there is no "Cult of Macintosh." No secret handshakes, no robes, no blood oaths; and although Steve Jobs has a lot of charisma, is Apple's leader and a genius, he is not a "charismatic evil genius."*[2]

So, as you review the evidence of cult building, keep in mind that Apple over the years has tended to blunder and improvise, as much as anything else. As Guy Kawasaki (who plays a prominent role in this chapter) famously commented in 1995: "Apple management. It's an oxymoron."[3] Real cults have far more consistent and effective management than Apple has had, by and large.

That being said, let's say that the "cult of Apple" took root way back in the late 1970s, when the company began sticking Apple decals in every outgoing Apple II box. Not just *one* decal, mind you, but a couple of decals, each suitable for sticking in your dorm room window, on the back window of your aging VW bug, or on your guitar case. Apple continued this practice through the 1990s. In fact, if you had called in the darkest days of the 1990s, Apple would have sent you fistfuls of the things.[4]

The odd thing is that it *worked*. People actually took the backing off those decals—featuring the logo with the horizontal rainbow stripes—and stuck them all over the place. Very few seem to have gone to the dump along with the packing materials. Again, people urgently wanted to demonstrate their affiliation with this new way of computing: the Apple II, the computer "for the rest of us."

But the cult didn't really get going along all of its future dimensions until the introduction of the Mac in 1984. Here's an interesting bit of Apple lore, as recounted by Apple historian Michael Moritz. As Moritz tells it, toward the end of 1983, Steve Jobs and Marketing Director Mike Murray were trying to come up with slogans to sell the yet-to-be released Mac:

> 'We don't stand a chance of advertising with features and bene-fits and with RAMs and with charts and comparisons,' Jobs said. 'The only chance we have of communicating is with a feeling.'
>
> 'It's got to be like a Sony Walkman or a Cuisinart. It's got to be a cult product,' Murray said.
>
> 'Yeah, we say, it's a cult, and then we say, hey, drink this Kool-Aid.' He strolled to the door and said, 'We want to create an image people will never forget. We've got to build it, and we've got to build it early.'[5]

In other words, lead with your strong suit. If soft stuff (imagery, feelings, and so on) is your strong suit, lead with that.

Guy Kawasaki joined Apple in the mid 1980s, charged with finding ways to persuade outside developers to write software for the Mac. In his book on the Macintosh culture—which he distinguishes from Apple culture, by the way—Kawasaki defined the "Cult" somewhat more narrowly. The Cult (which Kawasaki capitalizes) was that small band of fanatics who sold Mac to the community of consumers. Cult members didn't

> Bring the Jesuits around, and the rest of the Church will follow.

necessarily put Apple logos on their cars; they took it upon themselves to persuade *other* people to do that. These were the thought leaders: the high-end users, the savviest pundits, the well-connected dealers, and so on. These were the Jesuits of personal computing. "Bring these people around," Apple's marketers reasoned, "and the rest of the market will follow." It was far from a new idea in marketing, but Apple implemented it brilliantly.

One way they did so, Kawasaki argues, is through careful positioning of the product, and a careful choice of the words used to define the product. Apple defined the Mac as an "advanced personal productivity tool for knowledge workers." What did that mean, exactly? Not much, says Kawasaki:

*'Knowledge workers' delineated the target market for Macintosh.
Frankly, the phrase is marketing malarkey, but it worked because
it made people feel like part of a small, elite group. The phrase
caused people to align themselves to Apple's marketing, and they
persuaded themselves to buy Macintoshes. After all, who would
want to be an 'ignorance worker'? It is easier for the market to
align itself than for you to do it.*[6]

Another way that Apple influenced thought leaders was to put the
product in their hands, as inexpensively as possible. Dealer reps, in particular, were among those targeted by the company. The "Own-a-Mac"
program gave these reps rock-bottom prices on computers: $750, instead
of the suggested retail price of $2,495. This, presumably, helped get them
familiar with the product's features, which in turn made them far more
effective salespeople on the showroom floor.

It's probably time to remind ourselves that you can't build a cult sole-
ly, or even primarily, on a foundation of marketing malarkey. Apple has
had some great products over the years. They have been (reasonably)

> Eventually, your cult
> needs great products
> from you.

powerful, flexible, intuitive to use, pretty to
look at, virus-resistant, and affordable.
When those products have been good,
they've been better than anything else on
the market, and they've intersected with
users' lives—with livelihoods, works of art in the making, databases,
photo collections, and music libraries—with an intensity that few other
products could hope to match. "We love the computer so much,"
explained one otherwise restrained, not-over-the-top writer, "that Apple's
existence becomes very, very important to us."[7]

But Apple has also had bad spells—bad products, bad management—which have put the cult under pressure. The cult will can carry
you only so far. The cultists are willing to run to the ramparts, again and
again. Eventually, though, they need reinforcement from great products.

MUGs: Putting the Cult to Work

Go to any good-sized city in the developed world, or almost any college
campus in the United States, or certain visually oriented branches of the
U.S. federal government, and you are likely to find an interesting phenomenon: a Mac Users' Group (MUG).

User groups are a fairly standard way for a high-tech company to reach opinion leaders and create buzz. They are especially important to companies that: 1) don't have a lot of money to spend on creating buzz, 2) don't offer much technical support to their customers, and 3) create products that appeal to specialized users.

Apple has generally fallen into all three categories: no money, no support, and a customer base with lots of specific and esoteric product applications. So, Apple and MUGs have been something of a forced marriage: not necessarily anybody's first choice as to how to solve the problem at hand, but serviceable.

The origins of MUGs are lost in the mists of time, and are perhaps better left that way. Before Macs and MUGs, of course, came computers and computer clubs. Apple co-founder Steve Wozniak—and the "all around good guy" in almost any telling of the Apple story—was a member of the Homebrew Computer Club in Silicon Valley in 1975, and credits that informal group with helping to get Apple off the ground. (The club's leader, Lee Felsenstein, later designed the Osborne computer. Wozniak supposedly demoed the Apple I to his fellow Homebrewers.) The Apple II—a startling machine that in 1979 opened a lot of people's eyes to the potential of personal computing, but didn't have a lot of software or support available—prompted the organization of similar informal groups around the country.

One such group was AppleCore of Memphis, founded in September 1979. A group of, well, *nerds* got together at the office of the Memphis Jaycees and decided to organize a group of like-minded characters. They sponsored a dinner buffet at the local Holiday Inn, 30 people showed up (honor system: oops, they lost money), and thus began a conversation that continues to the present. "There was very little software available," recalls Steve Romeo, "and what was available was on cassette tapes that were very hard to use. We met to exchange ideas and to help each other."[8]

> Get your customers to provide their own technical support—and to keep saying nice things about you, too.

Lots of people needed this kind of help. By 1990, there was something like 750 such groups in the U.S., which counted some 200,000 people in their (informal) ranks. Geographically based MUGs appear to have reached their high-water mark in the U.S. in the mid 1990s, in part because of the arrival of the Internet. (Why join the Memphis group when you can join a worldwide virtual group aimed specifically at answering your questions about your applications?) But MUGs are still influential in certain cities and regions (new MUGs have recently been created in Beijing and South Wales) and among certain specialized user communities. The Apple website lists 15 MUGs located within federal government agencies, for example: little Mac islands ranging from NASA to the Pentagon to the Smithsonian.[9]

What's interesting about MUGs is how little Apple actually does for them. True, in the Sculley era, the company distributed a 128-page manual for setting up a MUG (*Just Add Water*), which you can still find online.[10] And of course, Apple says nice things about MUGs on its website. For example: "Apple recognizes the value of user group members and leaders who are passionate about using the best technology in the world and showing others what this technology could mean to them." But the next sentence, "Apple makes many attempts to support user groups in their mission," is a stretch at best.[11]

"Just ask any user group president how much support Apple gives them," writes Apple chronicler Scott Kelby. "They'll tell you that it ranges somewhere between zip and nil."[12]

Kelby goes on to scold Apple for its relative inattention to the MUGs:

> *Can you imagine how thrilled a company like Trane would be if each month, all around the world, groups of people who have Trane air-conditioning units would gather to help each other learn more about Trane compressors, blowers, and fans, and evangelize other Trane products? Trane would gladly pay millions to have a community like that...*[13]

Not Apple. To be fair, Apple does provide a list of MUGs on its website, hosts MUG events at Macworld, and steers new purchasers of Macs to local MUGs in a variety of ways. And, of course, the company supports the "Apple User Group Advisory Board," which serves as a sort of MUG ombudsman, standing between the MUGs and Apple. But note how Apple answers its own question—*What perks do board members get?*—in its FAQ on MUGs:

> *Not many. A nice dinner out, an occasional thank-you gift, a little recognition—that's about it. Board members pay their own way to trade shows and the many other events to which they travel. This is a volunteer position.*[14]

As suggested above, MUGs appear to be at a crossroad. Although geographically-based MUGs may be of declining importance—several have disbanded or gone broke in recent years—some of the reasons they were invented in the first place haven't gone away. (Apple still provides only limited technical support, for example.) The notion of a hardy band in Memphis fighting off the Windows-based Visigoths may be less compelling today than it was in the mid '90s, but if the "halo effect" of iPod lovers embracing Apple computers proves durable, there will be *more* people needing MUG-like help in the future. For example, an aging population of inexperienced Mac users might be better served by a geographically based network than a virtual network. And a geographically based MUG might be the best way to display (and learn) advanced new techniques in music and video editing, among other advanced applications.[15]

> Don't pay your advisory board's airfares. If they're *really* committed, they'll pay their own way.

In 1997, *Wired* magazine undertook to save Apple from itself. Number #18 of *Wired*'s 101 ways to save Apple read as follows:

> *Stop being buttoned-down corporate and appeal to the fanatic feeling that still exists for the Mac. Power Computing's 'I'll give up my Mac when they pry it from my stiff, dying fingers' campaign hits the right note. In the tech world, it's still a crusade. Support the Mac community, and the Mac community will support you.[16]*

No, thanks, said Apple. And like cacti and certain kinds of houseplants, MUGs have thrived on neglect. Who's to say that Apple has it wrong?

The EvangeListas

Guy Kawasaki, mentioned above, played an interesting role in the next phase of cult building. Kawasaki, a Hawaiian-born Christian, was an Apple marketer who at one point became interested in the techniques of evangelism. He attended one of the Reverend Billy Graham's traveling three-day "Schools of Evangelism" to get a better feeling of how the world worked at the intersection of faith and outreach—or, translated into our terms—at the place where the cult and corporate strategy converged.[17]

Kawasaki left Apple in 1987, and took a series of positions in the tech world. In those positions, he continued to be exposed to the evolving Apple story, and he was struck by the relentlessly negative spin on the stories about the former employer. When he returned to Apple in 1995, he brought with him a determination to counter what he saw as a drumbeat of anti-Apple stories in both the trade press and in general-interest publications.

Why this (alleged) anti-Apple bias in the press? One editor of a Mac-oriented journal, teetering on the very brink of cultspeak, gives his explanation:

> *Why? Because nearly every journalist everywhere uses a PC. These aren't Apple users, who really know Apple, reporting on the company. Instead, reporting on Apple is done almost exclusively by people who chose to use a competing product, reporting on the product that they didn't choose. It's like asking a salesman from the local Ford dealership to go on TV and tell America about the new line of Chevy trucks.*[18]

It's worse than that, actually: It's more like asking a Rosicrucian to pass judgment on the teachings of Scientology. But the other relevant fact, in the mid 1990s, was that Apple seemed to be on a long slow slide into oblivion, which only intensified (and, frankly, justified) the negative coverage.

To counter all this negativity, Kawasaki set up an Internet mailing list, the Mac EvangeList, in July 1996. Over the next three years, Kawasaki pumped out a steady stream of good news about the company, to a mailing list that grew to some 44,000 subscribers. At the same time, he exhorted his readers to head off to the local CompUSA store and hammer on the sales clerks to push Apple products. And finally, Kawasaki cited incidences of what he considered to be egregiously unfair coverage of Apple in the press, and urged his subscribers to complain to those reporters.

At least on this latter point, the cult responded. Journalists began complaining about the rough handling they were receiving at the hands

> Let the cult be your truth squad—within bounds. No zombies, please.

of Mac "fanatics." An editor at *MacWeek*, for example, said that the aftermath of being flamed on the EvangeList was like being "besieged by zombies."[19] Even Apple got uncomfortable with the stridency of the EvangeList, occasionally trying to get Kawasaki (and his successor) to tone it down. It's not smart, as the old political adage goes, to pick a fight with someone who owns a printing press. On the other hand, some reporters became a little less quick to write off Apple as a joke or an irrelevancy.

Mac EvangeList shut down in the spring of 1999. Steve Jobs was tall in the saddle once again, new Apple products (particularly the iMac) were burning up the marketplace, and Apple was back in the black. So did the cult save Apple? Probably not. Did it help the company stay afloat in its most sustained crisis? Probably.

Meanwhile, the phrase "Mac evangelist" has become a generic term. Search it on Google, and you get links to self-professed cultists, fanatics, zombies, and evangelists all over the world. And at Ibiblio's website, you can find the "Mac Evangelist's Oath (or how to co-exist peacefully with users of other platforms)"[20]:

1. I will seek to promote the notion that the person using the computer is the person with the greatest interest in what the computer is and what operating system it runs.
2. I will be patient with those who remind me constantly that my Mac won't run the thousands of software packages I don't want to run anyway (at least until I install Windows).
3. I will also be patient with those who do not understand that being able to color coordinate your computer system is a good thing.
4. I will seek to understand that Unix users are my distant kin, in that they want to get their work done too, it's just that their work is generally far different than my own.
5. I will not taunt Windows users, for they have chosen their own worst punishment.

Patience? *No taunting?* The cult matures!

The Cult on the Web

We've already touched on the web in the context of MUGs. The rise of the Internet has undercut the rationale for geographically oriented user groups, but it has led to an absolute explosion of special-interest Mac websites—close to a thousand, as of 2003, and presumably many more since the phenomenal rise of the iPod. Blogs and e-zines with Mac themes and subplots expand the cult-on-the-web horizons even farther.[21]

Surfing among these sites is a little like falling down a well, or venturing into a deep forest: You're not sure you'll ever get back out again. Rumormongering is a staple (see, for example, www.macrumors.com). So are sites devoted to deep-nerd technical fixes (for example, www.macfixit.com)—so much so, in fact, that your faith in Macs as relatively sturdy, stable, and safe machines may be shaken. So are dead ends and broken links. (Most survey sites still list www.macevangelist.com, for example, which died a half-decade ago, and is now for sale for $5,000.)

Trust me; the Mac cult is out there, in force, on the web. It is primarily small players, complemented by the occasional big publisher with strong opinions, *lots* of strong opinions. Which leads us to our final topic, in this chapter…

Why *Not* Build the Cult

Cults are double-edged swords. It comes with the territory: Lie down with a fanatic and, by definition, there's going to be a fanatic in the bed next to you.

Cult members compete for their leader's affection. Cult members feel neglected when their leader doesn't pay enough attention to them. Cult members are quick to perceive heresy, and to try and enforce orthodoxy. Author Scott Kelby says that Mac users are less like a *customer base*, and more like a *fan club*. And everybody knows how fickle a fan club can be. Fans don't like change. (Ask anyone from Bob Dylan to Britney Spears.) Kelby blames the failure of the Apple Power Mac G4 "Cube"—a highly stylized computer released in July 2000, which sold only 150,000 units before being taken off the market the following summer—on the strident disapproval of the Apple "fan club," which was expecting a 17-inch iMac and, instead, got a Cube:

> Beware the Jabberwock, my son. The jaws that bite! The jaws that catch!

> *What happened to the Cube is that it fell victim to our overzealousness to nail Apple on a product we (Mac fanatics) saw as a mistake. In effect, we "killed the Cube" even before Apple had a chance to. I can't blame the fans because they felt very strongly about the Cube—they feel strongly about everything Apple-related—and it's those people (you, me, we, they) that have kept Apple in business in spite of Apple management.[22]*

In other words, the cult can rise up and smite a product, just because the product doesn't meet its expectations. (The cracks in the Cube's casing didn't help, either.) The lesson here, it seems, is that building a cult is a little bit like raising baby alligators. Before you know it, they grow teeth—and strong opinions—and they can *bite* you.

Lessons in Cult Building

Let's pull together and summarize what might be called our lessons in cult building (and *not* cult building):

- **Bring the Jesuits around, and the rest of the church will follow.** You don't have to get everybody to join the cult. You just have to get the smartest, most connected, and most committed people to sign up. (Think Opus Dei.) They'll do the rest.
- **Eventually, your cult needs great products from you.** This is both the starting point and the sustaining point. Apple's cult has been willing and able to defend the company in its darkest hours, but grit and passion can only go so far. Eventually, you have to come up with the next reason to believe: the iMac, the iPod, and so on.
- **Get your customers to provide their own technical support—and to keep saying nice things about you, too.** It's very strange but true: Apple figured out (or backed into) a way to get people to pay high prices for computers, and then teach other people how to use them—and meanwhile, spend their spare time proselytizing in every direction about how great Macs were. (Which they *were*. But so are BMWs, and would you ever dream of joining a BMW users' group?)
- **Don't pay your advisory board's airfares.** If they're really committed, they'll pay their own way. Well, at least they will if they're members of the Apple User Groups' Advisory Board. In exchange for the occasional free dinner and a key chain, highly skilled people get to donate even *more* free time to Apple. It's an honor.
- **Let the cult be your truth squad—within bounds.** No zombies, please. First, hire a skilled evangelist. Then have that evangelist point your legions at individuals—particularly in the media—who appear to have it in for you. While not *really* annoying the Fifth Estate—for example, by not totally loosing the zombies on them— let the reporters know that you're watching their coverage. Let

them know when you think they're being unfair. Oh, go ahead; loose the zombies on them.

- **"Beware the Jabberwock, my son. The jaws that bite! The claws that catch!"** OK, so Lewis Carroll didn't have Mac fanatics in mind when he wrote of the Jabberwock. But remember that firing up a bunch of wired, committed fanatics tends to cut both ways. If you make a mistake, they may well come after you, eyes ablaze and pitchforks in hand. Or, they may come after you even if you *haven't* made a mistake, but you simply haven't met their expectations. Cultists can be like that.

Chapter 8

Get It Out There

Everyone lives by selling something.

—Robert Louis Stevenson

At 10:30 on a cool and cloudy Thursday morning in June 2005, the Chestnut Hill Mall in Newton, Massachusetts—an upscale suburb just west of Boston—was mostly asleep. The lunch crowd, still behind their desks in nearby suburban office parks, was at least an hour away. Seeing no competition for the pavement, delivery trucks blocked sidewalks and stuck their noses out into fire lanes.

Inside, the stores were all open, but the lack of foot traffic had clerks and cashiers reduced to either fussing with inventory—dusting glassware, sorting CDs, primping pillows—or giving up and reading newspapers behind their registers. The grand central staircase in the rotunda-like core of the mall sat deserted, except for a young mother shepherding twin toddlers who seemed determined to scale the great spiral, step by broad step. She trailed watchfully behind them, sipping a foamy Starbucks, and occasionally steering a toddler with an outstretched toe.

All was quiet.

Except in a ground-floor storefront, identified only by a backlighted white apple set into a grey, gunmetal backdrop above the store's glassed-in façade. Here at the Apple Store, things were *hopping*. A dozen black-suited 20-something sales clerks were all attending to customers. Another 30 or so people were waiting more or less patiently for a salesperson to get freed up.

Demure overhead signs indicated different sections of the store: Pro, Music, Software, and so on. Software—which tends to get packaged in garish, eye-catching colors—was all the way in the back by the cash registers. No doubt, it was safer back there than it would have been out by the front door. But, because the racks of gaudy packages were safely quarantined, they also were prevented from intruding upon the soft color palette of the store: white, Mac grey, blond wood, and black.

A cornucopia of products covered most of the available flat surfaces, and climbed up the walls as well. And, although there were plenty of computers in evidence—mostly laptops—the initial impression was that one had wandered into a highly disciplined RadioShack of the future: lots of cameras, digital music players, and other peripherals, mostly in the right colors (white, grey, etc.), all cabled and working, all well lit. No loose ends; nothing tacky; all tasteful.

Halfway toward the back of the store on the right, a chest-high wooden counter and a half-dozen bar stools jutted out into the pedestrian aisle. This, according to a retro-hip black logo on the wall behind the counter, was the "Genius Bar." (A grey-metal atomic diagram of electrons spinning in their tracks sat above the black words, underscoring the home-science-kit-from-the-'50s feel.) Every stool was taken, with people leaning forward, elbows on the counter. Behind the counter, two black-suited clerks who looked like they should be taking orders for green teas or fruit smoothies instead served up technochatter of varying levels of complexity. One customer, brow furrowed, took notes in a spiral-bound notebook.

The Apple website explains the Genius Bar:

> *Geniuses are always available for advice, insight, hands-on technical support, and repairs. You can even make a same-day appointment using the online Genius Bar Reservation System— visit your local Apple Store's web page for more details.*

And, according to the Chestnut Hill store's own web page, you can reserve a genius up to a week in advance if you buy a $99 "ProCare" package, which gives you benefits "over and above our standard level of service."[1]

It takes a certain amount of Applovian *chutzpah* to bill your floor-walkers as "geniuses." But, on this day at least, the concept—including the genius-reservation system—seemed to be resonating with customers.

A G4 PowerBook computer by the front door provided walk-ins with a way of signing up for a date with a genius. A check of

Sell your geniuses. At retail.

the machine's Genius Bar page revealed that the Chestnut Hill geniuses were all pretty well booked up until lunch time, and that a number of afternoon slots had already been given away (many, presumably, to ProCare customers).

Like the sales force, many of the customers in the Apple Store that day looked like college kids, or maybe recent grads—but not all of them. Over in the kids' corner—which featured a kid-high counter with kid-friendly software running on its machines, and substituted two-foot-diameter nerf balls for bar stools—a very young girl manipulated a mouse expertly and squealed happily when she got the squirrel to pop out of the hole in the tree. (When she squealed, she tended to lift her feet off the ground, setting the nerf ball in motion.)

Meanwhile, at a counter in the middle aisle, the store manager politely answered questions being posed to him by an elderly man about compatibility among various components. The manager gave the same answer several different ways: "They're all compatible, sir. They're designed to work together. They're what you call plug-and-play; absolutely no problem." His eyes occasionally flicked around the store, looking to see if any clerks were available to deal with the slowly mounting backlog of customers. (None were.) But he quickly focused again on the elderly man in front of him. "No problem at all, sir. In fact, we can help you set it all up."

The Chestnut Hill store is one of three Apple retail outlets in Massachusetts. All three are within 30 miles of each other, in the eastern part of the state, where most of Massachusetts's opinion leaders—and, not coincidentally, its money—are to be found. Not only will Wal-Mart and Apple never compete for the same retail space in Massachusetts, they're unlikely to wind up in the same town.

The first Apple Store opened in May 2001. Marketing experts were skeptical of the new distribution gambit. "No computer manufacturer has successfully branched into retail stores," as one such expert commented to a *New York Times* reporter. "It's completely flawed. They'll shut it down and write off the huge losses in two years."[2]

Well, judging from the state of Apple's growing retail empire four years later—109 stores in three countries, and counting—that wasn't the best prediction of 2001. But the experts had reasons aplenty for their

> Retailing experts are like any other experts: Sometimes they get it wrong. Really wrong.

skepticism. The computer retailing industry was reeling, in part because of a nasty recession, but also because, for the first time in decades, people were wondering whether personal computers were actually the wave of the future, after all. Maybe the PC would be subsumed into some sort of overgrown home entertainment center, as Bill Gates's strategic moves seemed to imply. Maybe some entirely new device—more portable, more personal—would emerge. Maybe selling PCs at retail was like selling buggy whips. The future seemed cloudy, at best.

One thing that *wasn't* cloudy, in the eyes of the critics, was Apple's record in the distribution game, right up to May 2001. That record, by most accounts, was downright dismal.

Nerds Go to Market

First things first: The thing to keep in mind about Apple is that it has always been "engineering-driven." This is a polite way of saying, "dominated by nerds."

Don't get me wrong; I like nerds. And I am mindful of one author's trenchant advice: *Be nice to nerds. Chances are you'll end up working for one.*[3]

Yes, nerds make the world go 'round, but they aren't usually great marketers. Engineers typically focus more of their attention on designing and building the best possible product, and less of their attention on *getting it out there*—that is, on cultivating the best possible distribution channels for those wonderful products. They believe, somewhat idealistically, that *if you build it* (the great product), *they will come* (the customers).

> Be nice to nerds, but don't let them do your marketing.

They would rather have customers "pull" these great products through more or less accidental distribution channels than take the trouble to create robust channels intended to foist products on unwitting or unwilling customers. Long-time Mac evangelist Guy Kawasaki summarizes this attitude—part of what he calls the "Macintosh Way"—as follows:

> *The status quo way of distribution is called Push. This means ramming large quantities of product on dealers and distributors because the status quo companies believe that the distribution pipe*

will sell whatever gets pushed on it. The Macintosh Way of getting products to customers is called Pull. Pull means creating demand so that customers will pull the products they want through the distribution pipe. Macintosh Way companies believe that the customer demand determines what sells, not distribution muscle.[4]

Yes, but the problem with the Nerd Way is that it's not enough, especially if you're frozen out of key distribution channels and if your overall volume is so low that those channels can simply choose to ignore you. You have to have *some* muscle.

Another kind of problem arises when you go to market inconsistently. For example, first you compete with your retailers, then you don't, then you do. Under these circumstances, retailers grow suspicious and lose their motivation to hawk your products.

And yet another kind of problem arises when the retail sector simply changes too fast for you to keep up, or changes in subtle ways that take a while to show up, but which ultimately work to your disadvantage.

Over the years, Apple has suffered from all of these problems, and more.

The Imperial Era: Apple Calls the Shots

We could start a quick scramble through Apple's distribution history way back when—for example, back when Steve Wozniak's first inventions were being sold through specialty electronics stores and hobby shops, operated mainly by and for nerds—but it probably makes more sense to begin in the early 1980s. At that point, Apple sold its computers (mainly its Apple Is and IIs) through about 1,300 full-service specialty stores, which were required to meet exacting service standards imposed by Apple.

Apple, then riding high, maintained an unusual degree of control over these chains. In 1982, for example, the company told Computerland that henceforth, Apple would decline to sell to the powerful retailer centrally. Instead, it would authorize and sell to Computerland franchises on a case-by-case basis. A store that didn't cut it—in Apple's estimation—would get no product.

This pattern was repeated when Apple decided to begin selling its products in selected department stores. An earlier foray into the department-store sector in the late 1970s had failed, mainly because the sales force in most department stores wasn't skilled enough to help customers purchase the right combination of parts to come up with a working Apple system.[5] But, taking a cue from the hi-fi industry, which was then moving toward preassembled rack systems, Apple in June 1982 came up with a novel Apple II starter-system package (including a disk drive, monitor, console/keyboard, manuals, and software). In theory, at least, this $2,000 soup-to-nuts system would make it more practical for less skilled salespeople to sell Apples. The Macy's in San Francisco's Union Square served as the beta site (in 1982) for the push into department stores; within a year, Apples were being sold in 21 locations in 12 North American department store chains.

But again: not in *all* stores in a given chain. Apple got to pick and choose. It also got to tell Macy's (for example) how the sales reps in the computer department would be compensated and exactly how a given store would spend the six months *preparing* for the grand opening of its computer department. The department stores grumbled, but complied.

Meanwhile, the specialty stores that up to this point had had a lock on Apple products also bristled. They resented the loss of their monopoly. They also pointed out that the sales staff in the department stores tended to know very little about computers assistance. Apple countered by pointing out that unskilled sales clerks were an *industry-wide* problem—meaning that even the specialty stores weren't immune to incompetence—and that having a presence in department stores was critical

> It's nice to be able to call the shots. But it won't last.

to Apple's plan to expand its presence in the "home market." People who might be intimidated by the computer specialty store, presumably including all those anticipated home users, were "more comfortable shopping in a department store environment."[6]

The next chapter began with the arrival of John Sculley at Apple in 1983. Sculley had earned a reputation during his years at Pepsi as a marketing whiz. He was the guiding light behind the "Pepsi Challenge" and "Pepsi Generation" campaigns, and he was hired by Steve Jobs in part to inject some discipline into Apple's marketing and distribution efforts.

But this emphasis on discipline went by the boards with the introduction of the Macintosh in 1984. You'll recall that Apple was justifiably excited about the Mac, Steve Jobs's baby, which it believed was finally going to deliver upon the potential of the ill-fated Lisa. So Apple launched several ambitious promotional schemes to get the word out.

These included, for example, a promotion called "Test Drive a Macintosh," which permitted Apple dealers to *loan* Macs to prospective customers, the theory being that no sentient being could fail to be wowed by Apple's amazing new machine, once exposed to it. They also included something called the "Apple University Consortium," which was a program designed to put half-priced Macs in the hands of students and staffers at carefully selected engineering schools (the Chestnut Hills of nerd academia).[7]

The problem was that by resorting to these promotional tactics, Apple was straining and aggravating its already shaky dealer network. The "Test Drive" program was launched shortly before the all-important Christmas season, when most retailers wanted nothing to do with a time-intensive loaner program. The 50 percent discount for Stanford students, among others, was even more annoying to retailers, especially when it became clear that at least some of these enterprising students were turning around and selling their discounted Macs at a profit.

John Sculley soon realized the perils inherent in competing with his retailers. In mid 1985, amid other corporate retrenchments, he announced that Apple would stop most of its direct sales efforts, and concentrate on making its dealers happier. At least some responsibility for marketing and advertising would be ceded to the dealers, along with a $250 "market development fund" for each Mac ordered by a dealer.[8] The imperial era at Apple was officially over; Apple's retailers now had the upper hand, and they knew it.

From Empire to Embarrassment

The world had changed around the proud computer-maker from Cupertino. Whereas in the early and mid '80s, retailers would do pretty much whatever Apple wanted to get their hands on the company's hot products, by the 1990s, the balance of power had shifted noticeably to the retailers. Although Apple's share of the PC market didn't actually peak until 1990, the handwriting was already on the wall: The vast majority of PC buyers wanted DOS, then Windows.

So, Apple took a fateful step. It opened the funnel, and authorized everyone and his brother to sell Macs. Macs started showing up in derelict chains like Montgomery Ward's, office-supply giants like Staples, and wholesale outlets like Sam's Club. Now, Macs were everywhere, but it wasn't clear that anyone would be better off for it. If service was bad when the retailer *cared* about Macs, things were likely to get far worse in stores where Macs were merely an afterthought, with declining market share, at that.

And so things did get worse. In their new and uncongenial homes, Macs were swamped in a sea of IBMs and Compaqs. Often relegated to dark and dusty corners, floor models might be broken, unplugged, or not hooked up to peripherals. Macs didn't sell, and so salespeople didn't try to sell them, and so Macs didn't sell. And, not surprisingly, more and more customers were steered toward Windows-based machines, which came in a broader array of choices, which operated on software that was both available and more or less familiar to the sales force, and which *worked*, right there on the store floor.

As was true for most aspects of Apple's existence, the bottom of the barrel came in the mid '90s. Apple's market share continued to plunge. Under financial pressure, the company circled the wagons, leading to further declines in service and support. The situation went from bad to worse, according to Mac historian Scott Kelby, as the company began to rely on volunteer labor to get to market:

> *It was a fairly common practice for some Macintosh fanatics from the local user group to get together on a Saturday and go to every Sears, Circuit City, Office Depot, etc., and quietly fix up the Macintosh section. They would restart all the computers, start the self-running demos on all the machines, and generally clean the place up and make it look respectable. They usually had to do this on the sly because as a general rule, the Macintosh department was staffed by—that's right—PC users.*[9]

Guy Kawasaki—whom we last encountered in the context of cult building—used his EvangeList to call out the troops, and help the beleaguered Apple tread water. "Kawasaki," writes Leander Kahney, "suggested subscribers tidy up displays, buttonhole salespeople, and counter pro-Windows sales patter."[10]

Again, it's always nice to have a cult to call upon. But, by the time Steve Jobs returned to Apple in July 1997, it was clear that the company was floundering on the distribution side—as in most other aspects of its operations—and that strong medicine was needed.

Fixing It—for Now

One thing that Jobs understood, from his prior experience at Apple, was that having machines sit on retail shelves was bad medicine. The older the unsold inventory got, the more likely that it would have to be heavily discount-ed, or even junked—and Apple chronically had higher levels of aging inventory than its Windows-based competitors. One reason was that it tended to ship too many clunky models, and not enough hot ones. Fixing this chronic prob-lem meant, first, the company had to get better at projecting sales, which it had never been particularly good at. It also meant that it had to get its products to move through the distribution channels faster.

> Move that inventory, based on better numbers!

Toward these two ends, Apple reduced from five to two the number of distributors it employed as middlemen between itself and its retailers. (The theory was that fewer distributors would lead to better sales projec-tions.) Many freestanding retail outlets were also dropped, in favor of national chain outlets. The company also added 100 sales and support reps to work with these outlets on the retail level—in part, again, to get a better handle on who might be selling how much of what.[11]

In an effort to put yet another finger on the retail pulse, Jobs announced (in November 1997) that Apple would start selling Macs directly to consumers through the company website. Although web cus-tomers wouldn't get a price break, they *would* be able to get a machine configured exactly to their specifications. There was no mystery about where Jobs got the idea for direct web sales: upstart Dell Computer, which had emerged from obscurity to become one of the world's most successful computer-makers. Dell had starting selling over the web the year before.[12] While announcing the new approach, Jobs projected a picture of Michael Dell on the screen behind him, with a bull's-eye across Dell's face. "We're coming after you, buddy," Jobs exclaimed.[13]

> Go after Dell. In fact, go after *anybody* with a great marketing idea.

But Apple continued to lose market share, year after year, and this contraction was reflected on the retail level. In 1998, the company announced that it was ending its relationships with Circuit City, Computer City, Tandy's, Office Max, and Sears, in favor of an exclusive deal with CompUSA. This may have been putting the best face on a bad situation,

since Best Buy had just announced—in January 1998—that it was dropping Apple's products due to poor sales. (Circuit City couldn't have been
far behind: between July 1996 and January 1997, that chain's Mac sales
had fallen from 6.5 percent to 0.6 percent of total computer sales.) And
dumping the chains also saved Apple, which had lost almost $2 billion in
the previous two years, as much as $75,000 per month for each chain that
was dropped.

"This doesn't represent a retreat from retail," said Apple VP of Sales
Mitch Mandich, bravely, "but instead a redefinition of what the retail buying experience will be for our customers."[14]

But others heard the clear signal of retreat being sounded. "It is
extraordinary evidence of Apple in retreat," said one industry pundit. "If
they can't sustain more than one national retailer, they are clearly still in
trouble."[15]

Jobs, not surprisingly, accentuated the positive. "We've also restruc-
tured our distribution channel," he told a conference of web publishers
in 1998, "and we've gotten rid of a lot of folks that were not interested in
investing in Apple. The buying experience was atrocious a year ago. It's
much better now, and we're pushing it to be better still."[16]

CompUSA had gotten the nod in part because that chain had dedicated extra floor space to Macs in several of its stores, a so-called "store
within a store." The experiment turned in good results: Mac sales had
jumped from 3 percent of overall computer sales to 14 percent. Was con-
centrating on one chain the best path out of the woods?

In a word, "no." The store-within-a-store concept only underscored
how puny Apple really was, when pitted against the Wintel giants that
took up the vast majority of CompUSA's aisles. (*Oh, yeah, the Apple stuff.
All the way in the back, on the right.*) And—at least based on experiences
in one CompUSA store in Eastern Massachusetts—few sales reps were
interested in, or skilled at, selling Macs. It was the same old story, all over
again: *Macs don't sell, so I won't push them, so they don't sell.*

Back to the Future

And that's how Steve Jobs found himself standing at the Tyson's Center
mall in McLean, Virginia, on May 15, 2001, being interviewed by CNBC's
Sue Herera. The event was the opening of the first Apple retail store.
Bluntly, Jobs admitted to Herera that 95 out of 100 people that set out to

buy a computer didn't even *consider* a Mac. "We're not even getting a chance to suit up," Jobs lamented. The new retail stores, he explained, would be located in high-traffic areas. "We're going to make it so that those customers only have to walk a few feet into our store. Once they get in our store, we're going to educate them as to what these products can do."[17]

Jobs denied that the new store—and the others that were soon to follow—would divert sales from existing Apple retailers. Instead, he stressed, they would give consumers an opportunity to see everything *working together*—computers, digital cameras, printers, websites, camcorders, and so on.

The company's independent dealers were quick to disagree with Jobs's assessment that no cannibalization would occur. When Apple opened its Glendale, California store shortly after the McLean, Virginia opening, sales at Pasadena-based Di-No Computers—an independent retailer with annual sales volume of about $4.5 million—fell precipitously. "Every time a customer in our area buys direct," complained Di-No Vice President Larry Moon, "it affects our business."[18]

> If all else fails, sell it yourself.

Moon had a point: The 7,700 people who visited the first two Apple retail stores bought $599,000 worth of merchandise in *two days*. And something else was going on, as well: the phenomenon of buzz. As Leander Kahney later put it:

> *At the first Apple Store opening [in McLean] in May 2001, the line broke into a chant of "Apple, Apple," according to people who were there. . . In August 2002, Apple held special late-night sales events to promote the launch of Jaguar, an update to Mac OS X. There were lines thousands strong at Apple Stores throughout the country. In Palo Alto, a queue of 2,000 to 3,000 people formed. The cops showed up to oversee crowd control, and the store didn't close until 2:30 a.m. when the crowds finally thinned out. Apple estimated that 4,000 people visited the store that night.[19]*

Apple's strategy, wrote the *New York Times*, was to "do for computer shopping what Starbucks did for coffee and what Barnes & Noble did for book browsing."[20] It was about creating a *shopping experience*, trading on Apple's legendary reputation for cool, flair, and style.

It was also a huge gamble. Computer sales were down, in part due to the nationwide recession. Gateway Computers—which had opened its

> Design a shopping experience that defines the *buyer* as much as the *seller*.

first retail stores in 2000—was already pulling back, pulling the plug on stores that weren't meeting volume expectations. Computerware, once one of the nation's largest Apple dealers (slogan: "We live Mac. We eat Mac. We sleep Mac. We dream Mac. All we do is Mac"), went out of business in April 2001, just before Jobs announced the Apple Store concept.

But, the gamble paid off. By the third quarter of 2004, Apple had opened 81 retail stores, which collectively were selling $1.2 billion in products annually, and making a profit. And it was an international phenomenon, as well: thousands of people stood in line when an Apple Store opened in Tokyo's Ginza district on November 30, 2003.[21] Steve Jobs said at a June 2005 developers' conference that a million visitors *per week* were trooping through Apple's 109 stores worldwide, where they were spending (he added pointedly, for the developers' benefit) a half-billion dollars on third-party products.[22]

In retrospect, of course, the roots of Apple's retail triumph can be traced back to the positive aspects of the CompUSA "store within a store" concept. Pay *attention* to Apple—play on the cachet and mystique of the Apple brand—and customers will beat a path to your door. Go a step further, and shape a shopping experience—one that defines the shopper as much as the seller—and you'll get a million customers a week, maybe even standing in line and chanting your company's name. But that would be selling Apple short. Somebody—presumably Steve Jobs—had a *vision*, and acted on that vision. The rest, as they say, is history in the making.

Lessons from Getting It out There

What does the tangled tale of Apple's distribution and retailing efforts tell us? It tells us that *consistency* is important in dealing with retail channels that you don't control. It tells us that selling personal computers can be harder than selling products in slower-moving industries like cars, even though selling cars is plenty hard. And it tells us that at the end of the day, cachet counts. And *inspiration* counts even more.

Eight specific lessons jump out of the preceding chapter:

- **Sell your geniuses at retail.** Spend the time and money to develop a sales force that's (at least) as good as your product. (Even the best products can't sell themselves, especially if they're intimidating.) Make your "geniuses" out to be scarce commodities, for example, with a sign-up sheet.

■ **Retailing experts are like any other experts. Sometimes they get it really wrong.** In May 2001, the pundits were predicting that Apple's retail gambit was going to prove an unmitigated disaster. Wrong!

■ **Be nice to nerds, but don't let them do your marketing.** Let's face it: engineers, for all of their many virtues, don't speak "marketing."

■ **It's nice to be able to call the shots. But it won't last.** Few products stay hot forever. Abusing your retail network today will almost certainly haunt you tomorrow.

■ **Move that inventory, based on better numbers!** If—like fish and computers—your inventory goes bad *real fast*, you have to move those goods ASAP. This means fixing the distribution chain in ways that give you better numbers, so you can make and ship more winners and fewer turkeys.

■ **Go after Dell. Go after anybody with a great marketing idea.** After 30 years of trying, Apple seems to have expunged the "not invented here" syndrome. They're prepared to copy Dell, Gateway, or whomever.

■ **If all else fails, sell it yourself.** The long sad saga of Apple in the retailing arena comes down to this: *The more special your product, the more likely you'll have to sell it yourself.*

■ **Design a shopping experience that defines the *buyer* as much as the *seller*.** Starbucks got there early, as did Barnes & Noble. This is also called "lifestyle shopping": Let the customer validate himself or herself simply by walking in the door. *I'm cool, therefore I am.*

Chapter 9

Keep Your Cool

Man is the only animal that blushes. Or needs to.

—Mark Twain

What does Apple really sell, at the end of the day? Well, in addition to its endless innovation, Apple sells *cool.*

It wasn't always this way. Back in the days of Woz and the Apple I and II, Apple actually sold *warm.* It sold an image of itself, and its products, as accessible, intimate, colorful, with no hard edges—the opposite of the cold-and-corporate IBM. The Apple logo underscored the point: In the icy and ominous world of computers, we're the people you'd like to hang out with, have a beer with. *Apple is the computer for the rest of us,* meaning, "us outsiders, fellow travelers, anti-establishment types." Yes, Apple was "cool" in the hipster sense of the word—as a rejection of mainstream values. Apple was cool in the same way that a VW bus was considered to be cool. (So what if it can't go more than 40 miles per hour uphill? It's *cool!* But overall, Apple was warm, fuzzy, even cuddly. Its early ad campaigns were playful, lighthearted, and offbeat.

Somewhere along the way, Apple changed. It left behind the hippies and its other countercultural roots. It left behind its rainbow-colored logo in favor of a sleeker, *cooler,* Apple. Yes, the new Apple still had a bite taken out of it, a winking reference to its playful past. But, instead of a fun, we're-in-this-together bite, it was now a *cool* bite. Apple was selling *cool.*

Part of being cool is having cool friends. Here's an interesting inter-lude from 1984, just after the spectacularly successful introduction of the Mac, as recounted by Apple observer Steven Levy:

> *And what was Steve Jobs doing? At first, he was busy delivering the Macintosh to various celebrities. He trekked to Mick Jagger's house with [software engineers Andy] Hertzfeld and [Bill] Atkinson; the Rolling Stone didn't show much interest so Andy and Bill gave a demo to his daughter Jade. Similarly, Jobs gave a Mac to Beatle offspring Sean Lennon for his ninth birthday. An interviewer for* Playboy *tracking Jobs watched as the Apple chairman and the boy slipped away from Yoko's A-list party to play with the comput-er. Looking over their shoulders were Andy Warhol and Keith Haring. Warhol himself sat down at the machine and moved his hand over the mouse. 'My God!' he said. 'I drew a circle!'[1]*

The coolest Rolling Stone, the widow and son of the coolest Beatle, Andy Warhol and fellow artist Keith Haring, all wrapped up in one pack-age—*cool,* at least in 1984 terms. You could question whether making house calls was the best use of Steve Jobs's time, but you can't argue with his choice of which doorbells to ring. Teaching Andy Warhol to draw cir-cles—*way cool.*

What happened to Apple? How did it go from the whimsy of Woz to the cool of Warhol?

The simplest answer is, "Apple grew up." Belatedly, the company saw that it had to change in order to grow—or even survive. Lots of com-panies begin with free-spirited or anarchic roots. But, if they stay that way—if they prove unwilling or unable to change—they stay stuck in their original pots, and get pot-bound. They languish, and eventually die.

Another piece of the answer is that the culture that spawned Apple—the Home Brew Club nerds, the revolutionaries, the countercultural avatars—dried up and blew away in the uncongenial '80s. Being the "computer for the rest of us" worked less well in the Reagan years, when there were fewer and fewer of the "rest of us." The "rest of us" were reduced to holding reunions.

And a third piece of the answer is that as Apple got less like one Steve, it became more like the other Steve. Steve Wozniak ("Woz") was, indeed, warm and cuddly, the type of guy you *would* like to have a beer with. Steve Jobs, by contrast, was an acetic: the kind of guy you

might take a vow of silence with. His
influence became especially pronounced
upon his return from the "wilderness."
When Jobs came back to rescue a desper-
ate company, people expected—even

> Don't get pot-bound.
> Don't be afraid to shed
> your skin—even if it's a
> comfortable skin.

demanded—that he put his cool stamp on the company, which, of
course, he proceeded to do.

One advantage of being perceived to be cool is that you sometimes
get to *define* cool. (If Apple's doing it, it *must* be cool.) But the flip side
is that you get held to a higher standard. The "cool police" scrutinize your
every move: *Is this up to the high standards of cool that we've come to
expect from Apple?*

When Apple does cool right, it looks effortless. Think of Steve Jobs
strolling around on a stage in front of the several thousand independent
software developers on whose good will the fate of the company ultimately depends. *No sweat.* Watching this,
you feel like you've happened into the
world's largest living room, where the hip
host—dressed in a black turtle neck and
jeans—tells cool stories while sipping on

> Cool is a double-edged
> sword. When the cool
> act uncool, it's disturbing.

bottled water, occasionally sitting down at the keyboard to dazzle his
friends. "We love you!" someone shouts. Some embarrassed laughter follows. Jobs barely breaks stride. "Thanks," he says, smiling slightly, nod-
ding. *Cool.*

But, when Apple loses its cool, it's disappointing, and offputting, and
confusing. It's like the maestro displaying a tin ear, or Santa Claus revealing a selfish streak. And nowhere is this more evident than in the marketing realms of media relations and advertising.

Influencing the Influencers

Early on, under the expert guidance of Regis McKenna, Apple learned the
importance of catering to the people who buy ink by the barrel.

McKenna, Silicon Valley's most prominent and successful marketing
guru, was recommended to Jobs and Wozniak by Intel, where McKenna
had previously done public relations consulting.[2] Among other contribu-
tions to Apple, McKenna's firm came up with the original Apple logo—
the technicolor one—and talked Jobs into adopting it. And later,

McKenna found himself on the ramparts when Apple started leaving behind its warm-and-fuzzy roots, in favor of cool:

> One of the things [that] people don't realize is that Apple wasn't happy with the name 'Apple' after they got going and growing. They actually looked at IBM and said, 'We don't look like IBM. We're not, you know, dignified. We don't look like a stable, large business organization.' And we had a big meeting at De Anza College in which I made a couple-of-hour presentations to all the employees at Apple, saying, 'That's exactly what you do want. You want to be different from IBM. You don't want to be the same. You don't want to emulate them. You want to do all of the things that distinguish you from them.' And they decided to continue with the name.[3]

Ultimately, of course, Apple went with a cooler logo (although the corporate name survived the transition to cool). But McKenna's firm made a far more enduring contribution in the realm of media relations. First, McKenna catered to the editors and reporters who put out trade publications. Where other companies tended to ignore those often underappreciated industry workhorses, Apple cultivated them with loaners, tips, and scoops.

> Cultivate your cool by cultivating thought-leaders.

And, going several rungs up the ladder of influence and respectability, McKenna also cultivated a local legend called Benjamin Rosen, who did things like help found Lotus, help found (and serve as chairman of) Compaq, and publish a highly influential technology newsletter. Rosen guarded his independence fiercely—which lent great credibility to his pronouncements, among both the press corps and the investment community—but he also owned and cherished an Apple II. Carefully staying on the right side of the line—*helping* Rosen, rather than appearing to manipulate him—McKenna earned Apple uncounted tons of positive ink.

"Then, remarkably," as Michael Malone relates, "Rosen went one step further":

> He began to play matchmaker between Apple and the press. He organized luncheons to introduce the company to publications like Time. Apple was now on its way to becoming a business phenomenon. In [Apple chairman Mike] Markkula's words:] 'We were

carrying the corporate image far out in front of the size and reputation of the corporation.[4]

By the time of the Lisa's introduction in late 1982, Apple had cemented its positive relationships with the national media corps, giving "sneaks"—sneak previews—of the powerful new machine to some of the nation's most powerful journalists at New York's tony Carlyle Hotel.[5]

Products counted, of course. But increasingly, as Markkula's comment implies, Apple was about *image.*

And increasingly, that image was about *cool.*

Advertising: Cool and Uncool

John Sculley tells a story about Steve Jobs coming to visit him at Pepsi's headquarters, back in the happy days in the early 1980s when Jobs was trying to woo Sculley away from soft drinks and into computers. Seated in his well-appointed office, Sculley talked to Jobs about how Apple should use advertising to create an "Apple generation," much as Pepsi had created a so-called "Pepsi generation." (There was some talk that they might even be the *same* generation.) Then Sculley showed Jobs a reel of Pepsi commercials, prepared by the ad agency BBDO. The ads, Sculley emphasized, were all about portraying Pepsi as number one, a necessary psychological prerequisite to *becoming* number one. Pepsi, said Sculley, had to *look* better than Coke, in order to be better than Coke; hence the emphasis on the *quality* of the production.

"That's just how we want it," Jobs reportedly replied. "That's really high-quality filming. That's what we want. We want to have the very best advertising, the highest quality possible."[6]

That, of course, was the thinking that went into the huge advertising coup scored by Apple in 1984, with the anti-Big Brother/anti-IBM ad that ran during the Super Bowl. Unfortunately, the same thinking also underpinned the "lemmings" ad that ran the following year. As recounted in an earlier chapter, the "1984" ad looked like the product of a proud, self-confident, forward-looking company, willing to take risks to convey a new kind of message. (It was easy to miss the fact, for example, that it was a *computer* that was being advertised so dramatically. Confident, and *cool.*) But the lemmings ad looked more like a product of the Brat Pack: condescending toward an audience it didn't really understand, and didn't *care* to understand. *Uncool.*

In the wake of that disaster, the company's advertising "got little." No more swings for the fences. Part of the reason was budgetary: As the company's fortunes began to decline precipitously in the mid '80s, Apple increasingly opted for cheaper outlets, including newspaper advertising.

But another part of the reason was a change in advertising agencies. In mid 1986, CEO John Sculley became frustrated by what he saw as unresponsiveness on the part of the TBWA Chiat/Day agency. In particular, he objected to a proposed commercial that depicted professional women happily using their Macs. What was going *on* here? At exactly the same juncture that Sculley was pushing hard to break through to the stubbornly Apple-resistant, male-dominated corporate IT market, his ad agency was pushing for a hip feminist message? Featuring Margaret Thatcher and Sandra Day O'Conner look-alikes? Featuring a walk-on by the real-life Gloria Steinem? Featuring Cyndi Lauper's "Girls Just Wanna Have Fun" as the background track?

Cool? Absolutely. On target, from a business-development perspective? Not in Sculley's eyes. He pulled the plug, and Apple ate the $600,000 that had been spent developing the ad up to that point.[7]

In the wake of this fiasco, Sculley decided to hold a winner-take-all shootout between TBWA Chiat/Day and BBDO, the agency that had served him well—with generally fluffy, upbeat campaigns—during his tenure at Pepsi.[8] Not surprisingly, perhaps, Sculley decided to go with BBDO, which impressed the Apple executives with a proposed campaign called "The Power to Be Your Best."

> If your product is all about being user-friendly, your ads should probably show your product being user-friendly.

BBDO certainly was limited by the resources at hand. (Ad spending plunged from some $90 million in 1985 to less than half that in 1987.) But the agency also seems to have been stumped by the product, and uncertain as to how to represent it. Inexplicably, the new generation of Apple ads rarely showed the product *being used*, which logically would have been a user-friendly computer's strong suit. Microsoft's advertising, by contrast, showed a variety of users happily at work, doing cool stuff with the help of their Windows-based machine, presumably backed up by legions of behind-the-scenes troubleshooters.

"For most of Apple's history," writes Scott Kelby, "many people would agree that [the company's advertising] fell somewhere between an absolute joke and a total disgrace."[9] The low point, according to Kelby, came in the mid 1990s, when Apple advertised the ill-fated Performa by showing a grandfatherly type using his computer to troll for babes online. Unseemly. Worse: *uncool*. What was Apple thinking?

Tin ears seemed to abound. Ad campaigns seemed irrelevant, even bizarre. Even people who loved their PowerBooks and had voyeuristic impulses didn't give a darn what was on a given (minor) celebrity's PowerBook. As *Wired* magazine put it, in its famous 1997 list of 101 things that should be done to "save Apple":

> **12. Light a fire under your ad agency.** *People don't need warm, fuzzy infomercials about the Mac family. And who cares what's on Todd Rundgren's PowerBook? People want to know about power (the CPU kind, not George Clinton's), performance, and price.*[10]

In this sad context, the returning Steve Jobs had nowhere to go but up. Of course, "up" was made infinitely more attainable by the arrival of some cool new products: first the G3 PowerMac line, and then—finally—the iMac!

Jobs more or less bet the farm on the iMac, launching a $100 million ad campaign in August 1998 in support of the futuristic-looking new computer. To do so, Jobs rehired TBWA Chiat/Day, which, as noted above, had produced Apple's ads back in the glory days of the Mac. This was to be the most expensive campaign in Apple's history, using a Rolling Stones soundtrack to thump the tub for the company's first breakthrough product since the arrival of the original Mac, more than a decade earlier.

"I think, therefore iMac," as the campaign's slogan put it. *Cool* was back. The fact that the most interesting thing about the appearance of the iMac—its transparent case—was a complete accident didn't deter Jobs from hawking that feature. (The cases used to field-test the iMac on school kids were clear, having come straight from the factory that way; kids were so excited about being able to see the *guts* of the machine that Jobs subsequently incorporated that accidental feature into the production run of the machine.) Five "fruit flavors," including the highly popular "blueberry," flooded the marketplace, snapped up almost as soon as

> Cool can be an accident. Exploit your accidental cool.

they hit the stores. Apple sold almost 300,000 iMacs in the first six weeks, and almost 800,000 before the end of the year.

Meanwhile, Apple and TBWA Chiat/Day finally began sounding the long-overdue note of direct product comparisons between the iMac (simple) and the PC (complicated). The celebrated "Un-PC" spot is a case in point. As the camera languidly trolls around the backside of an unidentified Windows machine, dodging cables along the way, the soothing male narrator says, in a poetic cadence:

> *The PC:*
> *Perpetually complicated?*
> *Profusely corded?*
> *Physically conspicuous?*
> *Particularly costly?*
> *Then there's the new iMac.*
> *Which is about as un-PC as you can get.[11]*

On the sales front, there was good news wrapped in the good news: something like 13 percent of iMac buyers were switching over from Windows machines—mostly a symbolic victory, given the relative sizes of the two operating systems' installed bases, but satisfying nonetheless. And more important, more than three in ten iMac buyers were first-time computer buyers. Evidently, the iMac was appealing to people who previously had found computers unappealing.[12] Some of this, surely, grew out of the machine's simplicity and the successful marketing of the "simplicity factor." But *cool* was another factor, as well. Apple was once again the *happening* computer company.

Think Different, and Switch

This success gave both Jobs and TBWA Chiat/Day some much-needed running room to work on the company's overall image. The "Think Different" campaign, launched in 1998, was based almost entirely on the concept of cool, featuring cultural icons like Picasso, Albert Einstein, John Lennon, and the Dalai Lama. (And note the overlap between this campaign and Steve Jobs's house calls, almost 15 years earlier.) No claim was made that these icons actually *used* Macs, of course—Amelia Earhart's plane crashed long before the two Steves went into that famous garage—but rather, that they had bucked convention, overcome long odds, and changed the world. "The people who are crazy enough to *think* they can change the world," intoned the narrator on the introductory "Think Different" TV spot, once again backed up by earnest piano chordings, "are the ones who *do*."[13] Just like a certain Cupertino-based computer company with a tiny market share, come to think of it.

Think Different hit some bumps in the road. Notably, when Think Different arrived in Asia, the Dalai Lama was missing from the line-up. Apple explained that in picking celebrity faces for the Asian market, it would be "sticking to those who are well known."[14] More likely, Apple didn't want to go out of its way to offend China, which was understandably sensitive about an ad campaign that celebrated the spiritual leader of beleaguered Tibet. This earned Apple some huffing and puffing from the *Wall Street Journal's* editorial page, which typically has not paid much attention to the company.[15] But generally, the high-profile campaign continued to buy back the "cool" turf that had been ceded during the Sculley years.

The "Switch" campaign—which followed Think Different, and urged people to switch from Wintel to Apple—took a sideways step away from celebrity cool. This campaign featured "ordinary" people telling horror stories about their experiences with Windows, and their subsequent happy Apple lives. But an odd thing happened in the summer of 2002: The campaign turned one of its subjects into a celebrity, of sorts. She was Ellen Feiss, a college student who appears to be a little

> If you're really cool, your cool may be transferable.

bit, well, *spaced out* as she tells the camera about her Wintel machine eating her term paper. "I mean," she says laconically—eyes half closed, looking as if no term paper will ever bother her again—"it's kind of a *bummer*."[16]

It's hard to believe that the dreamy Feiss won over many hard-nosed Windows users, but—as Leander Kahney reports—she surely captured the hearts of the Cult of Mac:

> *She became the subject of numerous newspaper stories, fan sites, icons, desktop wallpaper, and merchandise like T-shirts and Frisbees bearing her image. Talk show hosts David Letterman and Jay Leno requested interviews, and Hollywood called with talk of TV shows and movie roles.[17]*

The phenomenon of the iPod gave Apple an opportunity to get back into the business of celebrity cool. In the fall of 2004, in conjunction with the introduction of the new iPod Photo—which stores and plays back images, as well as music—Steve Jobs announced that Apple had struck a deal with U2, the Irish rock band fronted by the highly visible Bono. The *Wall Street Journal* explained the specifics of the deal:

> *Apple will sell U2's collected works, spanning more than two decades and 400 songs, for $149 as a 'digital box set' on Apple's iTunes Music Store. The deal, a steep discount over the more than $400 the songs would cost if purchased individually on iTunes, could stimulate sales of the band's older music. People who purchased the U2 iPod will get $50 off the box set, which includes U2's new album, 'How to Dismantle an Atomic Bomb.'[18]*

Jobs noted that Apple hoped to make similar arrangements with other high-quality artists. If the mass-market retailers couldn't or wouldn't stock older music by these kinds of musicians, Jobs said, Apple would. *Cool*, all around.

Wooing Hollywood: Right-Side-Up Cool

For at least three reasons, Hollywood and Apple would seem to be a natural combination. First, thanks in part to Regis McKenna's long-ago efforts to woo and win thought leaders over to the Apple cause, the West Coast's *glitterati* had always been predisposed toward the computer-maker up in Cupertino.

Second, there was that issue of cool. Stars—and the people who make them—have to worry about cool even more than the rest of us.

And third, the particular strengths of the Mac more and more overlapped with the needs of the creative community. As video editing, in particular, migrated away from huge Avid-like systems to PCs, the Mac more or less took over Hollywood.

Apple understood these happy trends, of course, and aggressively pursued "product placements"—cameo appearances in movies and TV shows by Apple products. The effort was highly successful: Macs showed up on the big or little screen more than 1,500 times in the last 20 years. Macs did everything from rescuing small children to getting cyberdates for Carrie (*Sex and the City*) and Ally (*Ally McBeal*) to saving earth from hostile alien invaders.

There was an interesting little subplot that emerged here, as well: The guys in the white hats (and the pretty girls) tended to use Macs, whereas the bad guys tended to use Wintel machines. Think *You've Got Mail*, a flick that featured personal computers in starring roles: corporate dirtball type Tom Hanks on Windows, beautiful earnest Indy bookstore operator Meg Ryan on Mac.

Same thing with the recent Kiefer Sutherland hit, *24*: everybody but the bad guy uses a Mac; the bad guy sports a Dell. Pure coincidence? Or was it nefarious conspiracy on the part of Apple and Hollywood to make Wintel look bad? You make the call.

All very cool, with one notable asterisk: In far too many of those TV shows and movies, the backlit Apple logo was *upside down*. That's right: Jeff Goldblum (or whoever) opens up his PowerBook to save the world, and the little detached stem on the backlit white Apple logo points downward. As Scott Kelby points out, it wasn't until Apple brought out the second-generation iBooks and first-generation G4 Titanium PowerBooks that the logo got flipped, and all those successful product placements could have their full impact.[19]

You could make the case that this weird saga of logo positioning reflected much deeper problems at Apple. (We cool people would rather talk to ourselves than to the masses. We'd rather connect with our installed base than with the other 98 percent of PC users.) But hey, they got it right, eventually. And little by little, thanks to a colorful cast of characters including the Dalai Lama, Ellen Feiss, Denzel Washington (government-issue Mac in *Courage Under Fire*), Tom Cruise (highly visible Mac in *Mission Impossible*), and a right-side-up logo, it gradually became less embarrassing to take out that PowerBook in business meetings. You could even earn a respectful nod, sometimes, by firing one up in first-class on the Red Eye. Cool.

> If your logo is upside-down, it may be symptomatic of bigger problems.

Oh, yes. And when Microsoft set up an internal task force in November 2002 to get more and better product placement for Microsoft products, what did they call the push? "Cool form factor," a nerd phrase meaning, roughly, "nice packaging."[20] *Not quite cool*, but aiming in the right direction.

The Uncool among the Cool

Now for the tin-ear part: Almost from day one, people like Regis McKenna advised Apple to take good care of thought leaders, especially *media* thought leaders, and those high-end opinion-makers would take good care of Apple.

But there's a problem: Apple has always seen itself as beleaguered. It has always seen itself as the little guy fighting the forces of darkness. It has even found some strategic advantage in seeing itself that way. (See the next chapter.)

At the same time, as noted in earlier chapters, Apple has always been an innovator—a *powerful* innovator, in fact. Wherever the computer world is going, Apple is likely to get there first.

So, you have a Little Kingdom under siege—at least in its own mind—and the Little Kingdom is full of valuable secrets. This combination has led to a certain, well, *paranoia*, out in Cupertino. And this, in turn, has led to a steady stream of lawsuits being filed by Apple against representatives of the Fourth Estate, broadly defined. In 2000, for example, Apple filed suit in Santa Clara County Superior Court against an "unknown individual" for allegedly revealing confidential Apple information on the Internet. The point of the suit, apparently, was to smoke out the Apple insider who was presumed to be leaking digital pictures of the dual-processor PowerMac.[21]

> Seige mentality + valuable secrets = paranoia (uncool).

The same scenario got replayed twice in 2005. First, in January, Apple sued a Harvard undergraduate, Nicholas M. Ciarelli, for disclosing details about unreleased Apple products. Ciarelli—Internet moniker "Nick dePlume," host of thinksecret.com—revealed the impending release of the $499 "Mac mini" computer two weeks before the 2005 Macworld. (Thinksecret was the first site to break the news—in 2001—that Apple was about to release a digital music player.) In an e-mail to the *Harvard Crimson*, Ciarelli protested his innocence: "I employ the same legal news-gathering practices used by any other journalist. I talk to sources of information, investigate tips, follow up on leads, and corroborate details. I believe these practices are reflected in Think Secret's track record."[22]

The following month, Apple sued three online journalists for publishing stories about "Asteroid," a product-in-the-making that supposedly creates an electronic link between musical instruments and Macs. Apple also sued the reporters' ISP, in search of e-mails that would, again, identify informants inside Apple.

Apple certainly has the right to protect itself against theft of its property, intellectual and otherwise. And because California's Uniform Trade Secrets Act deals harshly with what it calls "contributory infringers" (that is, people who help other people steal trade secrets), the stakes for Ciarelli and others in his situation could be high. On the other hand, skeptics have pointed to the fact that Apple made its moves against several Apple-rumor websites (2000), and then against Ciarelli (2005), just before the opening of Macworld in each of those years. Are these cases, they ask, in which protecting trade secrets might just possibly overlap with generating publicity?

One clear-cut case of simple retribution by Apple against opinion leaders came in the spring of 2005, when John Wiley & Sons published a book called *iCon Steve Jobs: The Greatest Second Act in the History of Biz*, by Jeffrey S. Young and William L. Simon. Not only did Apple ban *iCon* from its Apple Stores, but it reportedly also banned *all* Wiley books from its retail outlets. As a result, Bob LeVitus's popular *Macs for Dummies*, among other titles, disappeared from the shelves. "It stinks," LeVitus told the *Mac Observer*. And, as SiliconValley.com pointed out, banning books tends to be counterproductive, focusing more attention on the objectionable material than it would have gotten otherwise.[23]

And, in the wake of Apple's move against Harvard undergraduate Ciarelli, monthly page views at thinksecret.com doubled—from 2.5 million to 5 million.

What would Regis McKenna say? *Uncool.*

Lessons in Keeping Your Cool

Cool is an elusive quality. It's something that you can try to cultivate—in yourself, in your company—but at the end of the day, it really only exists in the eye of the beholder. Getting *cool* right, therefore, is hard. But blowing your cool is easy.

Here are eight Apple lessons in cool (and uncool):

- **Don't get pot-bound.** Even if you've got a good thing going today, in terms of your corporate image, it will almost certainly have to change tomorrow. If you have to migrate from warm to cool, migrate.

- **Cool is a double-edged sword.** If you cultivate cool, and then you act *uncool*, it's confusing and disturbing.
- **Cultivate your cool by cultivating thought-leaders.** This is one of the most important lessons that Apple learned early. If you want—like the Irish—to "fight above your weight," you need an oversized image.
- **If your product is all about being user-friendly, your ads should probably show your product being user-friendly.** Especially if your un-user-friendly competition is doing just that.
- **Cool can be accidental. Exploit your accidental cool.** The iMac was a classic case of accidental cool: The temporary transparent housings appealed to kids, so Apple made the temporary permanent. When Hollywood went looking for the coolest-looking computer to show on a desktop, guess which one got picked?
- **If you're *really* cool, your cool may be transferable.** If you can make nonentities into cult figures, you're probably firing on all cylinders.
- **If your logo is upside-down, it may be symptomatic of bigger problems.** Who really needs to see a right-reading logo: The tiny band of users in the process of firing up the computers they already own and love? Or everybody else in the galaxy?
- **Seige mentality + valuable secrets = paranoia (uncool).** One lesson that Apple occasionally forgets is that biting the hand that creates its outsized corporate image—suing Harvard undergraduates, banning books—is a bad idea. Remember the double-edged sword!

Chapter 10

Flog the Bad Guys

A man cannot be too careful in the choice of his enemies.
—Oscar Wilde

Build the cult, get it out there, tell the world about it: These are the (mostly) positive ways that Apple markets itself, leverages the fanatical devotion of its user base, and generally forces its nose under the tent even when it's not welcome in that particular tent.

But there's another side to the marketing of Apple—a darker side—which I'll summarize as *flogging the bad guys*. Simply put, this means identifying Somebody Out There as a villain and setting yourself up as a good guy, the cowboy in the white hat.

Why go to all that trouble? Well, it's a good way to build the cult, which we talked about in Chapter 7. It also sets up some good story lines for advertising campaigns and public relations ploys (Chapter 9). And finally, when you really screw things up badly, it's great to have Somebody Out There to blame for the mess. *It's not our fault*, you proclaim defiantly; *it was that guy in the black hat.*

There's almost always at least one bad guy in Apple's universe. Sometimes there's more than one. Sometimes the company picks a target that richly deserves the bad

> **Flog the bad guys**
> - To build the cult
> - For good ad copy
> - To obscure the fact that many of your problems are of your own making

guy treatment, and the campaign is productive and enduring. Other times, the target is less convincing, and the campaign fizzles. In this chapter, we'll look at examples of both.

The First Bad Guy: IBM

Maybe you had to be there.

In the 1960s, that is. Maybe you had to be a pot smoking, long-haired, college dropout in the summer of, say, 1969, preferably in the San Francisco Bay area, to really understand the roots of Apple Computer.

Of course, it would also help to have spent a little time in Armonk, New York, hanging around the world headquarters of IBM. There, you would have seen white-shirted, blue-suited legions with crew cuts and narrow ties—Tom Watson's boys—coming up with the next generation of mainframe computers principally designed to serve corporate America and the Defense Department. (OK, this is more than a little unfair—IBM was a truly innovative company, back then—but hey, we're painting a picture, here.)

IBM introduced its first commercially available scientific computer, the 701 "Electronic Data Processing Machines System," in 1952. It was slow, inflexible, not very powerful, and enormous. (Think "three-bedroom apartment.") Another milestone came on April 7, 1964, when the company released the "System/360," a family of computers that were faster and more flexible, and, on the smaller end, smaller. (Think "two-car garage.") The 360 revolutionized the course of computing. It made computers somewhat more affordable. It put more control in the hands of users, and took some control out of the hands of those white-coated lab technicians behind the thick glass windows. Yes, other companies competed—including GE, the upstart Digital Equipment Company, Honeywell, and Burroughs—but "Big Blue" dominated.[1]

IBM wasn't *exactly* congruent with corporate America. In fact, it was more forward-looking, design-conscious, and even a little more hip than most of the Fortune 500. (It hired graphic design superstar Paul Rand to design its new logo, for example, and paid careful attention to the look-and-feel of its flagship machines.) But the company was still a hard-edged, hard-nosed American monolith—expecting and enforcing conformity in its workforce, setting computing standards to which the rest of the world was expected to conform, and driving hard bargains among customers who didn't have a lot of other good choices. In the early '70s, for example, IBM introduced its "fixed-term plan," offering corporate customers reduced prices on disk drives if they would take longer leases on the company's equipment, thereby wedding themselves to Big Blue.

All of this didn't sit well with two college dropouts named Steve. On April 1, 1976, Wozniak and Jobs incorporated Apple Computer Company, and introduced the Apple 1 (list price: $666.66). From the start, the Apple was seen as the *alternative* to machines produced by the likes of IBM. Small, cheap, and friendly, it was, in Jobs's memorable marketing phrase, "the computer for the rest of us." Even Wozniak's choice for the start-up's name—*Apple*—underscored that this new company and its products were supposed to be something very unusual. Whatever an "Apple" was, it had to be different from an "International Business Machine."

At first, this was an indirect kind of competition: David over here serving little guys, and Goliath over there serving big guys. But this changed in 1981, when IBM introduced its first PC and began competing directly in Apple's markets. Suddenly—from Apple's point of view— Goliath had moved in next door and was looking to carry off David's daughters. The IBM PC (priced between $1,565 and $6,000, depending on features) sold 50,000 units in the six months. True, Adam Osborne introduced his Osborne 1 in that same year, but—at least in Apple's mind—the real war was between IBM and Apple.

It was a business war, to be sure, but it was also a *cultural* war. "The IBM PC was created by people who drank alcohol," as one journalist later commented. "The Mac was created by people who smoked pot."[2] Apple, of course, denied and downplayed reports of illicit drug consumption on its premises, but the larger point still stood. IBM was the old culture, handmaiden to the Department of Defense, the two-martini lunch: the *establishment*. Apple, meanwhile, was sex, drugs, and rock and roll—the anti-establishment.

But it wasn't until the introduction of the Mac that Apple decided to take on Big Blue directly, and to create its first full-fledged bad guy. On January 22, 1984, Apple ran a startling ad—a teaser for the forthcoming Mac—during the fourth quarter of the Super Bowl. It opens with an Orwellian rally: grey, zombie-like, shaven-headed men marching into a hall and seating themselves on benches, where they begin watching a Big Brother-like figure on an enormous black-and-white monitor at the front of a hall. *"Our unification of thoughts is more powerful a weapon than any fleet or army on earth,"* Big Brother is saying, haranguing his stupe-fied legions. *"We are one people, with one will, one resolve, one cause. Our enemies shall talk themselves to death and we will bury them with their own confusion. We shall prevail!"*

But wait! In sprints a young woman in a white athletic jersey (with an Apple logo prominently displayed, of course) and bright red shorts— the only splash of color in the entire hall. She is carrying a long-handled sledgehammer. Riot police in full clanking regalia are chasing her. She stops short in the center aisle, spins around three times, hammer extended, gathering momentum—police closing in—and with a shout of exaltation, hurls the sledge through the enormous screen. Crash! Big Brother disappears in a cloud of smoke! The zombies are set free!

> When flogging the Bad Guys, a combination of humor and terror is a good thing. Make people laugh. But make them worry, too.

"On January 24th," a new voice says, "Apple computer will introduce Macintosh, and you'll see why 1984 won't be like 1984."[3]

All across America, football fans sat stunned in their recliners. What was *that* all about? Was that a shot at IBM? (IBM, of course, was never mentioned.) Yeah, it must have been a shot at IBM. Wait a minute: IBM, American icon, as *Big Brother*?

The next day, speaking in front of 2,000 overheated Apple employ-ees and shareholders at DeAnza College in Cupertino, Steve Jobs con-nected the dots. He unveiled the Macintosh, which—amazingly—*spoke*. And the first words it said were:

> *Hello, I am Macintosh. It sure is great to get out of that bag. Unaccustomed as I am to public speaking, I'd like to share with you a thought that occurred to me the first time I met an IBM main-frame. Never trust a computer you can't lift. Right now, I'd like to introduce a man who has been like a father to me, Steve Jobs.*[4]

Thus began IBM's seven-year reign as Apple's first bad guy. The "1984" ad—directed by an unknown named Ridley Scott, just then finish-ing *Blade Runner*, and later the director of movies like *Alien, Thelma and Louise*, and *Gladiator*—created an absolute furor. (Furor was good; it ensured that the ad got played and replayed endlessly, for free, in sub-sequent months.) It was later named "ad of the decade" by *Advertising*

Age, and the "greatest commercial of all time" by *TV Guide*.[5] Although Apple never paid to air "1984" again, the spectacularly visible Super Bowl ad set a theme that was played out for years afterward. IBM was monochromatic, monolithic, lock stepping, and destructive of the human spirit. By extension, IBM PC *users* were a dull and grey breed.

Apple was liberating. Apple users were creative. They wore white hats.

Changing Hats

But fast-forward seven years and something *very interesting* happens.

On October 2, 1991, Apple and IBM signed a contract establishing a far-ranging collaboration between the two companies. The two companies would platoon hundreds of their star developers to work on ambitious joint ventures. The agreement, according to Apple and IBM, would "change the landscape of computing in the 1990s."

At the press conference, IBM President Jack D. Kuehler stood with John Sculley, CEO of Apple, behind a foot-high pile of documents that collectively made up the contract that the two corporate moguls would be signing. "Together we announce the second decade of personal computing, and it begins today," intoned Kuehler. Sculley seconded Kuehler's comments, saying that the Apple-IBM alliance would "launch a renaissance in technological innovation."[6]

No, the two leaders said, in response to questions; the Justice Department wouldn't object, and the cultural chasms between the two companies certainly weren't too large to jump. But on the second point, at least, some observers weren't so sure:

> *The nation's two largest producers of personal computers have long differed in style and philosophy ... Apple, based in Cupertino, California, has always styled itself as the upstart alternative to IBM, a pin-striped and staid company based in Armonk, New York. But executives of the two companies said they were confident the alliance would work because the negotiations were being conducted by the people who will now work together, rather than simply being decreed from the top.[7]*

So, IBM takes off its bad guy hat, and Apple throws its arms around Big Blue! What's going on here? In short: competitive necessity. Apple's position in its own markets was weakening, mainly due to the incompatibility of its operating system with the dominant DOS system then sold by Microsoft. IBM, having made the horrific blunder years before of giving up control over its operating system to the young Bill Gates, was now bleeding to death in the PC business as a result of the huge numbers of IBM-compatible, DOS-running PC clones then flooding the marketplace.

The arranged marriage was less a compelling vision of an exciting future, and more a salvage job. "Apple and IBM," concluded the *New York Times*, "have virtually nothing in common except a challenge: keeping the Microsoft Corporation at bay and shifting the power center of the industry away from software and back to hardware."[8] The two companies would work together to create a new computer called the "Power PC," designed to run on any operating system. This, the theory went, would allow customers to make their equipment choices based on *hardware*, rather than software.

> **Bad Guy wisdom:**
> • Don't burn that last bridge. Ever.
> • The enemy of my enemy is my friend.

What is the lesson in this strange saga? Well, first, don't burn any bridges when you make the other guy out to be the bad guy. (You may need to throw your arms around him in seven years.) And second, as the old Arab proverb puts it, *the enemy of my enemy is my friend*.

The Second Bad Guy: Microsoft

Here's a topic which, taken at its broadest cut, could fill a shelf full of books (and probably already has): the legendary ill will between Apple and Microsoft. So, we'll have to take a somewhat narrower cut.

The ill will began way back in the '80s, and only intensified throughout the '90s. In the late 1990s, for example, a 13-year-old PC user, for example, set up a website with the URL www.ihateapple.com. In response, a Mac fanatic launched a site called www.fuckmicrosoft.com. The operators of the latter site recently changed its name to www.microsuck.com, in a move intended to make it at least a little more family-friendly.[9] The bad blood persists today, despite regular efforts to bury the hatchet. The 2005 Macworld Expo, for example, featured prominently displayed banners for the new Tiger OS that read, "Redmond, start your photocopiers."

Apple started fitting out Redmond, Washington-based Microsoft as a bad guy way back in 1985, when Bill Gates's company released its "Windows 1.0" operating system. The new system was clunky and suffered dismal sales—but it represented a clear threat to Apple's main competitive advantage, which was a reasonably open and intuitive user interface. Inside and outside Apple, Windows 1.0 was seen as a blatant rip-off—and a "lame knock-off"—of the

> When in doubt, use cute kids and border collies against the Bad Guys.

Mac operating system. Here's how one self-professed Mac fanatic put it:

> So what's the real reason Mac people hate Microsoft? In my opinion, it's because they feel that Microsoft ripped Apple off. By that I mean that Apple was the company to bring icons, pull-down menus, folders, the little trash can, "point and click" using a mouse—in short, the whole GUI to computing. They didn't necessarily invent every piece of it themselves, but Apple is the company that brought it to personal computing, at a time when PC users were using the best operating system Microsoft had come up with to that point—DOS. PC users had no icons. No folders. No windows. No mouse! ...[10]

That, and the fact that much-despised Microsoft, with its inferior products and uncool leader, was actually winning. Year by year, percentage point by percentage point, Microsoft-powered machines were taking over the personal computer industry. This drove Mac fanatics *nuts*, to put it mildly:

> How could a lesser product rise to the stature and dominance that it now maintains? How could the vast majority of the PC world not see what happened? Not see the difference? Not demand something better, especially when it's out there on the Macintosh platform? This is at the core of what still really toasts Macintosh users to this day.[11]

Apple fanned these flames happily, especially after the 1991 rehabilitation and embrace of IBM (and after Apple's various lawsuits against Microsoft for alleged patent infringements were mostly thrown out of court). Throughout the 1990s, Apple ran ads belittling its competitors, all of which—of course—ran on Microsoft operating systems.

One of my personal favorites is a 1998 ad entitled "Simplicity Shoot-Out." It features a competition between a seven-year-old boy—Johann Thomas (assisted by his border collie, Brodie)—and a 26-year-old MBA from Stanford named Adam Taggart. The challenge: to be the first to unpack a brand-new computer from its box, set it up, and successfully connect to the Internet. Tow-headed little Johann and manic Brodie have an iMac to work with, while stolid Adam has an HP Pavilion 8250. We watch them start unloading their respective boxes on a split screen, with a counter ticking off the seconds under each of them. The cheerful narrator takes a few passing shots at the complexity of "Wintel" machines—*look at all those wires!*—and also at Windows 95. ("Wintel" is shorthand for "Windows machine powered by Intel chip.") No surprise: Johann and Brodie manage to connect to the Internet in 8 minutes and 15 seconds, and then go outside to play in the yard. Adam finally logs on at 28 minutes and 39 seconds.[12]

Steve Jobs showed the "shoot-out" ad at the Seybold San Francisco/Publishing conference in 1998. Amid much applause, he gloated about how much easier his machines were to set up and use than those powered by the loathsome Windows 95. *A boy and his adorable dog beat all those Wintel MBA types!*[13]

Equally important to our story, Apple in this period also aided—or at the very least condoned—the efforts of those Mac fanatics out in the world who sought to demonize the evil empire of Redmond, Washington.

Guy Kawasaki, whom we met in Chapter 9, played a central role in this effort. His "EvangeList" aimed squarely at the evil that was Microsoft. Mac chronicler Leander Kahney credits Kawasaki with (or blames him for) coming up with the "bad guys" strategy in the first place:

> *One of Kawasaki's central strategies was to identify and demonize a common enemy. In the early days, when he was dealing with software developers, it was IBM. Later, it was Microsoft, even though the company was, and still is, one of the biggest publishers of Macintosh software. During the EvangeList days, Kawasaki's rallying cry was, "Stop the Microsoft hegemony!"[14]*

But Kahney's assessment points to one of the big problems that Apple faced, in the Microsoft-as-bad-guy era. The two companies needed each other too much to really *clobber* one another. In the mid 1990s, when Kawasaki was doing his most urgent evangelizing, Apple was in deep, deep trouble. (That's the basic reason why Kawasaki was so energetic: Apple was on the ropes.) Apple desperately needed Microsoft to keep writing software—increasingly elegant software, by the way—for an operating system that seemed to have been left behind by much of the computer-buying public.

For its part, Microsoft was not going to launch a frontal attack on Apple. Even if Bill Gates and his legions were indeed bad guys, they weren't *stupid* bad guys. They wouldn't do anything that might risk killing off the billion-dollar Macintosh software market, a market that Microsoft already dominated. In fact, Microsoft was prepared to go to great lengths to keep Apple viable. Why? "Maybe if Apple caves in," wrote one observer in *Wired* in 1997, "Windows will get so much market share that the Department of Justice will intervene and break up Microsoft."[15]

Yikes! The dread "A" word, antitrust! This specter alone was enough to keep Microsoft's competitive juices somewhat contained. Apple and its zealots could say all they wanted to about Microsoft's hegemony (true) and its predatory instincts (not exactly untrue), but sensible observers knew that Microsoft would tread very carefully, vis à vis its small and cranky competitor down the coast.

In fact, Microsoft wound up doing far more than that. In August 1997, at the Macworld Expo in Boston, newly returned Apple co-founder Steve Jobs shocked his audience by announcing that Microsoft was investing $150 million in Apple. This translated into a 5 percent share in the company, a stake that Microsoft pledged to hold onto for a minimum of three years. This would give Apple enough time, and enough operating capital, to get back on its feet.

> If all else fails, sell yourself to a Bad Guy, and forget all that bad stuff you ever said about him.

Ouch! Jobs's announcement was greeted by a storm of hisses and catcalls—probably the only time that Jobs has ever been so roughly handled at a Macworld love fest. But the announcement was simply too much, for Apple buffs steeped in years and years of bad guy propaganda. And the imagery was all wrong, too. There was a little tiny Steve Jobs in person, taking abuse up on the stage, while above him loomed an enormous video image of Bill Gates. It was a little like the "1984" ad in reverse. This time, Big Brother drops the hammer on the woman in the red shorts, and the revolution comes to a sudden and sad end. Jobs, probably not too happy to find himself in this awkward position in the first place, didn't appreciate the crowd's reaction, and more or less told them off:

> *If we want to move forward and see Apple healthy and prospering, we have to let go of a few things. We have to let go of this notion that for Apple to win, Microsoft has to lose. OK? If we screw up and don't do a good job, it's not somebody else's fault. It's our fault.*[16]

This was easy for Jobs to say. He was only recently back in the fold. So, whoever screwed up, it was somebody else's fault, rather than his. Nevertheless, Jobs succeeded in making the bigger point. *No more demonizing the bad guys*, he was telling his shocked audience. *We have met the enemy, and he is us.*

In recent years, the anti-Microsoft ad guy campaign has cooled off a bit. This is in part because Microsoft—which, again, is not populated by dummies—maintained a studied cool toward the whole thing. (Being one of the world's most powerful quasi-monopolies gives you a certain kind of above-the-fray perspective.) And Apple's recent successes—not only with the iPod, but also in hardware and software—have gone a long way toward reassuring Mac users about the company's long-term viability. If you're not in danger of being overrun, you don't have to spend as much time

> Ultimately, you have to beat the Bad Guys at your own game. You have to own your problems, and fix them.

on the ramparts, looking out for the bad guys. And finally, it must be noted, Mac users have been distracted by internal doctrinal wars. (*Mac Classic will always be better than OS X! This new Tiger thing is way cool/totally bogus.*) A little internal heresy, and the related wars of purification, go a long way toward taking your mind off Bill Gates.

The Bad Guy that Flopped

Sometimes the bad guy impulse goes awry. Hard on the heels of its "1984" triumph—which formally launched the bad guy campaign against IBM—Apple opened another bad guy front. This time, the target was an unlikely one: the company's prospective customers.

The occasion, once again, was the Super Bowl—this time, the 1985 edition. And, once again, the campaign opened with an astonishing advertisement: "Lemmings." (It should be noted that the ad agency was once again Chiat/Day, which was also IBM's ad agency at the time.) "Lemmings" depicted a steady stream of blindfolded businessmen in suits, walking in single file off a cliff. The background music was a slow, corrupted version of the classic Disney tune, "Heigh Ho, Heigh Ho" (*it's off to work we go*). Finally, one human "lemming" steps out of line, raises his blindfold, and asks rhetorically, "Why am I doing this?"[17]

From the flog-the-bad-guy perspective, the answer is obvious. Businessmen are like lemmings: following the herd, failing to think for themselves. The evidence? Well, they were failing to "look into the Macintosh Office."

The ad was shown to the Super Bowl crowd at California's Stanford Stadium at the same time that it was being broadcast across the nation. Apple's vice president of operations, Jay Elliot, remembers sitting near Ford Motor Company's vice president of marketing. When the ad finished, the Ford executive turned to Elliot and said, "Hey, one out of two ain't bad."[18]

In other words, Apple had a bomb on its hands. "Rather than stunning the audience like '1984,'" Mac evangelist Guy Kawasaki later wrote, "it displayed Apple's self-delusions to millions of viewers."[19]

And, as Kawasaki also points out, Mac Office was missing some absolutely critical components, including a fileserver (which stores shared files and controls client access to the network). Apple promised in January 1985 that the fileserver would be available in March; in fact, it didn't hit the market until 1987. But even if it *had* turned up on schedule, it wouldn't have been fast enough for many office settings—operating at one-tenth of the speed of IBM's new PC Network, and one-fiftieth the speed of Xerox's Ethernet system.[20]

> Flogging your prospective customers tends to be self-defeating.

So, the lemmings weren't lemmings at all. They were simply savvy customers who were fully capable of finding the products (IBM products, Xerox products) that met their needs. And to the extent that they noticed Apple's short-lived bad guy campaign against them, they resented it.

The lesson: don't flog your prospective customers.

Lessons of the Bad Guys

There were other bad guys in Apple's past—notably Intel, the chipmaker that Apple loved to hate, but has recently embraced with a vengeance.

(That story pops up in Chapter 12, but for now, you can watch Steve Jobs and Intel CEO Paul Otellini bury the hatchet on the web.[21]) For now, let's pull together and summarize the lessons about flogging bad guys:

- **Flog the bad guys.** Why has Apple cultivated the notion that there are dark forces lurking out there in the world, against whom the company (and its supporters) must struggle? Easy: To reinforce the cult, to create interesting dynamics and good story lines in advertising campaigns, and—it must be said—to obscure the fact that many of the company's problems are of its own making. Sometimes that's a good strategy. Sometimes it's not.

- **When flogging the bad guys, combine humor and terror.** In other words, make people laugh even as you're making them nervous. (What if I woke up one morning, and my Mac was gone, and I was staring at a C-prompt on an old DOS machine?) It's an effective combination, like hot-and-sour soup.

- **Don't burn that last bridge.** Remember: The enemy of your enemy is your friend. If there's some chance that some day you'll have to climb into bed with IBM, it's best to flog IBM judiciously.

- **When in doubt, use cute kids and border collies.** What did W.C. Fields say? "Anyone who hates dogs and children can't be all bad"? Well, this is advice from the opposite direction. Enlist the forces of good and innocence in your struggle against the bad guys.

- **If all else fails, sell yourself to a bad guy.** Then be prepared to get booed and hissed by the people whom you've been steeping in bad guy philosophy.

- **Beat the bad guys at your own game, not theirs.** This is simply a nice way of saying what Steve Jobs had to tell the unruly crowd at the 1997 Macworld Expo in Boston: *Some of these problems are of our own making. Past a certain point, we can't blame it on the bad guys.*

- **Don't flog your prospective customers.** Depicting the people who aren't buying your products as small, mindless, suicidal, furry animals is a bad strategy, especially if the real problem is your products' shortcomings. Again, spend more energy fixing those problems than opening new bad guy fronts.

Chapter 11

Fix Your Leaders

∾୦∾

Since when was genius found respectable?
—Elizabeth Barrett Browning

Right after he signed on as CEO of Apple in 1983, John Sculley attended a three-day offsite meeting of Apple's executive team.

Sculley, then 44 years old, when the average age of an Apple worker was 27, was fresh from the paneled offices, the hierarchy, and the predictability of PepsiCo. He was here, at least in his own estimation, to help the still-youthful Steve Jobs grow up—to acquire the necessary skills and temperament to lead a billion-dollar corporation. It would be Apple's regency period: the seasoned old counselor exercising wise authority until the prince could grow into his rightful station.

So the meeting starts, and Sculley soon realizes that life on the Left Coast is going to be very different from life at PepsiCo. He has arrived with a formal agenda, which the group of young managers completely ignores. Instead, they engage in a "free-for-all," with insults flying in all directions. Not spared this abuse is the barefoot and blue-jeaned Steve Jobs, sitting in the lotus position on the floor of the conference room. When he ventures a critical opinion of something, his colleagues pounce on him, blisteringly, telling him that until he finishes the Macintosh and *gets it out the door,* he has no right to criticize *anybody.*

Throwing rocks at the prince!

Pepsi held its off-sites in the Bahamas. They were tightly scripted. There were no rocks thrown at the ultra-exclusive Lyford Cay Club (membership by invitation only). In fact, there were no surprises at all— except perhaps the muted elegance of it all. Here at Pajaro Dunes, it seemed, things would be different. Sculley found himself recalling a joke told by an executive at Apple's advertising agency: *What's the difference between Apple and the Boy Scouts of America? The Boy Scouts have adult supervision.*

But there were still more surprises to come, as Sculley relates:

We hadn't been in the meeting more than an hour and a half when the lights flickered and the building began to tremble. We were in the middle of an earthquake.

'Head for the beach,' someone shouted. We ran out the door, got fifty paces toward the beach, and someone else said, 'Wait a minute. The last earthquake, we got a tidal wave. Head for the land.'[1]

Personally, I like to picture Sculley pulling on his loafers and Jobs pulling on his sandals as the building starts to shake. (*We can't run out-side in our knee socks or our bare feet, right?*) For his part, Sculley later looked back on that meeting as a portent of things to come: arguments, passion, indecisive-ness, and natural disasters. And in a certain sense, he couldn't have been more right.

Run for the beach! No! Run for the hills!

But digging down another layer or two, Apple's real problem— thrown into sharp relief at regular intervals before and after the earth-quake at Pajaro Dunes—was a failure of leadership.

Followers and Leaders

Actually, the advertising executive was being a little unfair to the Boy Scouts. Certainly in the founding decade of the company, with the sweet smells of money and marijuana wafting through the California air, the kids from Apple didn't conduct themselves very much like Boy Scouts.

Nor is "conducting yourself like a Boy Scout" a key to success, espe-cially at the upper reaches of corporate America. The Boy Scouts, accord-ing to my dusty recollection, are supposed to be:

- Trustworthy,
- Loyal,
- Helpful,
- Friendly,
- Courteous,
- Kind,
- Obedient,
- Cheerful,
- Thrifty,
- Brave,
- Clean, and
- Reverent.

It's an interesting list, if you think about it. Collectively, these 12 attributes are a prescription not for leadership, but for *followership*. Yes, we'd like our leaders to be trustworthy and brave—and "clean" would be good, too; more on this below—but the rest of it seems secondary to leadership.

So, what would the comparable list for leadership be, and how often have Apple's leaders embodied it? Let's go with nouns, rather than adjectives, and put integrity and courage (trustworthy and brave) at the top of the list:

- Integrity,
- Courage,
- Consistency,
- Fairness,
- Experience,
- Wisdom,
- Tenacity,
- Flexibility,
- Empathy, and
- Vision.

If this list defines strong corporate leadership, then you have to look hard to find major companies (or universities, or churches) with strong leadership. And you could probably count on the fingers of two hands the number of major American companies that have had the benefit of two strong leaders in a row. Emerson Electric (Buck Persons and Chuck Knight) and General Electric (Reg Jones and Jack Welch) come to mind.

Unfortunately, Apple *doesn't* come to mind.

Before the Regency

Arguably, the first leader of Apple was a former Fairchild Semiconductor and Intel middle manager named Mike Markkula. It was Markkula who fell in love with the *idea* of the Apple Computer, wrote the business plan, put together the company's original financing—calling on venture capital friends like Arthur Rock, and taking a big piece of the business himself—and put the initial corporate scaffolding in place to support the two young genius Steves: Wozniak and Jobs. So when people marvel at the story of the two kids in the garage, they are overlooking the third person lurking in the background of that fable: Mike Markkula.

> Look for the adult supervision in the back of the garage.

Markkula also installed Apple's first CEO: a 32-year-old bachelor named Mike Scott, whom Markkula knew from their days together at Fairchild. The two Steves went along with the idea, with varying degrees of enthusiasm. (Woz, who from his tenure at Hewlett-Packard knew at least a little about corporate life, understood that Apple would need a full-time manager; Jobs knew that nobody else in sight—even including himself, at least for the moment—was prepared to lead the company.) One of Scott's first jobs, according to Apple chronicler Michael Malone, was to instruct Steve Jobs to take a bath. *A Scout is clean.* (Jobs had apparently heard that strict vegetarians like himself didn't need to bathe; his colleagues didn't agree.) Fortunately, Jobs acquiesced. But he didn't *have* to, did he? He, Wozniak, and Markkula held most of the stock in the fledgling company, and if Jobs had told Scott to go out and play in the traffic on Stevens Creek Boulevard, there wouldn't have been much that Scott could have done about it.[2]

> Note to would-be CEOs: If you don't control much voting stock, get a good bead on those who do.

A good lesson for future Mike Scotts: If other people hold most of the stock, check to see how ambitious those other people are. Particularly check to see if they're ambitious for your job.

Scott proved effective at creating an organization from scratch. He "hired up," meaning that he engaged managers, accountants, lawyers, and other professionals who might have appeared to be a little, uhm, too *important* to be signing up with the likes of Apple. But Scott was positioning the company for growth.

He also proved effective at stretching a dollar. In the company's first full fiscal year, it netted $775,000, an astonishing achievement, in the context of all those Silicon Valley start-ups that burned up their seed capital and went nowhere.

And finally, he proved effective at managing the mounting tension between Wozniak and Jobs. Both Steves were indispensable to the success of the company; but each thought the other was less indispensable than himself. When it came time to issue I.D. badges, for example, Scott gave Badge #1 to Wozniak—the technical genius, and the inventor of the Apple I. Jobs protested, saying that *he* should be #1. Or, if Wozniak *had* to be #1, then Jobs should be #0, and so on.

It's worth reminding ourselves that the Steves were only in their 20s, and Scott himself was only in his early 30s. Given how little seasoning there was on hand, it's amazing that Apple survived, let alone made a buck.

Let's fast-forward to December 12, 1980, when Apple made its fabled initial public offering. On that day, by Mike Scott's calculations, 104 people became millionaires, thanks in large part to Scott's own efforts over the previous three years. Now everyone was rich, and Scott's job became that much harder. Jobs (worth $256.4 million on December 13) became that much harder to control. Wozniak (worth $135 million) started losing his all-important focus on the company's technology; one result was a badly flawed Apple III. Now, more than ever, Scott found his time devoted to "babysitting the two founders."[3]

> Successful IPOs can make everybody that much harder to control.

The initial public offering (IPO), the most successful since that of the Ford Motor Company in the 1950s, turned out to be Scott's high-water mark. Encouraged by Wall Street to make Apple conform to the profile of a public company—and increasingly convinced that Apple's payroll had become padded—Scott initiated a small but symbolic series of layoffs in February 1981. Only 41 positions were axed, in a ritual bloodletting that became immortalized as "Black Wednesday," but the psychological damage was done An angry Apple manager confronted Steve Jobs and told him that *this was no way to run a company.*

"How do you run a company?" Apple's biggest shareholder mused, unhappily.[4]

Scott's health started to fail, and his behavior became increasingly autocratic and erratic. Perhaps seeing signs of his own unraveling, he asked Mike Markkula to step into an active management role, a move that Markkula had no intention of making. Instead, in March 1981, the Apple board sought and got Scott's retirement.

In retrospect, the forced transition seems to have been a mistake. Out the door went a skilled manager, and in his place came ... well, *nobody*.

> **Somebody is usually better than nobody.**

Mike Markkula, who had declined to take over operations when Scott asked for help, was now the nominal head of the whole company. Steve Wozniak, who injured himself seriously when he crashed his single-engine plane in February 1981, was effectively lost to the company for several years. Steve Jobs, bumped up to chairman, now had no one with both the power and inclination to make him bathe or otherwise behave himself. A $300 million publicly held company, growing like topsy, was effectively rudderless.

The Regency and Regicide

Here's a bad prescription for would-be company builders: give your brilliant, aggressive young leader-in-waiting—who happens to be your largest stockholder, and also chairman of your board—responsibility for managing a key division of your rudderless company. Then let him go hire a CEO to his liking.

That's what Apple did. Somewhere around January 1981—midway between the Day of the Riches and Black Wednesday—Steve Jobs took over the Macintosh division. This was in part because he had

> **Perceived inequities often come back to bite leaders.**

been largely frozen out of the Lisa project, and in part because the other division of the company—the Apple II division—was Woz's domain. And although the Apple II carried the company for years, racking up something like a billion dollars in sales, Jobs was contemptuous of both the product and the people who worked on it. "Clydesdales," he called them, suggesting a certain ponderousness. Or worse, "bozos." Eventually, the Apple II team was exiled to a remote building several miles down Highway 280 from the main campus—*bozos in absentia.*

Meanwhile, the team that Jobs assembled to build the next-generation Macintosh—the self-styled "pirates"—lived the good life in Bandley 3, which featured original Ansel Adams photography in its lobby and served up fresh-squeezed orange juice to its resident pirates. And, if a pirate had to take a flight of more than three hours on business, he or she got to fly first class (unlike, say, a Clydesdale).

The powerful, demanding, charismatic figure in the middle of this corporate passion play, of course, was Steve Jobs. He was, all at once, a scary, manipulative, brilliant, and impulsive leader. Far from an engineering genius, he nevertheless demonstrated a rare capacity to lead a team of geniuses. As marketing expert and former Mac acolyte Guy Kawasaki recalls:

> *Steve motivated us. He wielded a special ability to make you feel like a god or like a bozo. (In Steve's eyes, there are only two kinds of people.) ... Working for Steve was a terrifying and addictive experience. He would tell you that your work, your ideas, and sometimes your existence were worthless right to your face, right in front of everyone. Watching him crucify someone scared you into working incredibly long hours ...*
>
> *Working for Steve was also ecstasy. Once in a while he would tell you that you were great, and that made it all worth it. Watching him sanctify someone motivated you to exceed your capacities ...*
>
> *Steve's idea of management by wandering around (MBWA) was to go up to a person and say, 'I think Guy is a bozo. What do you think?' If you agreed, he'd go on to the next person and would say, 'I think Guy is a bozo. Mike agrees with me. What do you think?'*[5]

There was good Steve, and there was bad Steve. Both Steves, it seemed, aimed to instill a level of perfectionism into their workers, who—after all—were extensions of their perfectionist selves. The high praise and even higher-volume criticism made people try harder, jump higher, and work later into the night. One former colleague of Jobs, a graduate of medical school, realized he had seen this all before: in the surgeons who had trained him in the ways of the operating room.

> **Surgeons and leaders of creative teams are not necessarily nice guys.**

Surgeons on medical school faculties don't give a damn about being *liked*; they exist mainly to grow more people like themselves: relentless perfectionists.[6]

Into this strange and volatile mix came John Sculley, fresh from "selling sugared water" at Pepsi. The put-down was Jobs's, of course, who offered Sculley the choice between selling sugared water and changing the world. Arguably, Sculley made the wrong choice. At Pepsi, he was the golden boy, the heir apparent to chairman Donald Kendall, fresh from a major success at building Pepsi International Foods into a powerhouse division. In the sedate halls of Pepsi, he was even a bit of an *enfant terrible*.

At Apple, he was—at first—simply the regent. "In the back of my mind," he later wrote, "I wanted to learn from Steve just how he had [started a company], so that after I helped groom him to become Apple's president, I might move on to a start-up of my own."[7]

Despite the seeming naïveté of that personal mission statement, Sculley was no babe in the woods. He had successfully clawed his way up the Pepsi corporate ladder, presumably tangling with some tough characters along the way. But he had never run across anyone quite like Steve Jobs:

> *Steve was nothing short of exciting. He was arrogant, outrageous, intense, demanding—a perfectionist. He was also immature, fragile, sensitive, vulnerable. He was dynamic, visionary, charismatic, yet often stubborn, uncompromising, and downright impossible.*[8]

Although Sculley came into Apple fully intending to get along with Jobs—who was, remember, both his ultimate boss and the head of a fast-growing and powerful division within the company—the relationship soon went off the rails. Despite Jobs's promises and reassurances, the Mac wasn't selling, the new products weren't forthcoming, and Apple was a *products* company. The more Sculley challenged and questioned the elusive Jobs (*What product? When? At what price point?*), the rockier their relationship became. Apple's declining fortunes in the wake of stiff competition from the new IBM PC, as well as anemic sales of the dazzling new Macintosh, only compounded these woes. In a misguided effort to placate Jobs and keep him out of other people's business, Sculley folded the struggling Lisa division into the Macintosh division. Not exactly the right way to clip Jobs's wings, Sculley later admitted: "I had given Steve greater power than he had ever had, and I had created a monster."[9]

> Don't let your board chairman and biggest stockholder run your most important division.

In February 1985—only one sordid data point among many—Steve Wozniak quit the company in fury, claiming that Sculley and Apple were favoring the Mac division to an unnatural degree. (They were.) Belatedly, Sculley decided that he had to take action against his monster, who now happened to be the executive vice president of the company. On April 10, 1985, just about two years to the day after arriving at Apple, Sculley told his board that somebody had to get out of operations: him or Jobs. Reluctantly, the board gave Sculley authority to take the Mac division (and the EVP title) away from Chairman Jobs.

Typically, Sculley dragged his feet when it came to taking Jobs's operating responsibilities away from him, which he finally did at the end of May 1985. (Decisiveness was not Sculley's strong suit.) As the *New York Times* recorded the event:

> *The movement of Mr. Jobs out of line operations partly reflects the urging of the new cadre of managers [hired by Sculley], and part-ly Mr. Jobs's own recognition that he was better at developing new products and preaching the Apple gospel than at the nuts and bolts of running a major corp. Mr. Jobs, who is supposed to take some time off this summer in Europe, is trying to decide what to do next at the company, associates say.*
>
> *There have long been reports of friction between Mr. Sculley and Mr. Jobs, which may in part have stemmed from an awkward division of responsibilities. Mr. Jobs, Apple's largest shareholder and the chairman of the board, was Mr. Sculley's boss in a sense, but, as Macintosh division head, was also Mr. Sculley's subordi-nate. On the one hand, one former executive said, many at Apple were concerned that Mr. Sculley, a newcomer to the computer business, was not thinking independently from Mr. Jobs, and was getting too caught up in the old Apple structure.*[10]

In his memoir, Sculley told an uglier behind-the-scenes version of the same story: that Jobs had directly challenged his authority in May, telling Sculley in front of the entire executive staff that he himself could run the company better than Sculley. Sculley briefly considered resigning, then decided to fight back. He signed Jobs's walking papers, and told him he was out of operations.

After his summer vacation, Jobs returned to Cupertino—and summarily quit. Selling all but one share of his Apple stock, he took five top lieutenants with him, to compete—despite his protestations to the contrary—directly against Apple in the market that kept Apple's heart beating: the educational market.

The Interregnum: Sculley to Spindler to Amelio

John Sculley headed Apple for another eight years, leaving in October 1993. You could make the case that he was an effective leader. Between 1983 and 1993, Apple's sales grew from $800 million a year to $8 billion, and—at least for some of those years—Apple was one of the most profitable corporations in America. He applied some measure of discipline to product introduction and expanded the company's distribution system markedly.

Also on his watch, the personal computer made the transition from being a hobbyist's plaything to being an indispensable tool in business, education, and the home. The problem was, Apple did not make too many of those tools. Under Sculley, Apple's share of the PC market declined from 20 percent to 8 percent. Sculley's single-minded pursuit of margin protected the company's bottom line and provided the necessary cash for R&D, but also priced the Mac and other products out of the reach of the masses. Then there was that incompatibility problem: Apple proudly touted its unique operating system and its Motorola chips; the rest of the world embraced the ever-improving Windows (from the despised Microsoft!) and Intel chips (from the almost-as-bad Intel!). A failed joint venture with IBM in the early 1990s undercut Sculley's stature—as well as the company's performance—and his support of the ill-fated Newton personal digital assistant squandered still more corporate reputation and treasure.

> Trading market share for margin may be eating the seed corn.

The Newton episode underscored Sculley's lack of technical grounding, and also his confused embrace of the consumer electronics field. As former Apple PR consultant Regis McKenna later put it:

I think that one of the issues at Apple—this happens a lot to technical companies—is that they always [think] the grass is greener, and to be a consumer company is sort of Nirvana. They don't go back and trust to being technology-oriented, and they move to this consumer world, which has its own problems and difficulties. But if you don't understand the technology, I don't believe you can really run and build a business in this competitive world. You gotta make decisions too quick. You gotta rely a lot on your history; you gotta reach back and grab experiences out of your past and apply them; you gotta know who to call to pull together and [get] decisions made. And with all due respect to John [Sculley], when he reached back, he didn't have that experience, because he came out of a different world.

Now, he gained some of his knowledge later on, but it took about five years, and it was too late by the time he started really learning about the industry.[11]

Looking back from the vantage point of a decade after his own departure from Apple, Steve Jobs took an even less charitable view of the Sculley regime:

John Sculley ruined Apple and he ruined it by bringing a set of values to the top of Apple which were corrupt and corrupted some of the top people who were there....

They got very greedy, and instead of following the trajectory of the original vision—which was to make this thing an appliance, to get this out there to as many people as possible—they went for profits....

What that cost them was the future. What they should have been doing was making reasonable profits and going for market share, which is what we always tried to do....

The problem is this: no one at Apple has a clue as to how to create the next Macintosh ... They've just been living off that one thing now for over a decade, and the last attempt was the Newton, and you know what happened to that.[12]

Both critiques are fair, if a little harsh. Sculley, for his part, maintained throughout his tenure that it wasn't the job of the CEO to get down in the weeds and learn the technical details. (In fact, he prompted general scorn and derision when, in March 1990, he appointed himself Apple's chief technology officer, apparently in an effort to get a little more tech-nical traction.) And, as for values, others would say that it was Apple's *lack* of val-ues—from well before Sculley's arrival—that ultimately got the company into trou-ble. Apple, they say, was no Hewlett-Packard (HP) and never had been. Despite

> Great leaders instill great values. A company that lacks one lacks the other.

its brash and cocky image, Apple never enjoyed the kind of leadership that Dave Packard and Bill Hewlett gave their company—and therefore never had the benefit of the kinds of values that drove HP.

Meanwhile, Apple kept losing ground. For Sculley, the end came in June 1993, when he resigned as CEO. (He didn't step down as board chairman until October.) He was succeeded as chief executive by his operations head, the German-born Michael Spindler—nicknamed, not all that affectionately, "the Diesel"—who turned out to be the least effective of the CEOs who passed through Apple's revolving door in the 1990s.

To be fair, Spindler walked into a nearly untenable situation. Simply put, Apple was losing the war with Wintel, and there was almost nothing Spindler could do to get back up to his Holy Grail of 20 percent market share. He tried licensing the Mac OS—the long-deferred cloning strategy, first advocated by Bill Gates in 1985—but it was far too late. The increasing financial pressures on the company had already forced one round of layoffs in May 1991: 1,600 people (or 10 percent of the workforce). Now, facing a third-quarter loss that looked like it might approach $200—the largest in the history of the company—newly installed CEO Spindler had to cut another 2,500 more people (16 percent of the workforce) in the summer of 1993.[13] "There was a growing sense now that this would be Apple's future," wrote Apple historian Michael Malone, "an endless whittling away until there was nothing left."[14]

Morale plummeted. Apple was one of the companies featured in the 1984 edition of *The Hundred Best Companies to Work for in America*; it was conspicuous by its absence from the 1993 edition. Most of the good-ies and benefits that had made Apple a great place to work in the early 1980s were long since gone. No more cars, parties, or other perks: The bitter joke around headquarters was that when the last janitors were let go, the cubicle-dwellers would have to time-share the vacuum cleaners.[15]

Spindler was convinced that Apple's salvation lay in cutting costs and bringing down prices. The unintended consequence of this approach was the flooding of the market with low-quality, cheap Apple computers in the 1995 Christmas season, which didn't sell and led to a *billion-dollar* write-off early in 1996. In January, Spindler announced another round of 1,300 layoffs; by April, that number had risen to 2,800. (Spindler went to some lengths, unsuccessfully, to explain himself to the dwindling workforce.[16]) Spindler and the board were rumored to be negotiating a sale of the company to Sun—a deal that allegedly fell apart when Sun lowballed its final offer.

> Boards have to pull together—and in the right direction.

And by that time, Spindler himself was gone.

Before getting to Gil Amelio, our third CEO in three years, it's worth making two points about Apple's leadership. First, the board throughout this dark period was notably ineffective. Populated mainly by Sculley acolytes, it understood very little about Apple's products and prospects. It was slow to act, and—when it did act—likely to make bad decisions. The board should have known, for example, that Spindler was not the right man for the top job. He was temperamentally unsuited to the post; he was too closely allied with the failed Sculley regime, and he was ailing physically. The board failed to coalesce and pull together as a team; when it *did* pull together, it frequently pulled in the wrong direction. Toward the end of Spindler's regime, for example, the board became convinced that selling the company was the only way out; it therefore lost interest in trying to solve the company's urgent problems in the here-and-now.

The second point is that years of ineffective leadership at the CEO level had become a self-fulfilling prophecy: People paid no attention to the CEO, because they knew that—with the exception of delivering the dreaded pink slips—the CEO had little relevance to their lives. As Gil Amelio later wrote:

> *I came to recognize the fault lay not with the individual executives, but with the culture. They had learned over the years to view the CEO as a person who went out and made speeches, and left them alone to run (or ruin) the company God forbid the CEO should try to make a real business decision that they hadn't cooked up and put on his plate. I believe they had come to the con-*

*clusion that an Apple CEO was just another user-friendly icon—
a figurehead who shouldn't interfere with hard business decisions
that one of them hadn't initiated.[17]*

Unfortunately, Amelio didn't figure this out until *after* he himself had been put through the Apple meat grinder—a process that, as it turned out, required a scant 500 days.

> **Weak CEOs beget more weak CEOs.**

Amelio joined the Apple board in November 1994, and took over as CEO in January 1996. Somewhere in those intervening months of board membership, while he was still CEO of National Semiconductor, Steve Jobs paid him a visit. Jobs, Amelio recalls, put an interesting proposition on the table:

Steve wanted me to champion his return as CEO of Apple Computer. 'There's only one person who can rally the Apple troops," he said, "only one person who can straighten out the company ... Apple is on its way out of business. The only thing that can save it is a strong leader, somebody who can rally employees, the press, users, and developers.'[17]

The anecdote, if accurate, is telling for two reasons. First, it conveys Jobs's raw ambition. Despite his protestations to the contrary, Jobs very much wanted to get his hands on Apple, to rescue his baby, and to be *vindicated*. The prince wanted his long-delayed shot at the throne.

> **Thwarted princes tend to remember where they came from.**

Second, his analysis—and in deep retrospect, his prescriptions—were absolutely right. Michael Spindler, then CEO, couldn't save Apple. In fact, no one else could save Apple. Only Jobs could save Apple.

But first, Amelio, the alleged turnaround artist who had saved National Semiconductor, had to take a turn at the plate. He picked up the CEO bat on February 5, 1996, and started making the kinds of discoveries described above. He would make decisions and issue directives, and get yes'd to death. For example, he authorized a $5 million expenditure on a product tie-in, Tom Cruise using a Mac laptop in *Mission Impossible*, and then learned that the head of advertising (who supervised a $190 million annual budget) had vetoed the plan. Amelio had to issue the order again—this time more forcefully.[19] It was only one of many such incidents. Middle-level managers would simply nod their agreement at an executive decision, go away, and do nothing to implement the decision.

History tends to sell Gil Amelio a little short—in part because his tenure was so abbreviated, in part because he didn't *look* the part of an Apple CEO, and in part because he was so thoroughly eclipsed by the once and future king, Steve Jobs. But Amelio was more than simply a caretaker. A self-described "transformation manager," he cracked the whip over all those do-nothing managers, chasing many of them out of the company. He successfully refinanced Apple at a point when a failure to do so would have meant certain death. As noted in Chapter 6, he placed a renewed emphasis on quality, and started bringing back customers who had been driven away by product failures. He was the first Apple CEO ever who appeared to be entirely comfortable in his own skin, and although his galumphy appearance put some Macophiles off, his generally accessible and straightforward approach also won over many skeptics.

And, of course, he tackled the most mortal threat then facing Apple—the lack of a next-generation operating system, as described in Chapter 4. It was the purchase of NeXT that brought Steve Jobs back into the Apple fold and which helped precipitate the departure of Amelio in July 1997.

But also relevant to that departure, of course, was the fact that Apple managed to lose $1.6 billion between January 1996 and June 1997—almost exactly bracketing the dates of Amelio's tenure—and that by July 1997, Apple's stock price had sunk to a 12-year low.[20] "Today," Amelio wrote in his resignation letter, "we have a cost structure more in line with achievable results." This was an artful way of saying, in other words, that we're still bleeding—perhaps bleeding to death—but we're bleeding more *slowly*.[21]

Out there in the world, skepticism prevailed. "I'd shut it down," rival computer-maker Michael Dell said on CNET News.com, "and give the money back to the shareholders."[22]

But Dell was underestimating Steve Jobs, who didn't appreciate being underestimated. "CEOs are supposed to have class," he wrote to Dell in a stinging e-mail. "I can see that isn't an opinion you hold."[23]

The Return of the Prince

Here the story becomes almost exquisitely familiar, like a fairy tale remembered from childhood: The prince returns, swings his sword, works some magic, and the Little Kingdom is rescued from the forces of darkness.

And there's more than a little truth to the legend. Swinging his sword at his predecessors' pet project, Jobs immediately killed the cloning program (Spindler and Amelio) and the Newton (Sculley). He whacked away

> Good leaders swing their swords—but also bury their hatchets.

at the still-too-complicated Apple product line—which had resisted efforts by both Spindler and Amelio to simplify it—and began an intensive development of both next-generation Macs (the iMac family) and the long-delayed operating system (based almost wholly on the NeXT OS). He also broomed out the board stable, replacing almost every director with individuals more to his liking. Swept out in this purge, notably, was board member Mike Markkula, who had helped invent the company some 21 years earlier. "This is good news," opined a *Times* op-ed columnist, "since Mr. Markkula was the kingmaker at Apple who hired chief executive officers too quickly, then fired them too slowly."[24]

But Jobs also buried hatchets. For example, he made peace with Bill Gates, and sold Microsoft a $150 million equity stake in the company. So whatever motivated Jobs, it wasn't simply a yearning to return to the "good old days," back before there *was* a Microsoft. Jobs clearly had his eye on the future that, only a year or two earlier, he was publicly saying that Apple didn't have.

And he imposed *discipline* on Apple, a quality that the company hadn't enjoyed for many years. The company that used to be known as the "ship that leaks from the top" was soon transformed into a tightly controlled, team-oriented machine—to the point of being secretive, and even insular. "Jobs & Company"—another nickname that sprang up across the Valley in this era—would *not* be shooting itself in the foot or strangling on its own politics.[25]

It worked. By 1998, only a year into Jobs's tenure, Apple appeared to be turning the corner. The moderator of the Seybold publishing seminar held that year put it this way:

> *In the past 12 months and 12 weeks since Steve took over as interim CEO, I have had a lot of faith back in my blood that I won't*

have to give up my beloved Mac. Although you might not agree with all the decisions he's made, I think most of you would agree with me that he has done an awesome job of bringing Apple back from the brink of extinction.[26]

Jobs, for his part, didn't disagree:

The company is in the best financial shape it's been in years. It's on focus. The successful introduction of this cute little product called the iMac and the consumer product marketplace has resurrected Apple's reputation as an innovative design company and a powerhouse marketing company.[27]

By early 1999, Jobs had not only turned the company around, he had delivered five consecutive quarters of profits. And the most dramatic departures—and successes—were still to come. I've already told the amazing story of the iPod: Apple's first successful venture into consumer electronics, the field that almost every CEO of Apple had regarded longingly, from a great distance. (See the Introduction.) A management-consultant friend of mine works for a strategy boutique. One day, he confessed to me—not for attribution—that every single person in his firm would have told Steve Jobs to stay the hell out of consumer electronics. And, he continued, *everybody else at all the strategy boutiques in the world would have said the same thing.*

> Stay off alien territory—unless you're some kind of genius.

With one swing of his sword, therefore, Jobs conquered that vast and formerly hostile territory. The ghosts of Newton and Pippin could now be laid to rest, emphatically. Apple was selling more MP3 players than the rest of the world combined.

Apple was making more money than God.

Leadership Lessons

Extracting leadership lessons from this strange tale—40-plus years of roller coasters, intrigue, and management fog—is an interesting task. "Apple management," Guy Kawasaki said at an Atlanta gathering in 1995, at the bottom of the bottom of the company's fortunes: "It's an oxymoron."[28] Nevertheless, here are 15 conclusions we can make about leadership, based on the Apple experience:

- **Run for the beach! No! Run for the hills!** A lack of leadership can be a terrible thing, especially during natural disasters and man-made cataclysms.

- **Look for the adult supervision in the back of the garage.** Apple was made possible not only by boy geniuses, but also by seasoned pros. Strong leadership doesn't necessarily strut its stuff.

- **Note to would-be CEOs: If you don't control much voting stock, get a good bead on those who do.** You need to be the leader. Will you be able to lead, or will the 400-pound gorilla/major shareholder get in your way?

- **Successful IPOs can make everybody that much harder to control.** Rich guys don't take orders very well.

- **Somebody is usually better than nobody.** Is your CEO looking a little ragged? Does he or she really need to go? Wouldn't some R&R on a beach somewhere patch him or her back together?

- **Perceived inequities often come back to bite leaders.** One of the worst things a leader can do is create multiple classes of citizenship. If one group gets fresh-squeezed orange juice, *everybody* gets fresh-squeezed.

- **Surgeons and leaders of creative teams are not necessarily nice guys.** The relentless quest for perfection makes for good surgical outcomes and product launches. It doesn't make for great companions.

- **Don't let your board chairman and biggest stockholder run your most important division.** The possibilities for conflict are enormous—even if there *aren't* two huge egos involved.

- **Trading market share for margin may be eating the seed corn.** We know that John Sculley delivered the margins. We'll never know whether Steve Jobs could have delivered the market share.

- **Great leaders instill great values. A company that lacks one lacks the other.** This is at the heart of the leadership challenge: leading by value-laden example.

- **Boards have to pull together—and in the right direction.** In any recitation of a leader's strengths and weaknesses, the board *behind* that leader has to be taken into account. Do they cohere? Do they lead?

- **Weak CEOs beget more weak CEOs.** It's a self-fulfilling prophecy: If your last CEO was irrelevant, you're likely to make your next one irrelevant, too (if he or she lets you get away with it, that is).

- **Thwarted princes tend to remember where they came from.** It's usually a huge mistake to underestimate the emotional quotient of leadership. People with big brains often have big egos, and emotional investments, to go with those brains.

- **Good leaders swing their swords—but also bury their hatchets.** Steve Jobs did in his predecessors' pet projects, but didn't let the desire for revenge consume him. He sized up the outsized Bill Gates, and sued for peace.

- **Stay off alien territory—unless you're some kind of genius.** A great leader knows his or her limits, but also isn't intimidated by "expert" opinion. If you're a great broad-jumper, *leap*.

Chapter 12

Fix Your Plan

I claim not to have controlled events, but confess plainly that events have controlled me.

—Abraham Lincoln

"Planning for the future," wrote John Sculley in 1987, "at Apple, means just that. More than anything, we believe that the best way to predict the future is to invent it. We feel the confidence to shape our destiny."[1]

In his long and windy autobiography, Sculley was given to rhetorical flourishes, especially at the end of chapters. This particular flourish (at the end of Chapter 9) followed four pages of details about the Apple planning process. In those four pages, Sculley explained that Apple employed the same planning process used by MCI, Stanford University, and other great institutions: Look five years down the road, figure out what your industry is going to look like, and then figure out how you're going to get from today's reality to that imagined future.

Meanwhile—according to the tenets of this planning process—the company works on its "statement of identity," as well as "set of directions and values." And as soon as that effort is well underway, the company then pushes the visioning horizon out from five years to *ten* years. Throughout, says Sculley, the corporation encourages "unconstrained dreaming" (*wouldn't it be great if we could do so-and-so?*), and only gradually forces dreams to intersect with product and market realities.

That's the world as seen by John Sculley: the big picture. The view from 50,000 feet: planning for the future; shaping our destiny.

Evidently, the process didn't exactly wind up where it was supposed to wind up. A year after writing that cheery passage, Sculley implemented the second major reorganization at Apple in three years. Among other things, he created an "Advanced Technology Group," intended to serve as the unconstrained-dreaming side of the shop. At the same time, unfortunately, he also appointed Jean Louis Gasseé as the head of the new Apple Products Division. Even more than Sculley, Gasseé was determined to drive up Apple's margins, and in the next two years, the price of Apple computers increased an average *60 percent*. A "creeping elegance" mentality set in, across the Products Division; only the "perfect" portable could go on the market. When it finally arrived, it was a year and a half late and 10 pounds overweight.[2]

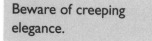

Beware of creeping elegance.

Meanwhile, of course, the price of IBM PCs and clones was *falling*, and dramatically. Belatedly, Sculley realized that the closed-architecture, "BMW-of-the-computer-industry" approach was unsustainable. Gasseé got the boot (in 1990) and Sculley, Michael "the Diesel" Spindler, and their colleagues came up with yet another new strategy for the 1990s. Simply put, this new strategy would make the company more market-driven. Time-to-market would be emphasized, and missed deadlines would mean reduced bonuses. Innovation would be put through the screen of *affordability*: Can we afford to build it, and can the customer afford to buy it? And finally, Apple would push its price/earnings (P/E) ratio up to an acceptable range. Apple then had a P/E ratio of around 10, while Microsoft's was around 45; why couldn't a great computer maker like Apple stand shoulder to shoulder with the still-despised Microsoft?

But wait! Even as this plan was being implemented, yet *another* planning exercise was lurching to life. In the spring of 1990, 60 of Apple's most senior managers huddled at the Pajaro Dunes conference center, site of John Sculley's welcoming earthquake, as described in Chapter 11. The assembled Apple brain trust came up with what they called the "Interdependent Business Model," aimed at breaking down the corporate "cowboy" mentality that still dominated Apple, and instead fostering teamwork and cooperation. And the "IBM" (note the unfortunate acronym) spoke directly to strategy problems:

At the level of corporate strategy, the model said that Apple had been very good at certain key tasks, such as defining powerful and unique personal computing standards, but less good in other areas. By maintaining control over the central tasks and joining with other companies with different areas of expertise, Apple could maintain control over the Macintosh environment while opening up the market to other companies. At the level of within the organization, the model said that the efforts of one group would be most powerful when joined with other parts of the organization ... The IBM became the focal point for strategic and organizational planning over the next few months....³

In September 1990, the new strategy was laid out to Apple's managers in a three-day meeting at the Worldwide Managers' Meeting in San Francisco. Affordable innovation, low-cost Macs, increased market share through the **Beware of the Strategy** seemingly imminent prospect of clones, no **of the Month.** more sacred cows, team players rather than cowboys: Perhaps this was a prescription for a new and improved Apple.

There's one more twist to the Sculley-Spindler planning story. In the fall of 1991, as described in Chapter 10, Apple, IBM, and Motorola announced the joint venture that would lead to the development of the "PowerPC", a new and more powerful microprocessor than anything then on the market. By this point, both Apple and IBM were anxious enough about the growing power of chipmaker Intel (as well as old nemesis Microsoft, of course) that they decided to make common cause. With a new generation of computers powered by the PowerPC, Apple and IBM could win back market share, rebuild their margins, and slay the beasts from Santa Clara and Redmond.

In an article describing the massive layoffs of July 1993, a Knight-Ridder reporter captured the essence of Apple's strategic dilemma:

Apple's R&D budget is far larger relative to its sales than any of its competitors'—double that of Compaq Computer Corp., for example. That's too big, in the minds of some analysts, who think that as CTO, [recently departed CEO John] Sculley launched far too many risky and expensive products.

Meanwhile, the company's main product line, the Macintosh personal computer, is aging, and the once-fat profit margins it

*delivered—in excess of 50 percent—have now fallen to less than
40 percent. They continue to decline in the face of a fierce price
war in the personal computer business.*

*The company's main hopes for the future, meanwhile, still
remain creatures of the lab and are unlikely to provide significant profits for years. The hand-held Newton "personal digital
assistant" is due to be shipped this year, but forecasts show little
demand for such devices until the mid-1990s. And personal computers built with a new microprocessor, called the PowerPC, won't
be available until next year....[4]*

In March 1994, the PowerMac 6100—based on the PowerPC chip—
hit the market. For a few months, the PowerMac ruled—several times
faster than the Motorola-chip-driven Macs, and both more powerful and
less expensive (on an apples-to-apples basis) than all those Wintel
machines out there.

But it didn't last. As Harvard Business School Professor David Yoffie
puts it:

*The big question is: Was it a failure of execution, or a failure in
strategy? And I say that fundamentally it was a failure in strategy. In the case of the IBM joint venture, which was intended to
attack Intel and Microsoft head-on, Apple greatly underestimated
the ability of two highly focused players to respond very effectively, which, in fact, they did. So from the outset, the strategy was
doomed to fail.[5]*

In other words, it was no longer enough to pull off a great engineering coup (which the PowerPC certainly was). Intel was too nimble to stay
beaten for long. Before the end of 1994, new Wintel machines that out-
performed the PowerMac—and cost $1,000 less—arrived on the market.
Meanwhile, the PowerMac still had that tendency to crash if you even
looked at it funny. The sales spike prompted by the arrival of the
PowerMac proved to be short-lived, and there were no more rabbits left
in anyone's hats.

Meanwhile, as noted in Chapter 4, Spindler was also venturing into
the realm of the clones, signing the first Mac OS licensing agreement with
Power Computing Inc. in 1995. But it was too little, too late, and
Spindler's plan to protect the high-end computers from clones didn't

work. Power Computing jumped into the education marketplace almost immediately. Instead of making $500 by selling a Mac to Stanford, Apple made $50 when Power Computing sold *its* Mac to Stanford.

And meanwhile, Apple's plans for international expansion were hobbled by the same kind of thinking that had gotten the company into trouble in the first place. Again, as David Yoffie puts it:

> *They* did *recognize China as a huge opportunity in the early '90s, when China had virtually no PCs and no installed base. This created an opportunity to think of China as a completely clean slate. The problem is that Apple's goal for the marketplace in China was, '15 to 16 percent a decade from now.' And when you think of it in those terms, you then say, 'If they've got 15 percent, who's got the other 85?' And the answer, of course, is Microsoft. And if it's 85 Microsoft, 15 percent Apple, how sustainable is that position? The answer is: It's not. You're back in the same predicament that you've had historically in the U.S.*[6]

So, in summary: Strategy #1—trying to go for volume, driving costs down, and making the Apple platform competitive again (the PowerMac, clones, etc.)—didn't work. International expansion, which would have contributed volume and advanced Strategy #1, got stuck in the mental hobbles of the past. Meanwhile, Strategy #2—trying to crank out hit products (the Newton, the PowerBook)—proved a hit-or-miss proposition, and the misses hurt the company dearly. Strategy #2 also worked at cross-purposes with Strategy #1, because the R&D required to crank out hit products is *expensive*.

> Pursuing multiple and internally contradictory strategies can't work.

When you are running two strategies at once, and neither of them works, it's probably time for another plan.

Where Did All the Plans Go?

It's almost exhausting, right—all this planning?

So, now let's look at the state of the strategic art at Apple in the early months of 1996: same company; new CEO. Gil Amelio—the down-home, plain-spoken, nose-to-the-grindstone guy who (as Michael Malone put it) looked like "your newly divorced uncle on his first date"[7] climbs into the saddle in February and starts hunting for Apple's strategic plan. He looks left, looks right, and *can't find anything*. Despite all that clanking machinery for strategic planning that Sculley and Spindler had supposedly put in place, despite all those thousands of people-hours devoted to mapping out the definitive strategy for the 1990s, there was no *there* there.

Of course, Amelio had an inkling of this situation, thanks to his prior year of service on the Apple board:

> *As a board member, I had complained repeatedly that Apple had no clear corporate strategy, no statement of direction that could be used as a basis for deciding which businesses the company should be in and which not, which markets we should be pursuing and which ignoring. Apparently, Apple had never had an official statement of strategy—which inevitably means that every executive, and most managers, design their own versions. Everyone pursues their own goals rowing frantically, but each pulling in a different direction. Definitely not a recommended formula for success.[8]*

But, from the vantage point of the corner office, it seems the situation was even more dire. And now Amelio owned the job of getting people to row in the same direction.

Before looking at Amelio's strategic diagnosis and prescription, though, it's worth asking an obvious question: *Where did the plan go?* And the answer is that it simply collapsed under the increasing competitive pressures being exerted on Apple. In 1990, the company had a billion dollars in the bank and no long-term debt, and all things (well, *many* things) still seemed possible. Within a short half-decade, however, the tide once again had turned against Apple. The Sculley-Spindler push for increased market share had succeeded briefly, increasing from 5 percent in 1990 to a peak of 12 percent in 1992. But between 1995 and 1996 (the year of the fiery 5300 series laptops, product recalls, and no salable inventory), it declined from 9 percent to 5 percent.[9] Now, instead of taking comfort from a billion dollars in the bank, Apple in 1996 had to announce a *billion-dollar write-off* of all those low-end computers that nobody bought during the disastrous 1995 Christmas season.

The strategic plan (or more accurately, "plans") had failed, and simply gone away. *Definitely not a recommended formula for success*, as

Amelio put it. Now, Apple—the perennially profitable company—was not only writing off its inventory, but also losing money (scads of money) every quarter. Once again, with failures littering the landscape of the recent past and the smell of disaster in the air, it was every man for himself. Of course, this fit nicely with Apple's anti-hierarchical, anti-authoritarian roots, and to a certain extent, people were simply reverting to form. But Amelio, to his credit, decided not to lay the blame at the feet of all those middle managers who surreptitiously put their cowboy hats back on:

> *I don't believe the Apple leadership were stonewalling; it's just that strategy is concerned with the future, and over so many years of changes and redeployments, these people, accustomed to the veneer of emergencies, could find no heart or time in their calendars for thinking beyond next month's products, next month's programs. Too many Apple people, I concluded, live only in the present and are so wrapped up in the present, so totally engrossed in fighting today's battles, that they live unaware of the past and the future. All today, no yesterday, no tomorrow.*[10]

So, Amelio had to *do* something—something that would get tomorrow back on the agenda—but what, exactly? He was beginning to understand that in a context of rapid and accelerating change, the mounting pressures from Apple's board to *figure out the plan and follow it* were fundamentally irrelevant, even dangerous. (Ironically, of course, Amelio had a been strong proponent of stick-to-it-tiveness during his own short tenure as an outside member of the board.) Board Chairman Ed Woolard—the highly respected former CEO of DuPont, and an Amelio appointment to the board—served as a case in point. The chemical industry was nowhere near as cyclical nor as volatile as the computer industry. Based on that stable, predictable industry background, wrote Amelio, "Ed believed in making a plan, announcing the plan, and sticking to it. The adaptations and swift-footed changes required in high tech were essentially foreign to his method of management."[11]

Nevertheless, Amelio promised his board that he would come up with an interim plan within two weeks—a staggeringly unrealistic commitment, at a company like Apple in the early months of 1996. Most of the senior managers, either wary or burned-out or both, simply declined to cooperate with the crash planning process, which quickly went from cooperative to confrontational. Amelio soon concluded that he had to protect the planning process from leaks, and even sabotage. Only one

A bloody battlefield does not a good planning process make.

person had a key to the "War Room" in which the strategic deliberations took place. Managers who had declined to participate in the early rounds were denied access to the War Room. The planning process became, in Amelio's words, a "bloody battlefield."

Not surprisingly, two weeks turned into two months. The result, delivered to the board in April 1996, was a 40-page white paper that arrived with multiple disclaimers attached. According to its preamble:

> *This White Paper is a strategic framework. You might wish to think of it as the top couple of layers for a company-wide strategic plan, which doesn't yet exist. While it has been written quickly and is a working document, it sets forth the basic directions, strategies, priorities, and the like for Apple Computer over the next few years. It is a framework for providing a structure for future detail and implementations.*[12]

But this strategic planning effort, too, went nowhere—drowned in a sea of red ink. Apple was not only writing off inventory, it was losing hundreds of millions of dollars every quarter. So, it was all well and good to talk about changing the product mix, except that Apple couldn't afford to give up a single product that was making any money at all. Amelio's somewhat hazy vision of a Mac that would run Windows applications (maybe even on an operating system designed by arch-nemesis Microsoft!) went nowhere, mainly because Bill Gates demanded too high a price to cooperate with the flopping and flailing Apple.

And, while Amelio fully understood that the company's future depended on innovation, his main focus was (and had to be) cost-cutting and restructuring. He killed the notably unsuccessful eWorld, a Macintosh-users-only online service, something like today's AOL, that had been introduced in January 1994. He killed Pippin, the proprietary Internet box that briefly had appeared to be Apple's long-anticipated leap into the consumer electronics field. With an eye toward the future, he *didn't* kill the hapless Newton personal digital assistant, even though it was costing Apple $15 million a quarter to keep Newton on life support.

None of these decisions, apparently, was easy. "Had I made the correct decision?" agonized Amelio, regarding his stay of execution for the Newton. That $60 million a year, he acknowledged, could have kept a lot of employees on the payroll—maybe even somebody, somewhere in the system, who could figure out how to keep the floundering company alive.

"Newton," Amelio concluded, "was a tough call."[13]

It was a tough call because nobody had a crystal ball clear enough to see exactly what the arrival of the Palm Pilot 1000 and Pilot 5000 organizers in March 1996 portended. (Looking into the future is *difficult.*)

But just as important, it was a tough call because Apple had no *plan.* If you don't know where you're going—to paraphrase the Cheshire Cat's advice to Alice—there will be a lot of tough calls along the way.

The Jobs Strategy

It's June 7, 2005, and Steve Jobs is once again prowling around on a dramatically lit stage in front of one of Apple's most important constituencies: the independent software developers attending the Worldwide Developers' Conference. Dressed in his trademark black turtleneck and blue jeans, occasionally taking a swig from a bottle of spring water, he finishes up telling the developers about the stunning success of the growing network of Apple Stores. (See Chapter 8.)

He moves on to the even more astounding success of the iPod and the iTunes Music Store (iTMS): *76 percent worldwide market share of all MP3 players; 430 million songs downloaded through iTMS.* The developers applaud heartily.

Now, Jobs moves on to a new topic—podcasting—which he describes as "Wayne's World for radio." If you're a person or organization with something to say (or *not*, as the case may be), you can piece together some sort of audio programming, mount it on a server, and let the whole world listen to your "podcast" by downloading it to their PCs. It's the "hottest thing in radio," says Jobs (although it's not really "radio," in any strict sense of the word), with some 8,000 podcasters already out there, and more every day. And yes, there are a lot of Waynes out there—but companies like Disney, Procter and Gamble, and General Motors have also discovered the power of podcasting.

As a consumer of podcasts, Jobs explains further, you can subscribe to your favorites and have them downloaded automatically by your Mac.

And the next time you dock your iPod to your computer, the podcast gets downloaded automatically to your Mac.

"Meanwhile," continues Jobs, sitting down at a keyboard, "Apple wants to make this easier for you. We have built all the necessary software into iTunes and the iPod, so that subscribing and downloading is effortless." Now, as he continues his narration, his fingers start to move across the keyboard:

> *But one of the most important things is, how do you* find *these podcasts? Do you want people typing URLs into iTunes? Well, they could do that, but we're also going to build right into the iTunes music store ... a podcast directory. So that we're going to list thousands of podcasts. And you'll be able to click on them, download them for free, and subscribe to them right in iTunes. So I'd just like to give you a quick peek of what this is going to look like.[14]*

Jobs scrolls through what's clearly an enormous index of podcasts and settles on a show by Adam Curry. After a quick sample, he goes back to the menu, and selects *The Treatment*, a show on LA's public radio station KCRW. And, not to be outdone, Jobs says slyly, "Apple is in the process of putting together its *own* podcast, called *New Music Tuesdays,* which will feature music that's recently become available through iTMS."

Jobs fires up the prototype of *New Music Tuesdays*, and continues to talk as he pecks at the keyboard:

> *And the nice one about this one is that, as we scroll along, you'll see that the artwork changes, too. Right? [Applause] And you can go to different chapters in this thing ... So very, very simple. [Applause] And we think it's going to basically take podcasting mainstream, to where anyone can do it, and really easy to find these podcasts, [and] really easy to listen to them. So we're very excited about this, and this can be one more way in which iPod, and the iTunes digital music community are really at the forefront of this stuff, bringing the innovation into the marketplace.[15]*

Some people have bemoaned the fact that in recent years, half of Apple's revenues have come from iPod/iTMS. (Most is from iPod, of course; Apple only makes about a dime for every 99-cent song that's downloaded through iTMS.) They worry that every R&D dollar invested in the iPod is a dollar not invested in the Apple computer lines.

Not the people assembled at the WWDC. For the most part, these developers couldn't be happier about the success of Apple's venture into the music arena. No, they don't make their money from this side of the Apple Empire. But they *do* understand the "halo effect"— happy iPod users switching from Wintel machines to Macs—and they understand that any development that makes Apple look stronger is likely to lead to increased computer sales, which will lead to increased software sales, which will benefit them directly. *More power to the iPod!*

> The friend of your product is your friend.

It's probably not safe to say that from Day One—way back in September 1997, when he took over the reins at the floundering Apple— Steve Jobs knew that he was steering toward complementing his computers with an array of allied computer electronics. After all, the Apple landscape was still strewn with Pippins and other failed ventures in this realm. Jobs, moreover, killed the Newton as soon as he got his hands on it, suggesting that he wasn't interested in distractions from the core computer product lines. But certainly by late 1998, he had an inkling that he might be able to leverage his company's technical and design skills in new and exciting ways. "The consumer business is pretty cool," he told one interviewer, "because it's high-volume and you really get to interact with individual consumers."

And—perhaps remembering those days a quarter-century earlier when he used to haunt the Sony regional sales office, trying to figure out exactly how the Japanese giant worked its particular consumer magic— he added: "The whole strategy for Apple now, is, if you will, to be the Sony of the computer business."[16]

The Yoffie Prescription

David Yoffie, professor and strategy expert at the Harvard Business School, talks about Apple Computer with equal parts of detachment, frustration, admiration, and amusement. And he knows whereof he speaks: He was a close advisor to John Sculley in the early 1990s and was well connected in the high-tech community in general. Today, he sits on Intel's board, so he knew sooner than most of the world that in the spring of 2005, Steve Jobs would startle the Apple community once again by embracing Intel chips for the next generation of Apple computers.

In fact, Yoffie himself had tried to broker exactly the same marriage more than a decade earlier. In his role as wise counselor, he arranged a meeting between Intel's Andy Grove and John Sculley, hoping that a face-to-face encounter with the legendary Grove finally would force Sculley to come to terms with some harsh realities. "There is no way," Grove told Sculley, as the grim slides rolled by, one after another, "that IBM can make the microprocessors you need. Only Intel can do that. Look at our range of products versus theirs. Look at our volume versus theirs. It's not even close."

Sculley was clearly shaken by Grove's presentation, which included graphic summaries of Intel's enormous chip volume. He promised Yoffie that he would think hard about what he had just heard.

A week later, Yoffie had dinner with a group of senior Apple managers, who—although they hadn't been in the room with Sculley and Grove—had since seen a version of Grove's presentation. "Intel must be selling a lot of microprocessors into toasters," one of the managers said offhandedly.

Yoffie was puzzled. "What do you mean?"

"Well," responded the manager, "God forbid that they're selling them all into *computers*! If they were, well, that would be bad news for us!"[17]

> Remember all those flying toasters? Nope; no Intel inside.

But of course all (or almost all) of those microprocessors were going into computers—millions and millions of Wintel computers—and Apple was already en route to its marginal position in the PC industry.

Which leads us to the first of six strategic lessons that Yoffie draws from the long and turbulent saga of Apple Computer:[18]

- **Figure out the true competitive landscape.** This, of course, is easier said than done. But more than most companies, Apple was insulated from reality. What happened when Apple managers and technical experts actually went out and talked to customers? They had a love-fest. See no Wintel, speak no Wintel, hear no Wintel. Somehow, you have to break through the adoration of those closest to you—or those with a stake in the status quo—and figure out what reality looks like. If someone brings Andy Grove in for a chat, take good notes.
- **Don't bank on being "the best."** Business history is littered with the corpses of companies that counted on being the *absolute best*

in their business and letting the market come to them. Being the best is not sufficient insurance against being overwhelmed by the *second*-best, especially if that other player has higher volume and lower prices.

- **Standards will prevail, especially in high tech.** This lesson grows out of the previous one. Crown Cork & Seal, a venerable old manufacturer of bottle-sealing devices, got away with being "only the best" for decades in part because there were no external standards driving that industry. Not true for high tech, where consumers want the benefit of compatibility and interoperability. Standards favor the high-volume players (Wintel) and punish the oddballs (Apple).

- **Timing is everything.** Yoffie points out that Apple actually figured out almost everything that it needed to do, strategically; it just *acted* on that understanding two or three years too late, time after time after time. In 1985, Bill Gates told Sculley that Apple had to license its software, *in a hurry*, if it wanted to stay competitive. *Ten years later*, Michael Spindler took the first baby steps toward permitting cloning. Both Sculley and Spindler understood the appeal and power of the consumer marketplace; neither moved fast enough or effectively enough toward it.

- **Competitive advantages go away over time.** Let's say your competitive advantage is the world's easiest-to-use operating system (ETU/OS). That's great (assuming that it's not the kind of oddball that lives too far outside the realm of standards, as described above). But let's also assume that there's somebody out there— like, say, Microsoft—that's steadily closing the ETU/OS gap. Now let's also assume that every year, almost the *entire population* of relevant consumers is getting more and more comfortable with technological complexity. As Boston-based IT guru Seth Miller points out, even if you can maintain the ETU/OS gap (no easy job, with the barking hounds of Gates on your heels!), that advantage is simply going to become less important over time.[19]

What is the lesson of this lesson? *Innovation* is critical. We began this chapter with a quote from John Sculley, to the effect that the best way to predict the future is to invent it. Exactly right, but the inventing has to take place in the company's wheelhouse, both in terms of production and distribution. People are eagerly awaiting the Apple cell phone, but Yoffie, for one, thinks Steve Jobs will shy away from plunging full-bore into the cell phone business, because the distribution side of cell phones is nightmarishly complicated.

A related lesson is that the smart company *innovates across the value chain*. For years, Apple turned up its nose at the low end of the PC field—and got killed, as a result. For about a year after the introduction of the iPod, it looked like Apple might be making the same mistake again: inventing only high-end solutions for Mac users. All of a sudden, though, Apple attacked the other 98 percent of the computer world by bringing out a Windows-compatible iPod. At the same time, it grabbed the low-end MP3 player market (with the flash-memory-based Shuffle) and also introduced moderately priced iPods to cover the middle market segments. Meanwhile, it looked back at the computer business, realized its past mistakes, and brought out the Mac Mini.

- ■ **Success begets success.** Except for a few unshaven contrarians on the fringes of the stock market and the occasional mobster who figures out how to rig a horse race, nobody bets on a loser. When Apple looked like it was sinking beneath the waves in 1995–96, developers stopped developing and consumers stopped consuming. When first the iMac and then the iPod caught fire, people started thinking that *just maybe* the Little Kingdom would survive, and that buying a Mac might just be a good bet.

Place Your Bets!

Yes, Virginia; there *is* a Santa Claus. But there may not always be an Apple.

Here's one more bit of competitive analysis from David Yoffie: It used to take about a billion dollars, give or take, to come up with a new operating system. (The next Microsoft OS, Longhorn, is expected to cost something like *twice* that, all in, but for now let's stick with the $1 billion number.) If Microsoft sells 150 million copies a year at $60 a unit, on average, it takes Microsoft only about *six weeks* to break even on its billion-dollar investment.

The Apple calculations are more complicated, since the company makes money on both its hardware and software. But, let's unbundle those two prices, and let's arbitrarily say Apple makes a few hundred dollars every time it sells an operating system. If Apple sells 4 million units a year, it takes Apple something like three years to earn back *its* billion.[20]

Which company are you going to bet on?

But before you answer that seemingly obvious question, let me complicate the calculation by pointing to four things that Apple has going for it.

First, of course, it has *Steve Jobs*. It doesn't much matter whether he's actually mellower, or only *pretending* to be mellower; or whether he's overly aggressive toward books that are critical of him; or whether he's imposed a lock-down mentality on the Little Kingdom; or whether that Photoshop demonstration at the 2005 WWDC might have had the benefit of a little, hum, electronic *enhancement*.[21] That's all chatter and noise at the margins. What matters is that Jobs is some kind of genius. As Scott Kelby puts it:

> *There's one thing I am absolutely certain of: Steve's the right man to lead Apple. There's never been anyone at Apple who has had the impact that Steve has had since his return. He may be a tyrant, demanding, unforgiving, and the worst boss ever. But he's also a visionary. A genius. A man that gets things done. And the man that kept Apple afloat when a host of other nice guys couldn't.[22]*

Of course, being dependent on one person's genius is a risky position for an $11 billion corporation. Is Jobs taking the necessary steps to clone himself? Is he teaching other people how to lead creative teams as skillfully as he does? For the sake of Apple's shareholders, let's hope so. For the moment, though, he's reasonably young and healthy, he seems to be enjoying himself, and he keeps pulling those huge fat rabbits out of his hat.

Second, Apple has some *running room*. It's real nice to have, say, $5 billion in the bank. But more important, for the first time *ever*, Apple has significant multiple income streams. In the early 1990s, John Sculley couldn't make any meaningful moves because he couldn't risk upsetting the Mac income stream, even though everyone (including Sculley) knew that the aging Mac alone couldn't carry Apple much longer. Steve Jobs's most recent dramatic moves, including the introduction of OS X, the plunge into consumer electronics, and the announced shift to Intel chips are only possible because Apple has the benefit of running room. If Jobs has more rabbits to fund, he knows where to get the money.

Third, Apple has a *powerful and revitalized brand*. As noted in earlier chapters, Apple has one of the most instantly recognizable brands in the world. With the success of the iMac and iPod, that brand has been reinvested with the authority of a winner—for the first time in 20 years.

And finally, Apple has *good luck* going for it. Apple is lucky that Bill Gates is a patient man, and one who had the Justice Department on his tail at a critical juncture in Apple's history. Steve Jobs is *very lucky* that just as the spiffy new iMac hit the market, the computer industry in general was entering into the

> Understand and play to your strengths.

most spectacular two-year run in its history (1998–99). He and Apple are both lucky that when computer sales cratered in the early 2000s, the iPod was there to keep the pins in place beneath the company.

Maybe not quite enough reason to buy a big slug of Apple stock—maybe it would be wise to see how Steve Jobs will solidify his consumer-electronics foray, and tie that effort ever more tightly into his computer core—but certainly four good reasons not to bet against the Little Kingdom.

And having prompted chest pains across the legions of the Mac Faithful—by suggesting above that there may not always be an Apple—I should also say that *there will always be a Something that plays the role of an Apple*. I have heard this from too many smart people to discount it.[23] Too many people depend on having a *really smart bunch of people* out in Cupertino, or somewhere, working to supply them with great tools.

That's what Apple has always done, and—if it plays its cards right—will continue to do.

Lessons in Planning

Apple has had its hot strategies and its ice-cold strategies. Here are a few lessons derived from both:

- **Beware of creeping elegance.** This is my shorthand for, "Don't let your products start to exaggerate themselves." Also, don't put people in positions of power who are likely to endorse creeping elegance behind your back.
- **Beware of the Strategy of the Month.** From the viewpoint of the trenches, nothing is more exhausting or demoralizing than to have your leadership bouncing from one strategy to the next.

- **Pursuing multiple and internally contradictory strategies can't work.** You can't go both east and west at the same time.
- **A bloody battlefield does not a good planning process make.** Take it from Gil Amelio: If you have to lock the doors to keep your senior managers *out* of the planning process, you're not going to wind up in the right place.
- **The friend of your product is your friend.** Cheer heartily for any development that makes the Mother Ship more secure.
- **Remember all those flying toasters? Nope; no Intel inside.** Businesspeople—just like other humans—see what they want to see, and hear what they want to hear. This is dangerous, from a strategic perspective.
- **Follow the Yoffie Prescription.** Figure out the true competitive landscape. Don't bank on being the best. Standards will prevail, especially in high tech. Timing is everything. Competitive advantages go way over time. Success begets success.
- **Understand and play to your strengths.** Apple will succeed (or—gasp—fail) based on its competitive advantages, including: Steve Jobs, running room, and a powerful and revitalized brand. And throw some good luck in there, too.

Notes

Notes for Introduction

1. See the interesting write-up of the Lisa, and also a picture of the two-floppy-port version of the machine, at www.oldcomputers.net.
2. Much of this history is taken from: Linzmayer OW. *Apple Confidential 2.0*. San Francisco: No Starch Press; 2004:73-83. Linzmayer's book is aptly subtitled "the definitive history of the world's most colorful company." Also good is David T. Craig's homage to the Lisa at lisa.sunder.net/mirrors/Simon/Lisa/Index.html. Craig's paper is based in part on an article by Lisa co-designer: Tesler L. "The Legacy of the Lisa." *MacWorld*, September 1985.
3. Lisa's GUI was *like* the Alto's, but it was also substantially different. In fact, according to one insider, much of the Lisa's operating system had been developed before the fateful visit to PARC, but the Xerox machine upped the ante. See the discussions at www.apple-history.com/frames/body.php?page=gallery&model=gui.
4. And it had much more than can be summarized here. For more details, see Craig DT. "Lisa Technology," lisa.sunder.net/mirrors/Simon/Lisa/LisaLegacy/LisaTechnology.html.
5. The picture is reproduced in: Linzmayer OW. *Apple Confidential 2.0*. San Francisco: No Starch Press; 2004:80.
6. I don't intend to fuel the Apple/Microsoft wars in this book. (They're overblown, in any case.) But I can't resist including what Bill Gates supposedly said when Steve Jobs accused Microsoft of pirating Apple's GUI and incorporating it in Windows 1.0: "No, Steve, I think it's more like we both have a rich neighbor named Xerox, and you broke in to steal the TV set, and you found out I'd been there first, and you said, 'Hey, that's no fair! I wanted to steal the TV set!'" See "Graphical User Interface (GUI) at www.apple-history.com/frames/body.php?page=gallery&model=gui.

7. Manjoo F. "OK Mac, What's So Special Now?" www.wired.com/news/technology/0,1282,47710,00.html.

8. See Meikle E. "Sony Loses Exclusive Walkman Rights." June 24 2002, www.brandchannel.com/features_effect.asp?pf_id=103.

9. www.wired.com/news/gizmos/0,1452,47805,00.html. Note the quotation marks around "breakthrough."

10. See "Key Milestones in the Life of the iPod," www.ipodlounge.com/articles_more.php?id=4280_0_8_0_M.

11. Walker R. "The guts of a new machine." *New York Times*, November 30, 2003, www.nytimes.com/2003/11/30/magazine/30IPOD.html?ei=5070.

12. Paczkowski J. "Rio takes a dirt nap." August 30, 2005, *Good Morning Silicon Valley*, blogs.siliconvalley.com/gmsv/2005/08/first_move_adva.html.

13. Anderson M. "Apple 'Silhouettes' Do the iPod Shuffle." www.mediaweek.com/mw/search/article_display.jsp?schema=&vnu_content _id=1000752897.

14. "Apple reports second quarter results," April 13, 2005, www.apple.com/pr/library/2005/apr/13results.html.

15. Burrows P, Crockett RO, Green H. "Apple's phone isn't ringing any chimes." *BusinessWeek*, September 19, 2005:58. Technically speaking, it's a Motorola product that supports iTunes.

16. Suroweicki J. "All together now." *The New Yorker*, April 11, 2005:26. The HP partnership has since been dissolved.

17. Craig DT. "Lisa Technology." lisa.sunder.net/mirrors/Simon/Lisa/LisaLegacy/LisaTechnology.html.

18. Walker R. The guts of a new machine." *New York Times*, November 30, 2003, www.nytimes.com/2003/11/30/magazine/30IPOD.html?ei=5070.

Notes for Chapter 1

1. Levy S. *Insanely Great*. New York: The Penguin Group; 1994:27.

2. Malone MS. *Infinite Loop*. New York: Doubleday; 1999:3. Malone's book, subtitled "How Apple, the world's most insanely great computer company, went insane," is one of the best Apple books out there.

3. I am indebted to Professor David Yoffie, strategy expert at the Harvard Business School, for these and other perspectives that will be presented in this book. Yoffie, currently a member of Intel's board of directors, worked with Apple's senior management for many years, and wrote a series of best-selling HBS cases on the company. These include *Apple Computer: Building a Worldwide Strategy*, case #9-495-045; *Reshaping Apple Computer's Destiny 1992*, case #9-300-002; *Apple Computer 1999*, case #9-799-1088; and *Apple Computer 2005*, case #9-705-469.

4. This gives me an opportunity to introduce another resource consulted in the course of writing this book: J. David Allred. Allred has been working with Apple and Macs since the mid 1980s, and my companies have employed his firm, Photon, Inc. (www.photoninc.com), in a number of consulting capacities.

5. Kelby S. *Macintosh: The Naked Truth*. Indianapolis: New Riders Publishing; 2002:160.

6. Orlowski A. "Wintel—the next generation's horoscope." February 28, 2002, at *The Register*, www.theregister.co.uk/2002/02/28/wintel_the_next_ generations_horoscope/.
7. Markoff J. "Apple faces challenge to its role as innovator." *New York Times*; August 10, 1990:D1.
8. Markoff J. "Apple faces challenge to its role as innovator." *New York Times*; August 10, 1990:D1.
9. Markoff J. "Beyond the PC: A's Promised Land." *New York Times*; November 15, 1992.
10. Harvard Business School, *Reshaping Apple Computer's Destiny 1992*, case #9-300-002; November 23, 1999:9.
11. "Observer comments," May 21, 2001, www.themacobserver.com/comments/ commentindivdisplay.shtml?id=3511. Steve also disputes the Mac = BMW analogy, saying that Mac is less like a BMW and more like a Chevette: "95% of people don't own a Chevette because they DON'T WANT to own it, even though they CAN afford it. Chevettes, in their mind, are junk. And same with Apple Computers."

Notes for Chapter 2

1. Moritz M. *The Little Kingdom: the Private Story of Apple Computer*. New York: William Morrow; 1984:14.
2. "Happy Birthday PowerBook!" www.pbzone.com/tenyear.shtml.
3. Markoff J. "Beyond the PC: A's Promised Land." *New York Times*; November 15, 1992.
4. *Silicon Genesis: Oral Histories of Semiconductor Industry Pioneers*. Interview with Regis McKenna, August 22, 1995. www.stanford.edu/group/mmdd/ SiliconValley/SiliconGenesis/RegisMcKenna/McKenna.html, p. 16.
5. Kelby S. *Macintosh: The Naked Truth*. Indianapolis: New Riders Publishing; 2002:122-3.
6. For nerds in search of technical specs, see Apple's website: www.apple.com/ au/macmini/specs.html.
7. Gibson B. "Cagey Apple sold 138,000 Minis in Q2, analyst believes." *The Mac Observer*; April 15, 2005, www.macnewsworld.com/story/42346.html.
8. Pollack A. "A's growing office line." *New York Times*; January 23, 1985:D1.
9. Kawasaki G. *The Macintosh Way*. Glenview, IL: Scott, Foresman & Company; 1990:22-3.
10. Kelby S. *Macintosh: The Naked Truth*. Indianapolis: New Riders Publishing; 2002:91.
11. Markoff J. "Stakes high in Apple's bet on PC." *New York Times*; July 30, 1993:D1.
12. Malone MS. *Infinite Loop*. New York: Doubleday; 1999:501.
13. Malone MS. *Infinite Loop*. New York: Doubleday; 1999:528.
14. Harvard Business School, *Apple Computer (B)* (Abridged): Building a Worldwide Strategy, case #9-495-045, revised July 14, 1995, p. 3. Sculley's first hit product to result from this program was the PowerBook, introduced in October 1991. It generated $1 billion in sales in its first year on the market.

15. O'Connor RJ. "Apple Computer to cut workforce by 2,500 people." *Knight Ridder/Tribune News Service*; July 7, 1993.
16. Markoff J. "Where the cubicle is dead." *New York Times*, April 25, 1993:F7.
17. Harvard Business School, *Apple Computer 1999*, case #9-799-1088, revised May 24, 1999, p. 6.
18. Amelio G. *On the Firing Line: My 500 Days at Apple*. New York: HarperCollins; 1999:220.
19. Longitudinal summaries of Apple's R&D spending are hard to come by. This one is from Henry Norr's August 3, 1998 *MacInTouch* column, "On the eve of iMac: Apple's challenge," as www.macintouch.com/norr021.html. Norr also includes a revenue chart from the same period, showing that R&D spending roughly tracked revenues (i.e., downward) in this period.
20. Burrows P. "Commentary: how to milk an Apple." February 3, 2003, *BusinessWeek Online*, www.businessweek.com/print/magazine/content/03_05/b3818063.htm?chn=tc&.
21. Nesbitt P. "Anderson predicts accelerated growth for Apple," *MacUser*, www.Pcpro.co.uk/macuser/news/46956/Anderson-predicts-accelerated-growth-for-apple.html.
22. From a MacNN summary of a Gilder Technology report, "Apple retail provides upside," April 10, 2003, macnn.com/print/18720.
23. Amelio G. *On the Firing Line: My 500 Days at Apple*. New York: HarperCollins; 1999:50.
24. "Special Keynote: Steve Jobs," transcript of the Seybold San Francisco/Publishing 1998 Web Publishing Conference, http://seminars.seyboldreports.com/1998_san_francisco/ETAPE_02.html.
25. "Special Keynote: Steve Jobs," transcript of the Seybold San Francisco/Publishing 1998 Web Publishing Conference, http://seminars.seyboldreports.com/1998_san_francisco/ETAPE_02.html.
26. Sales statistics from Dan Knight's "MacMusings: Apple takes it on the chin in FY 2001," December 28, 2001, www.lowendmac.com/musings/01/1228pf.html.
27. "Oral History Interview with Steve Jobs," by Daniel Morrow, Executive Director, the Computerworld Smithsonian Awards Program, April 20, 1995, www.geocities.com/franktau/interviewpart4.html.
28. "Oral History Interview with Steve Jobs," by Daniel Morrow, Executive Director, the Computerworld Smithsonian Awards Program, April 20, 1995, www.geocities.com/franktau/interviewpart2.html.
29. "Special Keynote: Steve Jobs," transcript of the Seybold San Francisco/Publishing 1998 Web Publishing Conference.

Notes for Chapter 3

1. From the Apple website, at www.apple.com/environment/design/awards.html.
2. These and other product details are from "History of computer design," www.landsnail.com/apple/local/design/design.html, which is organized by era and device.
3. Deutschman A. *The Second Coming of Steve Jobs*. New York: Broadway Books; 2000:28-9.

4. "History of computer design," www.landsnail.com/apple/local/design/ design.html. Jobs's name is one of three on the design patent, along with Manock and Oyama.
5. Sculley J. *Odyssey*. New York: Harper & Row: 1987:165.
6. Deutschman A. *The Second Coming of Steve Jobs*. New York: Broadway Books; 2000:28-9. Deutschman's study of the Jobs aesthetic—and of Jobs in general—is brilliant.
7. Sculley J. *Odyssey*. New York: Harper & Row; 1987:156-7.
8. The Esslinger/frogdesign story is from "History of computer design," www.landsnail.com/apple/local/design/design.html.
9. Moritz M. *The Little Kingdom: the Private Story of Apple Computer*. New York: William Morrow; 1984:16.
10. Interview with Jonathan Ive, Design Museum, 2003, www.designmuseum .org/design/index.php?id=63.
11. Amelio G. *On the Firing Line: My 500 Days at Apple*. New York: HarperCollins; 1999:36.
12. Amelio G. *On the Firing Line: My 500 Days at Apple*. New York: HarperCollins; 1999:135.
13. Interview with Jonathan Ive, Design Museum, 2003, www.designmuseum. org/design/index.php?id=63.
14. Deutschman A. *The Second Coming of Steve Jobs*. New York: Broadway Books; 2000:268.
15. Kelby S. Macintosh: *The Naked Truth*. Indianapolis: New Riders Publishing; 2002:100.
16. Kahney L. *The Cult of Mac*. San Francisco: No Starch Press; 2004:48.
17. Patton P. "The Apple Cube entered the museum as it exited stores." *New York Times*; August 16, 2001:G.3.
18. Apple's blueprint for genius," by Peter Burrows, *BusinessWeek* online, April 21, 2005, www.businessweek.com/print/magazine/content/05_12/b3925608 .htm?chan=mz&.
19. Deutschman A. *The Second Coming of Steve Jobs*. New York: Broadway Books; 2000:307-8.

Notes for Chapter 4

1. And a real accomplished person, at that. Google him for a general flavor, then visit his web site at www.differnet.com.
2. Sculley J. *Odyssey*. New York: Harper & Row; 1987:163-165.
3. Biersdorfer JD. "Apple breaks the mold." *New York Times*; September 14, 2000:G.1.
4. Actually, something called "Windows 1.0"—originally announced by Microsoft in November 1983—went to market in November 1985 after experiencing multiple delays. But this was only a slightly souped-up DOS program, with a marginally better user interface. Windows 2.0, although still hideous, pointed directly at a troubling future, from Apple's point of view. See the history of Windows at members.fortunecity.com/pcmuseum/windows.htm.
5. Amelio G. *On the Firing Line: My 500 Days at Apple*. New York: HarperCollins; 1999:94-5.

6. Amelio G. On the Firing Line: *My 500 Days at Apple*. New York: HarperCollins; 1999:150-1.
7. See Lewis PH. "The brave new world of IBM and Apple." *New York Times*; October 13, 1991:F8, and Markoff J. "Big loss and revamping at Apple." New York Times; July 16, 1993:D1.
8. See pictures of the professor and Phil at work at webzone.k3.mah.se/ k3jolo/Sketching/sk51.htm, which summarizes a November 2, 2004 talk by Jonas Lögren at Stockholm University. John Sculley's business autobiography, *Odyssey*, goes on for many pages talking about the Knowledge Navigator—from page 403 on—but Phil is conspicuous by his absence.
9. See "Microsoft Bob," at toastytech.com/guis/bob.html. This site also has a great GUI timeline, at toastytech.com/guis/guitimeline.html.
10. Flynn L. "The Executive Computer: When, oh when, will computers behave like people?" *New York Times*; January 1, 1995:3.8.
11. June 25, 1995 memo from Bill Gates and Jeff Raikes to John Sculley and Jean Louis Gassee, www.scripting.com/specials/gatesLetter/text.html.
12. Markoff J. "Stakes high in Apple's bet on PC." *New York Times*; July 30, 1993:D1.
13. Amelio G. *On the Firing Line: My 500 Days at Apple*. New York: HarperCollins; 1999:172-5.
14. Amelio G. *On the Firing Line: My 500 Days at Apple*. New York: HarperCollins; 1999:151.
15. Amelio G. *On the Firing Line: My 500 Days at Apple*. New York: HarperCollins; 1999:94-5.
16. Renaming the OS would also make it easier to renegotiate those one-sided licensing agreements.
17. Gomes L. "Apple to release Copland system in increments." *Wall Street Journal*; August 8, 1996:B.4.
18. Gomes L. "Apple, seeking new operating system, holds discussion with co-founder Jobs." *Wall Street Journal*; December 16, 1996:B.6.
19. Amelio G. *On the Firing Line: My 500 Days at Apple*. New York: HarperCollins; 1999:193.
20. Jobs also happened to own Pixar Inc., the animation studio that he bought from George Lukas, and which was in the process of making it big with the release of *Toy Story*. But that's a whole other soap opera. Suffice it to say that, throughout the early months of 1997, Jobs said that his heart belonged to Pixar, not Apple.
21. Markoff J. "Steven Jobs making move back to Apple." *New York Times*; December 21, 1996:1.37.
22. A particularly colorful account is contained in Alan Deutschman's *The Second Coming of Steve Jobs*, New York: Broadway Books; 2000:238-46. For obvious reasons, Jobs disliked this book intensely. Also good is Michael S. Malone's *Infinite Loop*, New York:Doubleday; 1999:538-61.
23. Harvard Business School, Apple Computer 1999, case #9-799-1088, revised May 24, 1999:12.
24. Ierna T. "Unix and the Macintosh: having it all." This interesting piece is undated, but appears to be from about 1997. Online at www.mackido.com/ Software/UnixNMac.html.

25. Gomes L. "Apple's next step is a software gamble. *Wall Street Journal*; December 23, 1996:B.1.
26. Markoff J. "Unsung success in revamping software holds a clue to the turn-around at Apple." *New York Times*; October 11, 1999:C.1. Markoff's articles on Apple were consistently among the best, in this period.
27. Tam PW. "Why Microsoft wants Apple's new software to be a hit—developers of Macintosh programs say slow takeoff of OS X system could put their products at risk." *Wall Street Journal*; July 15, 2002:B.1.
28. Biersdorfer JD. "Apple breaks the mold." *New York Times*; September 14, 2000:G.1.
29. Dalrymple J. "Apple making big inroads in business with OS X." www.macworld.com/news/2005/07/21/osx/index.php.
30. From Jobs's keynote to Worldwide Developers' Conference, June 7, 2005.

Notes for Chapter 5

1. Bekker S. "Microsoft rises in Fortune 500 ranking." April 5, 2005, redmond mag.com/news/article.asp?EditorialsID=6635.
2. Emmanuel's comment is from the online discussion that follows "Beginning Mac development," by Justin Williams, *MacZealots*, May 2005, maczealots.com/articles/development.
3. Interview with David Yoffie, June 9, 2005.
4. See Weyhrich S. "Apple II History," apple2history.org/history/ah18.html.
5. See Bricklin's own account, including why he didn't patent his invention, at www.bricklin.com/history/saiidea_m.htm.
6. See the ad at www.aci.com.pl/mwichary/computerhistory/ads/international/visicorp/pics/percon7909.
7. VisiCalc sales figures from: Malone MS. *Infinite Loop*. New York: Doubleday; 1999:161. Malone quotes an Apple source as saying that VisiCalc was responsible for 20 percent of Apple's sales in FY 1980.
8. See Jeremy Reimer's wonderful "Personal computer market share: 1975-2004" chart at www.pegasus3d.com/total_share.html.
9. Pirated versions of MacBASIC continued to float in the ether, however, and two published books on MacBASIC mysteriously sold very well for a few years. See Hertzfeld A. "MacBasic," folklore.org/StoryView.py?project=Macintosh&story=MacBasic.txt.
10. From written comments by David K. Every, who wrote "History of Visual BASIC," 06.02.05, www.igeek.com/articles/History/VisualBasic.txt), and also answered some of my very elementary questions.
11. Sculley J. *Odyssey*. New York: Harper & Row; 1987:202.
12. From Every's "History of Visual BASIC," June 2, 2005, www.igeek.com/articles/History/VisualBasic.txt.
13. Sculley J. *Odyssey*. New York: Harper & Row; 1987:127-8.
14. Kawasaki G. *The Macintosh Way*. Glenview, IL: Scott, Foresman & Company; 1990:101.
15. Kahney L. *The Cult of Mac*. San Francisco: No Starch Press; 2004:81-2. Kahney is quoting statistics from *Infoworld*.

16. Amelio G. *On the Firing Line: My 500 Days at Apple*. New York: HarperCollins; 1999:107-9.
17. Kahney L. *The Cult of Mac*. San Francisco: No Starch Press; 2004:83. This strange detective story, starring a New Jersey-based systems analyst named Arun Gupta as the detective, originally appeared in a *MacWeek* series. In the wake of the critical *MacWeek* articles, SPA discontinued the "sales reports."
18. Malone MS. *Infinite Loop*. New York: Doubleday; 1999:498.
19. Every DK. "Developers are leaving." 1999, www.mackido.com/Myths/dev_leaving.html.
20. "Developers finally get a break," by Don Crabb, in the April 1996 issue of *MacTech*, www.mactech.com/articles/mactech/Vol.12/12.04/Apr96Crabbs Apple.
21. "Heidi Roisen: I survived small biz—and Corporate America," www.businessweek.com/1997/23/b353056.htm.
22. Deutschman A. *The Second Coming of Steve Jobs*. New York: Broadway Books; 2000:291.
23. Harvard Business School, Apple Computer 1999, case #9-799-1088, revised May 24, 1999, p. 13.
24. Norr H. "Mac OS X: it makes sense," www.macintouch.com/norr006.html. Norr was commenting on the *Macintouch* coverage of the May 1998 WWDC. See "Mac OS X introduction," May 11, 1998, www.macintouch.com/m10.html.
25. "Special Keynote: Steve Jobs," transcript of the Seybold San Francisco/ Publishing 1998 Web Publishing Conference, http://seminars.seybold reports.com/1998_san_francisco/ETAPE_02.html.
26. Special Keynote: Steve Jobs," transcript of the Seybold San Francisco/ Publishing 1998 Web Publishing Conference, http://seminars.seybold reports.com/1998_san_francisco/ETAPE_02.html.

Notes for Chapter 6

1. Kawasaki G. *The Macintosh Way*. Glenview, IL: Scott, Foresman & Company. 1990:22-3.
2. Malone MS. *Infinite Loop*. New York: Doubleday; 1999:342.
3. Sculley J. *Odyssey*. New York: Harper & Row; 1987:228-9.
4. Pollack A. "Apple's growing office line." *New York Times*, January 23, 1985: D1.
5. Sculley J. *Odyssey*. New York: Harper & Row; 1987:228-9.
6. Markoff J. "John Sculley's biggest test." *New York Times*, February 26, 1989: F1.
7. Amelio G. *On the Firing Line: My 500 Days at Apple*. New York: HarperCollins; 1999:126. We'll be quoting Amelio a lot in this chapter because he, more than any other Apple CEO, tried to come to grips with the issue of promise-keeping.
8. Malone MS. *Infinite Loop*. New York: Doubleday; 1999:467.
9. Harvard Business School, Apple Computer 1999, case #9-799-1088, revised May 24, 1999:6.

10. Harvard Business School, Reshaping Apple Computer's Destiny 1992 (Abridged), case #9-300-002, November 23, 1999:10.
11. Schmit J. "Apple chief marketer quits, signals discord." *USA Today*, September 18, 1997:B2.
12. Amelio G. *On the Firing Line: My 500 Days at Apple*. New York: HarperCollins; 1999:132.
13. Malone MS. *Infinite Loop*. New York: Doubleday; 1999:539.
14. See the settlement write-up at www.appleipodsettlement.com.
15. As reported in the February 10, 2004 *MacForum*, at forums.maccentral.com/wwwthreads/showflat.php?Cat=&Board=general&Number=618987.
16. Daly J. "101 ways to save A." *Wired*, June 1997, http://hotwired.wired.com/collections/computers/5.06_apple_pr.html.
17. Amelio G. *On the Firing Line: My 500 Days at Apple*. New York: HarperCollins; 1999:113.
18. Amelio G. *On the Firing Line: My 500 Days at Apple*. New York: HarperCollins; 1999:113.
19. Amelio G. *On the Firing Line: My 500 Days at Apple*. New York: HarperCollins; 1999:133.
20. Daly J. "101 ways to save Apple." *Wired*, June 1997, http://hotwiredwired.com/collections/computers/5.06_apple_pr.html.
21. See, for example: Thurrot P. "Microsoft responds: there are not 63,000 Win2K bugs." February 16, 2000, www.windowsitpro.com/Article/ArticleID/19131/19131.html.
22. See Foley MJ. "Somebody call an exterminators: Can Microsoft squash 63,000 bugs in Windows 2000?" February 11, 2000, www.oops-web.com/FoleyOn2000.html.
23. Kelby S. *Macintosh: The Naked Truth*. Indianapolis: New Riders Publishing; 2002:45.
24. Kahney L. *The Cult of Mac*. San Francisco: No Starch Press; 2004:87.

Notes for Chapter 7

1. Kahney L. *The Cult of Mac*. San Francisco: No Starch Press; 2004.
2. Kelby S. *Macintosh: The Naked Truth*. Indianapolis: New Riders Publishing; 2002:208.
3. Kelby S. *Macintosh: The Naked Truth*. Indianapolis: New Riders Publishing; 2002:102.
4. Kahney L. *The Cult of Mac*. San Francisco: No Starch Press; 2004:8.
5. Moritz M. *The Little Kingdom: The Private Story of Apple Computer*. New York: William Morrow; 1984:115.
6. Kawasaki G. *The Macintosh Way*. Glenview, IL: Scott, Foresman & Company; 1990:78.
7. Kelby S. *Macintosh: The Naked Truth*. Indianapolis: New Riders Publishing; 2002:4.
8. See "The History of AppleCore," memphisapplecore/applecorehistory.html.
9. See "Federal user groups," www.apple.com/federal/usergroups.html.
10. "Just Add Water," www.adobe.com/support/usergroup/pdfs/commedued.pdf.

11. Questions and Answers about the Apple User Group Program," www.apple.com/usergroups/questions/program/.
12. Kelby S. *Macintosh: The Naked Truth*. Indianapolis: New Riders Publishing; 2002:47.
13. Kelby S. *Macintosh: The Naked Truth*. Indianapolis: New Riders Publishing; 2002:47.
14. "Questions and Answers about the Apple User Group Program," www.apple.com/usergroups/questions/program/.
15. See Chaffin B. "Mac User Groups in the age of the iMac," www.themacobserver.com/columns/thebackpage/2000/20000718.shtml.
16. Daly J. "101 ways to save Apple," June 1997, hotwired.wired.com/collections/computers/5.06_apple_pr.html.
17. This fascinating story is from Leander Kahney's *The Cult of Mac*, pp. 76-82.
18. Kelby S. *Macintosh: The Naked Truth*. Indianapolis: New Riders Publishing; 2002:23.
19. Kahney L. "Mac EvangeList bites the dust," April 16, 1999, www.wired.com/news/technology/0,1282,19175,00.html.
20. "The Mac Evangelist's Oath," www.ibiblio.org/macsupport/oath.html.
21. Kahney L. *The Cult of Mac*. San Francisco: No Starch Press; 2004:85. Kahney steers you to www.macpicks.com, which is as good a place as any to start this journey.
22. Kelby S. *Macintosh: The Naked Truth*. Indianapolis: New Riders Publishing; 2002:86.

Notes for Chapter 8

1. www.apple.com/retail/procare/.
2. Lee JB. "To cash in on a lifestyle, Apple hits the mall." *New York Times*, July 12, 2001:G.3.
3. This is often misattributed to *uber*-nerd Bill Gates, who supposedly delivered it in a high school commencement address. In fact, it's from a book called *Dumbing Down Our Kids*, by conservative education commentator Charles Sykes.
4. Kawasaki G. *The Macintosh Way*. Glenview, IL: Scott, Foresman & Company; 1990:112.
5. Much of this story is derived from Brochstein M. "Apple: a carefully planted seed." *Retailing Home Furnishings*, March 7, 1983:C22.
6. Brochstein M. "Apple: a carefully planted seed." *Retailing Home Furnishings*, March 7, 1983:C22.
7. These programs are described in Kawasaki's *The Macintosh Way*, pp. 20 and 103, respectively.
8. Pollack A. "Apple seeks supplier links." *New York Times*, June 27, 1985:D5.
9. Kelby S. *Macintosh: The Naked Truth*. Indianapolis: New Riders Publishing: 2002:96.
10. Kahney L. *The Cult of Mac*. San Francisco: No Starch Press; 2004:79.
11. See "Apple Computer Inc.: Terms changed on dealings with resellers and retailers," *Wall Street Journal*, September 27, 1997:B.2; and "Apple Computer

Inc.: Computer firm will use two distributors for PCs." *Wall Street Journal*, November 4, 1997:1.

12. "Dell at a glance," www1.us.dell.com/content/topics/global.aspx/corp/ background/en/facts?c=us&l=en&s=corp&~section=004.

13. Harvard Business School, *Apple Computer 1999*, case #9-799-1088, revised May 24, 1999.

14. "Apple picks CompUSA as national retail outlet." *New York Times*, February 3, 1998:D.6.

15. Carlton J. "Apple to focus its retail efforts on CompUSA." *Wall Street Journal*, February 3, 1998:1.

16. "Special Keynote: Steve Jobs," transcript of the Seybold San Francisco/ Publishing 1998 Web Publishing Conference, http://seminars.seyboldreports .com/1998_san_francisco/ETAPE_02.html.

17. Chaffin B. "Steve Jobs interviewed on CNBC, touts Apple Stores using BMW analogy," May 16, 2001, www.themacobserver.com/stockwatch/200a/05/ 16.1.shtml.

18. Gross J. "Apple stores sow seeds of discontent." *VARBusiness*, August 20, 2001:48.

19. Kahney L. *The Cult of Mac*. San Francisco: No Starch Press; 2004:20-1.

20. Lee JB. "To cash in on a lifestyle, Apple hits the mall." *New York Times*, July 12, 2001:G.3.

21. For a truly amazing video showing people lining up for the event, see "The Longest Line," at homepage.mac.com/masanorif/iMovieTheater23.html.

22. Cohen P, Snell J. "WWDC 2005 keynote live update," June 6, 2001, www.macworld.com/news/2005/06/06/liveupdate/index.php.

Notes for Chapter 9

1. Levy S. *Insanely Great*. New York: Penguin Books; 1994:203.

2. To read McKenna on McKenna, see www.regis.com/about.

3. *Silicon Genesis: Oral Histories of Semiconductor Industry Pioneers*. Interview with Regis McKenna, August 22, 1995. www.stanford.edu/group/mmdd/ SiliconValley/SiliconGenesis/RegisMcKenna/McKenna.html, p. 17.

4. Malone MS. *Infinite Loop*. New York: Doubleday; 1999:177-8.

5. Sculley J. *Odyssey*. New York: Harper & Row; 1987:68.

6. Sculley J. *Odyssey*. New York: Harper & Row; 76.

7. This background, as well as a long write-up of the "shoot-out," can be found in Sculley's *Odyssey*, pp. 348-355.

8. Malone MS. *Infinite Loop*. New York: Doubleday; 1999:396.

9. Kelby S. *Macintosh: The Naked Truth*. Indianapolis: New Riders Publishing; 2002:208.

10. Daly J. "101 ways to save A," June 1997, http://hotwired.wired.com/collections/ computers/5.06_apple_pr.html.

11. www.theapplecollection.com/Collection/AppleMovies/mov/un_pc.html

12. Harvard Business School, *Apple Computer 1999*, case #9-799-1088, revised May 24, 1999:12.

13. It's worth watching, at www.uriah.com/apple-qt/think-different-one.html.

14. "The two sides of Apple," *The Tibetan Bulletin*, March-April 1998, www.tibetnews.com/bulletin/98Issue2/page5.html.

15. See, for example, "Bitten Apple," the *Wall Street Journal* editorial of April 24, 1998.

16. Feiss says she was not stoned, but taking allergy medications. See Feiss at work: www.ellenfeiss.net/movie.php?movie=movies/ellen_feiss.mov. The other Feiss "Switch" ad (www.ellenfeiss.net/movie.php?movie=movies/ellen_feiss_02.mov) also shows the allergy medicines having their impact.

17. Kahney L. *The Cult of Mac.* San Francisco: No Starch Press; 2004:42.

18. Wingfield N. "Apple introduces iPod that displays photographs; digital-music leader also launches promotion with the rock bank U2," *Wall Street Journal*, October 27, 2004:D10.

19. Kelby S. *Macintosh: The Naked Truth.* Indianapolis: New Riders Publishing; 2002:85.

20. Olsen S. "Geeky Microsoft wants a TV makeover," CNET News, news.com.com/Geeky+Microsoft+wants+a+TV+makeover/2100-7343_3-5086260.html.

21. Fried I. "Apple sues over alleged leak of trade secrets," August 2, 2000, http://news.com.com/2102-1040_3-243972..html?tag=st.util.print.

22. Tartakoff JM. "Apple sues student," *The Harvard Crimson*, January 12, 2005, www.thecrimson.com/printerfriendly.aspx?ref=505326. For thinksecret's perspective, see www.thinksecret.com/news/antislapp.html.

23. Murrell J. "Look, Steve, you've made your point; besides, I think book burning breaks some ordinance," April 26, 2005, *The Mac Observer*, blogs.siliconvalley.com/gmsv/2005/04/look_steve_youv.html.

Notes for Chapter 10

1. For a great timeline of the telecom/computer age, see Lars Aronsson's "Telecom History Timeline," at http://aronsson.se/hist.html.

2. Quoted in Kahney L. *The Cult of Mac.* San Francisco: No Starch Press; 2004. See pages 32-34 for an insightful summary of this culture war.

3. See the ad and ad copy at www.uriah.com/apple-qt/1984.html.

4. Kawasaki G. *The Macintosh Way.* Glenview, IL: Scott, Foresman & Company; 1990:16.

5. www.answers.com/topic/1984-television-commercial.

6. Pollack A. "IBM now Apple's main ally." *New York Times*, October 3, 1991:D1.

7. Pollack A. "IBM now Apple's main ally." *New York Times*, October 3, 1991:D1.

8. Lewis PH. "The brave new world of IBM and Apple." *New York Times*, October 13, 2001:F8.

9. See *The Cult of Mac*, pp. 91-92. Curiously, you can't get into the Apple-bashing site without a password. And there is no obvious way to get a password.

10. Kelby S. *Macintosh: The Naked Truth.* Indianapolis: New Riders Publishing; 2002:156.

11. Kelby S. *Macintosh: The Naked Truth.* Indianapolis: New Riders Publishing; 2002:157.

12. This one's a little harder to find on the web. I found it at translate.google.com/translate?hl=en&sl=it&u=http://www.mylothlorien.com/modules.php%

3Fname%3DNews%26file%3Darticle%26sid%3D38&prev=/
search%3Fq%3D%2522ultimate%2Bmac%2Bversus%2Bwindows%2B
challenge%2522%26hl%3Den%26lr%3D%26ie%3DUTF-8. Look for the
"Simplicity shootout" link.

13. "Special Keynote: Steve Jobs," transcript of the Seybold San Francisco/
Publishing 1998 Web Publishing Conference, http://seminars.seybold
reports.com/1998_san_francisco/ETAPE_02.html)

14. Kahney L. *The Cult of Mac*. San Francisco: No Starch Press; 2004:82-3.

15. Attributed to Milo Medin, president of @home, in: Daly J. "101 ways to save
Apple," *Wired*, June 1997, hotwired.wired.com/collections/computers/5.06_
apple_pr.html.

16. Lorimer D. "Mac faithful begin to see light after the dust settles," vnunet.com,
August 21, 1997, at www.pcmag.co.uk/analysis/34329.

17. Friedman T. *Electric Dreams: Computers in American Culture*, February 28,
2005.Online at www.tedfriedman.com/book/2005/02/apples_1984.php. The
description of the "Lemmings" ad is in Chapter 5.

18. Hesseldahl A. "The Mac @ 20: Selling Steve's vision," www.forbes.com/
2003/12/16/cx_ah_1216adapple.html.

19. Kawasaki G. *The Macintosh Way*. Glenview, IL: Scott, Foresman & Company;
1990:22.

20. Pollack A. "A's growing office line," *New York Times*, January 23, 1985:D1.

21. See Jobs's keynote address at www.apple.com/quicktime/qtv/wwdc05.

Notes for Chapter 11

1. Sculley J. *Odyssey*. New York: Harper & Row; 1987:129-30.

2. Malone MS. *Infinite Loop*. New York: Doubleday; 1999:112-20.

3. Malone MS. *Infinite Loop*. New York: Doubleday; 1999:201.

4. Moritz M. *The Little Kingdom: The Private Story of Apple Computer*. New
York: William Morrow; 1984:261.

5. Kawasaki G. *The Macintosh Way*. Glenview, IL: Scott, Foresman & Company;
1990:18-9.

6. Deutschman A. *The Second Coming of Steve Jobs*. New York: Broadway
Books; 2000:61.

7. Sculley J. *Odyssey*. New York: Harper & Row; 1987:138.

8. Sculley J. *Odyssey*. New York: Harper & Row; 1987:157.

9. Sculley J. *Odyssey*. New York: Harper & Row; 1987:240.

10. Pollack A. "The restructuring of Apple Computer," *New York Times*, June 1,
1985:35.

11. Silicon Genesis: Oral Histories of Semiconductor Industry Pioneers.
Interview with Regis McKenna, August 22, 1995. www.stanford.edu/group/
mmdd/SiliconValley/SiliconGenesis/RegisMcKenna/McKenna.html, p. 18.

12. "Oral History Interview with Steve Jobs," by Daniel Morrow, Executive
Director, the Computerworld Smithsonian Awards Program, April 20, 1995,
www.geocities.com/franktau/interviewpart4.html.

13. O'Connor RJ. "Apple Computer to cut workforce by 2,500 people." July 7,
1993, Knight Ridder/Tribune News Service; Markoff J. "Visionary Apple
chairman moves on." *New York Times*, October 16, 1993:39.

14. Malone MS. *Infinite Loop*. New York: Doubleday; 1999:462.
15. Harvard Business School, *Reshaping Apple Computer's Destiny 1992* (Abridged), case #9-300-002, November 23, 1999, p. 6.
16. See a meandering and maundering memo from Spindler to the troops at www.interesting-people.org/archives/interesting-people/199602/msg00006.html.
17. Amelio G. *On the Firing Line: My 500 Days at Apple*. New York: HarperCollins; 1999:88.
18. Amelio G. *On the Firing Line: My 500 Days at Apple*. New York: HarperCollins; 1999:x.
19. Amelio G. *On the Firing Line: My 500 Days at Apple*. New York: HarperCollins; 1999:51-2.
20. Harvard Business School, Apple Computer 1999, case #9-799-1088, revised May 24, 1999, p. 6.
21. From Amelio's July 11, 1997 letter of resignation, online at www.resignation.com, which is an interesting archive of dashed hopes.
22. Dell's comment was made to Jai Singh, CNET News.com, October 6, 1997.
23. Deutschman A. *The Second Coming of Steve Jobs*. New York: Broadway Books; 2000:246.
24. Cringeley RX. "Apple's worst enemy no more," op-ed. *New York Times*, August 7, 1999:A.31.
25. Markoff J. "Apple and PCs, both given up for dead, are rising anew." *New York Times*, April 26, 1999:C.1.
26. Comments by Maggie Canon, moderator, August 31, 1998, Seybold San Francisco/Publishing 1998 Web Publishing Conference, http://seminars.seyboldreports.com/1998_san_francisco/ETAPE_02.html.
27. "Special Keynote: Steve Jobs," transcript of the Seybold San Francisco/Publishing 1998 Web Publishing Conference, http://seminars.seybold reports.com/1998_san_francisco/ETAPE_02.html
28. Kelby S. Macintosh: *The Naked Truth*. Indianapolis: New Riders Publishing; 2002:102.

Notes for Chapter 12

1. Sculley J. *Odyssey*. New York: Harper & Row; 1987:297.
2. Harvard Business School, *Reshaping Apple Computer's Destiny 1992* (Abridged), case #9-300-002, November 23, 1999, p. 5.
3. Harvard Business School, Apple Computer (B) (Abridged): Building a Worldwide Strategy, case #9-495-045, revised July 14, 1995, p. 2.
4. O'Connor RJ. "Apple Computer to cut workforce by 2,500 people." July 7, 1993, Knight Ridder/Tribune News Service.
5. Interview with David Yoffie, June 9, 2005.
6. Interview with David Yoffie, June 9, 2005.
7. Malone MS. *Infinite Loop*. New York: Doubleday; 1999:531.
8. Amelio G. *On the Firing Line: My 500 Days at Apple*. New York: HarperCollins. New York: 1999:25.
9. Market share data from www.pegasus3d.com/totalshare0.gif.

10. Amelio G. *On the Firing Line: My 500 Days at Apple.* New York: HarperCollins; 1999:70.
11. Amelio G. *On the Firing Line: My 500 Days at Apple.* New York: HarperCollins; 1999:167-8.
12. Preamble to the Apple strategy White Paper, from: Amelio G. *On the Firing Line: My 500 Days at Apple.* New York: HarperCollins; 1999:65.
13. Amelio G. *On the Firing Line: My 500 Days at Apple.* New York: HarperCollins; 1999:89-90.
14. From Jobs's remarks to the June 7, 2005 Worldwide Developers' Conference, www.apple.com/quicktime/qtv/wwdc05.
15. From Jobs's remarks to the June 7, 2005 Worldwide Developers' Conference, www.apple.com/quicktime/qtv/wwdc05.
16. Both Jobs quotes are from page 14 of Harvard Business School's *Apple Computer 1999*, case #9-799-1088, revised May 24, 1999, which in turn cites Kirkpatrick's *The Second Coming of Apple*.
17. These quotes, and much of the rest of the section that follows, are from my June 9, 2005 interview with Yoffie. Once again, I am indebted to Yoffie for sharing his insights with me.
18. Yoffie gets credit for the lessons; I take responsibility for the *explanations* of the lessons.
19. Seth Miller, founder and CEO of Boston-based Miller Systems, Inc., an IT consulting and web development shop, contributed this insight. Miller was a rabid Apple fan—he admits to owning an autographed copy of Guy Kawasaki's *The Macintosh Way*—who gave up and moved over to Windows because he could no longer get his work done on Macs. From my July 8, 2005 interview with Miller.
20. Again, thanks to David Yoffie for these orders-of-magnitude calculations.
21. This was the scuttlebutt at the MIT Mac Users' Group (MUG) that I attended right after the WWDC.
22. Kelby S. *Macintosh: The Naked Truth.* Indianapolis: New Riders Publishing; 2002:189. And this, it should be noted, was before the scope of the iPod triumph became clear.
23. One of these is J. David Allred, of Cambridge-based Photon, Inc. (www.photoninc.com), who has regularly reassured me that: 1) Apple is here to stay, and 2) something will succeed Apple, if worst comes to worst.

Index

Note: Boldface numbers indicate illustrations.